Greening through Trade

Greening through Trade

How American Trade Policy Is Linked to Environmental Protection Abroad

Sikina Jinnah and Jean-Frédéric Morin

The MIT Press
Cambridge, Massachusetts
London, England

© 2020 Massachusetts Institute of Technology

All rights reserved. No part of this book may be reproduced in any form by any electronic or mechanical means (including photocopying, recording, or information storage and retrieval) without permission in writing from the publisher.

This book was set in ITC Stone Serif Std and ITC Stone Sans Std by Toppan Best-set Premedia Limited. Printed and bound in the United States of America.

Library of Congress Cataloging-in-Publication Data is available.

ISBN: 978-0-262-53872-5

10 9 8 7 6 5 4 3 2 1

For Doug and Isabelle, with our deep gratitude for watching the kids while we wrote this book.

Contents

Acknowledgments   ix
List of Abbreviations   xi

1   **Introduction**   1
2   **The Evolution of Environmental Provisions in US Trade Agreements**   23
3   **Why Link Trade and Environmental Politics?**   53
4   **Can Trade Agreements Enhance the Effectiveness of Multilateral Environmental Agreements?**   73
5   **Can Preferential Trade Agreements Diffuse Environmental Norms?**   103
6   **Do US Preferential Trade Agreement Provisions Become Global Standards?**   129
7   **Conclusions**   153

Notes   177
References   183
Index   203

Acknowledgments

We are especially grateful to the impressive cadre of graduate and undergraduate research assistants who have supported our work on this book over the last decade. These include Zachary Dove, Layla Farhat, Mathilde Gauquelin, Julien Katchinoff, Julia Kennedy, Noémie Laurens, Abby Lindsay, Micaela Samodelev, Dimitri Thériault, and Samantha Wapnick. We are also incredibly appreciative of the many government and NGO staff who took the time to speak with us about their work on trade-environment issues, some of them multiple times. Finally, we are immensely grateful to the organizations that have contributed to funding portions of this work over the years, including American University's School of International Service, the University of California, Santa Cruz, and the Canadian Social Science and Humanities Research Council.

List of Abbreviations

CAFTA-DR	Central American Free Trade Agreement
CEC	Commission on Environmental Cooperation
CEPA	Canadian Environmental Protection Act
CITES	Convention on International Trade in Endangered Species of Wild Fauna and Flora
COP	Conference of the Parties
CPTPP	Comprehensive and Progressive Trans-Pacific Partnership
CWA	Clean Water Act
DSM	dispute-settlement mechanism
ECA	environmental cooperation agreement
EIA	Environmental Investigation Agency
EO	executive order
EPA	Environmental Protection Agency
GATT	General Agreement on Tariffs and Trade
IUU	illegal, unreported, and unregulated fishing
MEA	multilateral environmental agreement
NAAEC	North American Agreement on Environmental Cooperation
NAFTA	North American Free Trade Agreement
NGO	nongovernmental organization
PTA	preferential trade agreement
TPA	Trade Promotion Authority
TPP	Trans-Pacific Partnership
TREND	Trade and Environment Database
USMCA	United States, Mexico, and Canada Agreement
USTR	United States Trade Representative
WTO	World Trade Organization

1 Introduction

The World Trade Organization (WTO) is on life support. Its continued relevance has come into question as the Doha Development Round has staggered through nearly two decades of unsuccessful negotiations. The WTO's 164 member states have been unable to reach agreement on core trade issues such as non-agricultural market access and agricultural subsidy reform. Despite the ailing WTO, countries are still actively pursuing international trade liberalization. Increasingly, they are turning to preferential trade agreements (PTAs) between smaller groups of countries, often just two, as an alternative to the stagnant multilateral process.[1] Indeed, PTA numbers have been exploding in recent years, creating a massive network of overlapping rules and norms in what economist Jagdish Bhagwati has famously termed the "spaghetti bowl" phenomenon (Bhagwati 1995a). Figure 1.1 below shows that over 688 PTAs were concluded globally between 1947 and 2016, with 87 of these PTAs agreed after the WTO Ministerial meeting collapsed in 2008.[2]

In parallel to this explosion of PTAs, skepticism has also increased regarding the feasibility and efficacy of environmental treaties to solve global environmental problems. Despite an impressive level of international cooperation on these issues, with over 1,200 environmental treaties currently in force, environmental problems continue to worsen (Mitchell 2018; UNEP 2012). One explanation for this lack of progress is that global environmental governance operates on the basis of consensus. In trying to bring all countries on board, a consensus-based approach often results in lowest-common-denominator agreements that do little to actually solve environmental problems (Susskind and Ali 2015). Another explanation is that global environmental governance is weak because it lacks enforcement

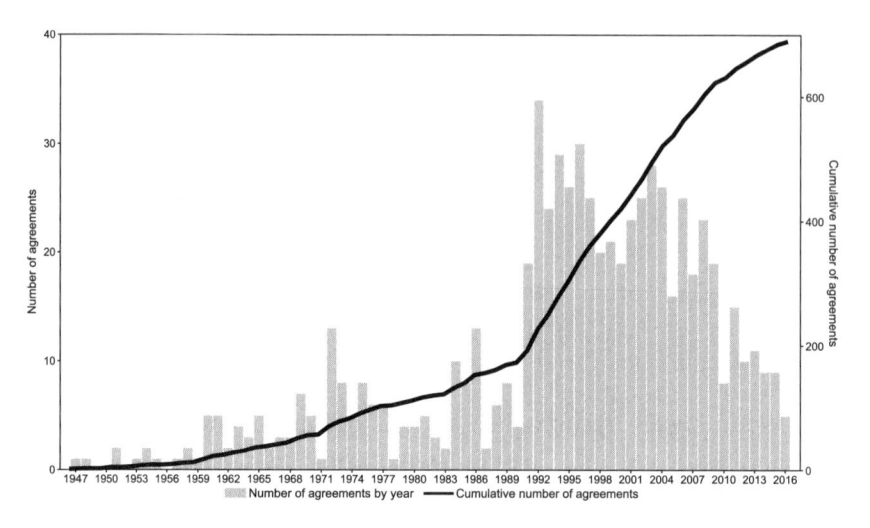

Figure 1.1
Growth of PTAs over time

power. This deficit can, among other things, create incentives for some countries to free ride on the actions taken by others (Chasek, Downie, and Brown 2018). This has catalyzed interest in alternative options to protect the global environment. In particular, there has been a recent resurgence of interest in using trade agreements, and their relatively stronger enforcement mechanisms, as tools for environmental protection.

Attempts to link trade and environmental policies are not new. Environmentalists have long attempted to leverage the economic benefits of liberalized trade (e.g., lower tariffs and increased market access) for more effective environmental governance. For example, environmental organizations have lobbied WTO member states to legalize the use of tariffs on products whose manufacturing process is deemed harmful to the environment.[3] The WTO agreements also contain environmental provisions providing for exceptions to trade rules under certain circumstances. WTO members can implement environmental policies that would otherwise conflict with their obligations under WTO agreements if they are related to the conservation of natural resources or are necessary for the protection of human, animal, or plant life or health. Although these exceptions sound permissive, they have historically been interpreted quite narrowly, often hinging on whether the environmental policy was applied in a manner that constitutes arbitrary or unjustified discrimination.[4] More recent developments at the intersection of trade and environmental governance are tethering these two domains even more closely and in new and innovative ways. This book explores this largely uncharted terrain of trade-environment linkages in PTAs.

PTAs are at the forefront of this innovation. Our analysis of 688 global PTAs reveals that about 86 percent of all PTAs globally now incorporate environmental provisions. Some of them are only vague references to the goal of reaching sustainable development, or are exceptions similar to the ones found in the General Agreement on Tariffs and Trade (GATT) of 1947. But many other provisions are more far-reaching than those pursued in the WTO context. Since at least the mid-1980s, many PTAs globally have included not only the WTO's environmental exemptions but also provisions requiring, for example, that trading partners implement multilateral environmental agreements (MEAs); cooperate on environmental issues; strengthen and/or enforce existing environmental laws; protect endangered species; regulate fishing activities; and address climate change. Importantly, as we discuss in chapters 2 and 4, some of these environmental provisions enjoy the full range of remedies available under the PTA's dispute-settlement procedures. This level of enforceability for international environmental policy includes access to sanctions, and is thus far stronger than anything available under contemporary environmental treaties.

The United States has long been at the vanguard of these efforts. On September 15, 1992, William Reilly, then administrator of the US Environmental Protection Agency (EPA), testified before the House Ways and Means Committee about the recently concluded North American Free Trade Agreement (NAFTA). He confidently predicted to the House Representatives that, "for some time to come, when other nations negotiate with their neighbors to open up markets, NAFTA will be their model for dealing with related environmental issues" (Ludwiszewski 1993, 706). Reilly's prediction was overconfident. NAFTA has never been a static model, even for subsequent US PTAs. However, he was certainly right to think that NAFTA's environmental provisions would have a profound impact on the entire trade governance system, as they have since diffused into dozens of PTAs beyond the United States, providing a foundation for what have become some of the most far-reaching environmental provisions in trade agreements globally.

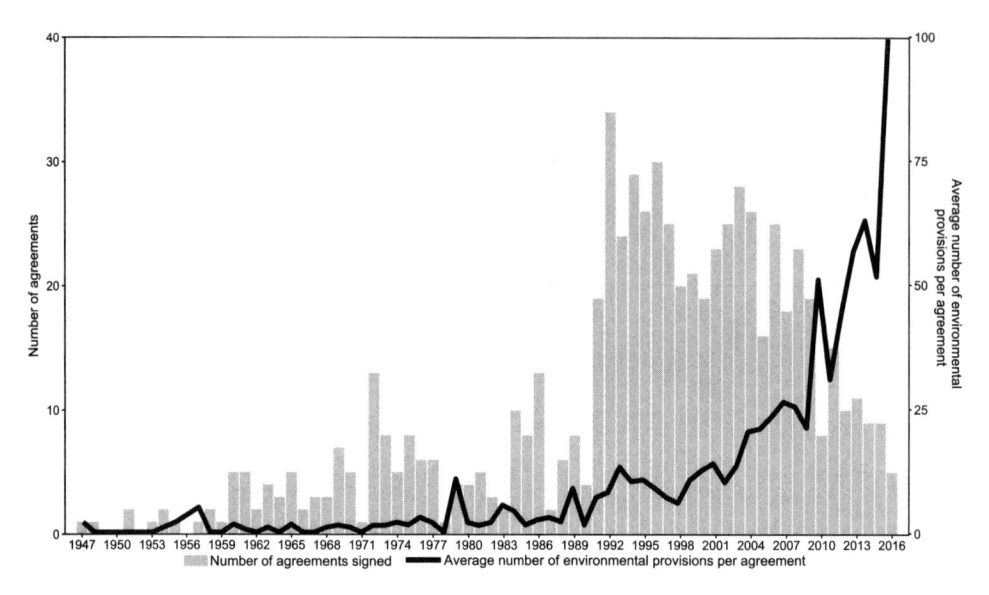

Figure 1.2
Growth of environmental provisions in global PTAs over time

Indeed, the United States is a global leader in terms of linking environmental and trade policies through PTAs. By "global leader," we mean a country that is a pioneer and moves forward before other countries, that takes on commitments that go beyond other countries, and that generates momentum and incentives for other countries to follow suit (Young 1991; Skodvin and Andresen 2006; Chasek 2007). To be sure, the United States is a laggard on a number of environmental issues, most notably climate change (Andresen and Agrawala 2002; Parker and Karlsson 2018). In recent decades, the European Union is frequently presented as a global leader on environmental policies, at least in regard to climate change (Vogler and Stephan 2007; Kelemen and Vogel 2010). However, the role of the United States on the trade and environment linkage is clearly one of leadership.

Indeed, the United States has been a front-runner in terms of substance, number of these provisions in its agreements, and influence over the global trade system. On substance, the United States is the most innovative country in designing environmental provisions in trade agreements, when calculated by the number of *new* environmental provisions included in its PTAs (Morin, Pauwelyn, and Hollway 2017). Figure 1.3 shows the most

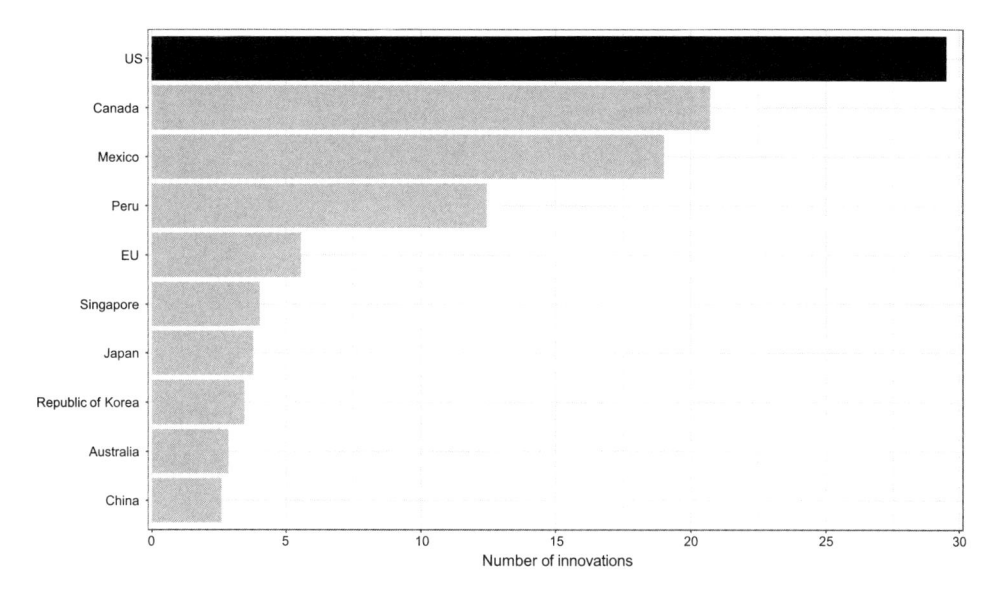

Figure 1.3
Total number of innovations per country (innovations per PTA divided by number of contracting parties)

innovative countries as measured by the number of environmental provisions that were unprecedented at the time of their introduction in a PTA. We first calculate the number of innovations for each PTA and then divide these innovations equally among contracting parties of these agreements. When innovation is measured this way, the most innovative PTA ever concluded is by far NAFTA, followed by the US-Peru agreement. In fact, NAFTA and US-Peru are so innovative compared to other PTAs that they bring Mexico, Canada, and Peru up to the second, third, and fourth ranks of innovative countries, even if other Canadian, Mexican, and Peruvian PTAs do not include many unprecedented environmental provisions.

For example, as we detail in chapter 4, the United States was the first country to make environmental provisions fully enforceable in its PTA with Peru, and it was a pioneer in linking PTA compliance to that of various MEAs, such as the Convention on International Trade in Endangered Species of Wild Fauna and Flora (CITES). Indeed, some US PTAs lead the world in terms of the sheer number of environmental provisions they contain. The United States has included more than 100 environmental provisions in

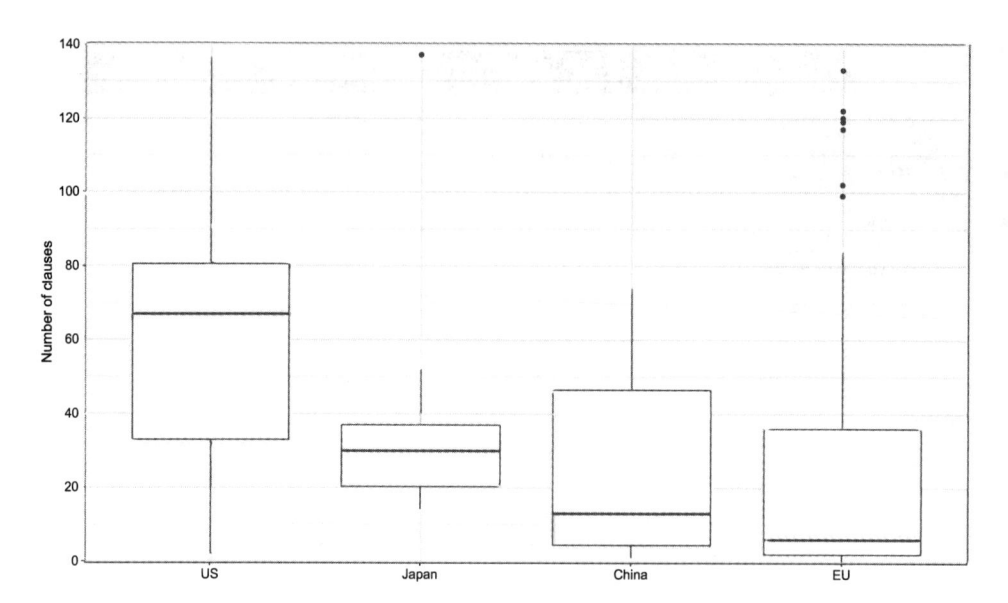

Figure 1.4
Number of environmental provisions in US, Japanese, Chinese, and European PTAs (1946–2016)

some of its recent PTAs and, as figure 1.4 indicates, on average has far more environmental provisions per trade agreement than do other major players in the global trade regime, such as the European Union, Japan, and China (the lines represent median values).[5]

The United States has also had prolific influence on trade-environment politics internationally, with much replication of US provisions across global agreements. Further, even as the Trump administration has retracted US engagement in international trade policy, the United States continues to influence how many other countries approach trade-environment linkages. This is nowhere more evident than in the Trans-Pacific Partnership (TPP). Although the Trump administration withdrew the United States from the TPP in 2017, many of the TPP's environmental provisions remain in the Comprehensive and Progressive Trans-Pacific Partnership (CPTPP) among the remaining 11 TPP countries.[6] As such, recent estimates that 90 percent of the TPP's environment chapter was derived from prior US PTAs reflect US influence on the CPTPP as well (Morin and Beaumier 2016). We discuss this global influence in more detail in chapters 5 and 6.

Introduction

Therefore, in the WTO's shadow, as more and more countries are turning to PTAs, the United States has increasingly incorporated innovative environmental provisions into these bilateral and regional agreements. This raises a host of questions related to the politics surrounding these trade-environment linkages. For example, we know little about the factors that enable and constrain how the United States identifies environmental issues through trade agreements, the character and extent of environmental provisions included in US trade agreements, the way US PTA environmental norms and policies impact domestic and international policy making in trading partner nations, or the impact of PTAs on MEAs' implementation and effectiveness. These questions are at the heart of this book.

Centrally, this book asks: *what are the impacts of the environmental provisions in US PTAs on environmental policy in trading partner nations and on the effectiveness of MEAs?* We illuminate answers to these questions through a series of case studies. We argue that US trade agreements serve as mechanisms to diffuse environmental policies and norms to both trading partner nations and third-party countries. Further, we argue that environmental provisions in US PTAs can play an important role in enhancing the effectiveness of MEAs by strengthening the enforcement capacity of the latter through linkages to PTA dispute-settlement systems.

The next section briefly summarizes the history of global trade-environment politics, primarily focusing on the WTO's activities in this area. This is followed by an overview of the scholarly literature, which emerged in response to those historical developments, and positions this book within that literature. We then explain our methodological approach to answering these questions before providing a detailed roadmap for the book, which also summarizes the book's main findings.

A Brief History of Global Trade-Environment Politics

Despite some half-hearted efforts to develop so-called "win-win" scenarios, trade and environmental issues have historically been viewed in opposition to one another. At the core of this understanding is the idea that increased trade necessarily means increased production and consumption, which in turn means increased resource use and environmental degradation. Balancing this environmental reality is the trade community's concern that environmental policies will be used as a form of protectionism. For example, domestic subsidies for development of solar panels could be used to protect fledging domestic industries by making foreign imports of such products less competitive in the market. In chapter 3, we map the literature on linkage politics and, in particular, that on why states choose to link trade and environmental issues. In this section and the next, we cover the empirical history between these two topics in contemporary policy and law, as well as the literature that has grown out of that linkage.

Daniel Esty's foundational book, *Greening the GATT*, captures this opposition well in describing these issues as a clash of cultures, paradigms, and judgments between "free traders" and environmentalists, who tend to approach governance issues quite differently (1994). The "free trader" ideal type is more outcome-oriented, utilitarian, sees solutions as rooted in proper economic pricing, and tends to see environmental problems as indeed solvable. The environmentalist on the other hand, is more process oriented, concerned with moral imperatives, sees solutions as based in law, and tends to see environmental problems as far more severe. As Esty aptly quips, "the word 'protection' warms the hearts of environmentalists, but sends chills down the spines of free traders" (1994, 36). This dichotomy is clearly a simplification and has evolved substantially over time, especially with, for example, the growth of market mechanisms (e.g., emissions trading, carbon taxes) being used for environmental protection. Recent survey-based empirical studies have demonstrated, for example, that those who are more concerned with the environment also favor more protectionist trade policies, due to their concerns about trade impacts on the environment (Bechtel, Bernauer, and Meyer 2012). Further, despite political leaders in the Global South opposing linkages between trade and environment, recent empirical studies show this feeling is not shared by citizens. Namely, Bernauer and Nguyen (2015) find that citizens in the Global South do not view economic integration and environmental protection as a trade-off. Nonetheless, even if they are more simple than contemporary politics fully supports, the motivations undergirding Esty's ideal types are still helpful in understanding the underlying politics at the heart of trade-environment issues in politics today.

Contemporary trade-environment politics can be traced back to the famous "tuna/dolphin" dispute (Kulovesi 2011). In 1991, a panel under the 1947 GATT upheld Mexico's challenge to a provision of the US Marine Mammal Protection Act. The provision prohibited the import of yellow fin tuna from the Eastern Tropical Pacific Ocean if that tuna was caught using commercial fishing technologies, which result in the incidental killing of dolphins. The GATT panel's decision in the "tuna/dolphin" dispute was never formally adopted. However, the case sparked much controversy and discussion, including by putting pressure on newly elected US President Bill Clinton to include environmental provisions in NAFTA, which was recently agreed under his predecessor, George H.W. Bush, but had not yet passed through the US Congress when Clinton took office (Houseman and Orbuch 1993). Clinton was ultimately successful in negotiating an environmental "side agreement" to NAFTA, officially called the North American Agreement on Environmental Cooperation (NAAEC). The NAAEC greatly expanded NAFTA's environmental provisions over the WTO's status quo. For example, the NAAEC created a citizen enforcement mechanism that allowed citizens to hold their governments to account if they were not enforcing existing environmental laws. NAFTA's environmental provisions, though critiqued strongly by groups on both sides of the issue, opened the door for what would become a long history of environmental linkages in PTAs. We discuss the NAAEC's provisions in more detail in chapter 4.

It is worth noting here, however, that NAFTA also included an investor-state dispute settlement mechanism that had important implications for environmental politics. This mechanism has been heavily critiqued by environmentalists and others, who argue that allowing foreign investors to sue governments if domestic (environmental) policies hinder their investments is a significant threat to environmental sovereignty (Neumayer 2017). Indeed, at least 18 disputes have been heard under this mechanism that have directly challenged environmental protection measures.[7]

Shortly after NAFTA entered into force, the WTO was created to succeed the 1947 GATT. The WTO adopted many aspects of the 1947 GATT, including its environmental exemptions (contained in GATT Art. XX). Importantly, however, the WTO framework made GATT rules, including environmental exemptions, fully enforceable. No longer would both parties to a dispute have to agree to adopt a panel's decision; decisions were now adopted automatically and an appeals process was put in place. Moreover, panel and appellate body decisions could include sanctions or other retaliatory measures for violations of WTO rules. This new enforceability within the WTO dispute-settlement process drew additional attention to the WTO's decisions surrounding environmental provisions.

Particularly important to the trajectory of trade-environment politics was the 1998 "shrimp-turtle" dispute, wherein Malaysia, Thailand, India, and Pakistan challenged US domestic policies that were designed to protect sea turtles from being inadvertently killed in the drift nets commonly used in commercial fishing operations. Despite US claims that the environmental policy was permissible under the WTO's environmental exemptions (GATT Art. XX), the WTO dispute-settlement body ruled against the United States in this dispute. This triggered outrage in the environmental activist community, who saw this as the WTO again striking down domestic environmental laws. The most public manifestation of this outrage was the so-called "Battle in Seattle," wherein upwards of 40,000 environmental and pro-labor activists joined forces to shut down the 1999 WTO Ministerial meeting with large-scale street protests (Seattle Police Department 1999). The media was flooded with images of activists in sea turtle costumes carrying signs that read "Teamsters and Turtles—Together at Last!" and chanting

Figure 1.5
Environmental protesters in sea turtle costumes at the 1999 WTO Ministerial Conference
Source: Wikimedia Commons, https://commons.wikimedia.org/wiki/File:WTO_protestors,_1999_(20680767813).jpg#/media/File:WTO_protestors,_1999_(20680767813).jpg.

"We don't want you! We didn't elect you! And we don't want your rules!" (Cooper 1999).

The WTO has since heard several environment-related disputes on issues ranging from gasoline to retreated tires to asbestos. Of central importance in these disputes is whether or not a specific domestic environmental policy that would otherwise violate WTO rules qualifies for an environmental exemption. These exemptions require that the domestic measure either "relate to the conservation of a nature resource" (GATT Art. XX(b)), or "is necessary for the protection of human, animal, or plant life or health" (GATT Art. XX(g)). If either of these conditions is met, it further requires that the policy was "applied in a way that does not constitute arbitrary or unjustified discrimination" (GATT Art. XX chapeau). As of the most recent WTO Secretariat summary report of WTO cases, the WTO has heard nine such disputes to date (WTO Secretariat 2019). Of these nine disputes, the WTO has ruled more often than not that a domestic environmental policy did indeed meet the requirements of Article XX(b) or (g). Nonetheless, the WTO has only granted an environmental exception once in a new dispute. This is because it has otherwise ruled that the domestic environmental policies in question did not meet the requirements of the Article XX chapeau. There has been one additional instance of an environmental exemption being granted. However, this involved a challenge to a party's compliance with a previous decision. As such, in that instance, the WTO appellate body told the United States what to do to comply, and the United States followed those instructions to the appellate body's satisfaction. Table 1.1 summarizes the Article XX disputes heard under the WTO since its inception in 1995.[8,9]

The most recent decision, adopted on January 11, 2019, after more than a decade of consultations, panel hearings, and appeals, was the US-Tuna II (Art. 21.5) dispute, in which Mexico challenged US policies related to the use of the "dolphin-safe" label. Both sides have won battles along the way, with, for example, a US win in a late 2017 ruling that US "dolphin-safe" labeling policy had been amended in such a way as to now qualify for an environmental exception. Although Mexico appealed this decision on December 1, 2017, on December 14, 2018, the appellate body issued its decision upholding the panel's 2017 assessment.

In the last decade, the focus of environment-related dispute settlement at the WTO has moved away from Article XX exemptions. Rather, disputes

Table 1.1
Summary of WTO Article XX Disputes

Case	Adopted	Issue/Challenge	XX(b) or (g)?	Chapeau?	Exemption Granted?
US: Gasoline[a]	5/20/96	US Clean Air Act rules for gasoline standards; favored domestic producers	g	No	No
US: Shrimp[b]	11/6/98	US policy to protect sea turtles pursuant to Endangered Species Act; illegally restricted shrimp imports from some countries	g	No	No
EC: Asbestos[c]	4/5/01	French restrictions on imports of asbestos-containing products; favored French substitutes	b	Yes	Yes
US: Shrimp (Art. 21.5)[d]	11/21/01	Challenged US compliance with US-Shrimp I (1998) panel decision	g	Yes	(Yes)[e]
Brazil: Retreaded tires[f]	12/17/07	Brazil's prohibition on imports of retreaded tires	b	Yes	No
China: Raw materials	2/22/12	China's export restraints on certain raw materials (e.g., bauxite, silicon metal)	No	NA	No
EC: Seal products[g]	6/18/14	EU import restrictions on seal products, including from indigenous hunts	NA[h]	No	No
China: Rare earths[i]	8/29/14	Export restrictions on rare earths, tungsten, and molybdenum	No	NA	No

Table 1.1 (continued)

Case	Adopted	Issue/Challenge	XX(b) or (g)?	Chapeau?	Exemption Granted?
US: Tuna II (Art. 21.5)[j]	1/11/19	Challenged US "dolphin-safe" labeling rules	g	Yes	Yes

[a] *United States—Standards for Reformulated and Conventional Gasoline.*
[b] *United States—Import Prohibition of Certain Shrimp and Shrimp Products.*
[c] *European Communities—Measures Affecting Asbestos and Asbestos-Containing Products.*
[d] *United States—Import Prohibition of Certain Shrimp and Shrimp Products. Recourse to article 21.5 by Malaysia.*
[e] Noted in parentheses because, as explained above, this case was not new but merely involved a challenge to US compliance with a prior decision.
[f] *Brazil—Measures Affecting Imports of Retreaded Tyres.* Appellate Body Report.
[g] *European Communities—Measures Prohibiting the Importation and Marketing of Seal Products.*
[h] This issue was not considered by the appellate body because the measure failed to meet the requirements of the chapeau. However, it should be noted the panel found that the measure was not consistent with Article XX(b).
[i] *China—Measures Related to the Exportation of Rare Earths, Tungsten and Molybdenum.*
[j] *United States–Measures Concerning the Importation, Marketing and Sale of Tuna and Tuna Products–Recourse to Article 21.5 of the DSU by the United States.*

have surrounded issues related to subsidies for renewable energy technologies. Eight such disputes have been heard since 2012.[10] For example, in 2013, the United States (later joined by several third parties) challenged the WTO compatibility of India's local content requirements for solar cells, and in 2010 Japan challenged the local content requirements of Canada's feed-in tariff program. These disputes have provided little clarity about when such subsidies are permissible and when they are not, which has in turn prompted calls for legal reform to clarify this issue (Asmelash 2015).

In addition, more than 40 WTO disputes concern the Agreement on the Application of Sanitary and Phytosanitary Measures. The most well known of them is the dispute regarding the moratorium on genetically modified organisms. This dispute revealed more than any previous disputes the ambiguous relation between WTO agreements and MEAs, in this case the Cartagena Protocol on Biosafety. However, several other disputes related to sanitary and phytosanitary measures concern more directly public health than environmental protection. In parallel to the dispute-settlement process, but having received far less attention, is the WTO's environmental negotiations track. Defined by the 2001 Doha Development Agenda, WTO delegates have been negotiating issues such as how to enhance the mutual supportiveness of WTO and MEAs, enhance the patentability of plants and animals, and increase market access for "environmental goods and services" by cutting or eliminating tariffs on such products. This has been a particularly active aspect of environment politics in the WTO, with negotiations surrounding the development of an environmental goods and services agreement ongoing since 2014.[11] If concluded, the environmental goods and services agreement could greatly increase market access for products like wind turbines, solar panels, and water filtration systems.

Until quite recently, the WTO has really been the epicenter of trade-environment politics. Despite the growing number and strength of environmental provisions in PTAs globally, and in particular in US agreements, comparatively little media, activist, and/or scholarly attention has been directed to these agreements. This is surprising, because PTAs often include far more detailed and far-reaching environmental provisions than anything under the WTO. For example, the United States, Mexico, and Canada Trade Agreement (USMCA) contains the most detailed environmental provisions of any trade agreement to date (Laurens et al. 2019). It includes many provisions replicated from prior agreements, related to, for example, citizen enforcement, public participation, and MEAs. However, it also includes new provisions related to plastic pollution, wildlife trafficking, and food waste. As we explain in chapter 2, the re-negotiation of NAFTA has not changed much in terms of the environmental substance compared with the TPP. Negotiators remain, at least for now, in a holding pattern with respect to the future of trade-environment politics in PTAs.

What Do We Know about Trade-Environment Politics?

The WTO disputes detailed above have also catalyzed a wave of scholarly discussions surrounding trade-environment politics at the WTO. Much of this work has dissected the WTO's approach to environmental dispute settlement under the GATT Article XX. In contrast to the environmental activist community's strong critique of the WTO's handling of environmental disputes, much of the scholarly literature is more measured in their assessment. Several scholars have argued that the WTO's record is not as bad as its critics make it out to be, highlighting, for example, poor decision making by the United States and others in implementing environmental policies in ways that are unnecessarily discriminatory, even if the environmental policies in question were in line with Article XX exemptions (Charnovitz 2007; Desombre and Barkin 2002; Howse 2002; Jinnah 2003; Neumayer 2004). Others have been more critical, including Joel Trachtman (2018), who characterizes the WTO appellate body's approach to environmental jurisprudence as incoherent and ineffective in addressing environmental exemptions. Still others have highlighted that the WTO's approach to environmental and other social issues has led to an organizational "legitimacy crisis," and a "chilling effect" on environmental policy development (Axelrod 2011a; Conca 2000; Eckersley 2004; Esty 2002; Stilwell and Tuerk 1999).

WTO-focused trade-environment scholarship has also delved into the empirical politics of trade-environment linkages, exploring, for example, how the WTO Secretariat has influenced trade-environment decision making at the WTO (Jinnah 2010; 2014), and the conditions under which the WTO has linked to environmental issues at all (Johnson 2015).[12] Most recently, scholars have examined what Wu and Salzman have called the "next generation" of WTO environment conflicts, which have been largely related to renewable energy subsidies and industrial policy (2013). This work has explored, for example, the implications for low carbon development (Lewis 2015); why renewables have been challenged even though fossil-fuel subsidies have not (Asmelash 2015; Meyer 2017; de Bièvre, Espa, and Poletti 2017); and the domestic coalition politics that lead to protectionist policies for renewables (Hughes and Meckling 2017). These connections at the intersection between trade and climate change are sure to be an important locus of trade-environment politics for years to come (e.g., Kulovesi 2014). We discuss some of this work in more detail in the context of the broader linkage politics literature in chapter 3. There is indeed quite a bit of overlap between these two areas of scholarship, with trade-environment cases serving to demonstrate linkage politics dynamics for many scholars.

There is also a more limited body of work that looks at the WTO's Committee on Trade and Environment, wherein delegates discuss environmental issues, including those outlined in the Doha Development Agenda, such as tariff reductions for environmental goods and services.[13] Scholarship is divided on the effectiveness of the committee's work, with some seeing important contributions to environmental cooperation and others responding more skeptically.[14]

Few scholars, however, have explored these questions as they relate to PTAs. The existing literature on PTAs has been largely focused on NAFTA and the novel set of environmental provisions it introduced in the mid-1990s, which went beyond the WTO's environmental exceptions. Much of the NAFTA literature focused on the negotiation process (e.g., Hogenboom 1998; Markell and Knox 2003; Steinberg 1997); the environmental impacts of NAFTA writ large (e.g., Gallagher 2004; Hufbauer 2000); NAFTA's novel Commission for Environmental Cooperation (Betsill 2007; Raustiala 2003); and how the NAFTA experience can inform environmental governance moving forward (Deere and Esty 2002).

The 687 other global PTAs currently in force have received surprisingly little attention. Aside from our own work leading up to this book, there has been very little analysis of the rapidly expanding politics of environmental governance through PTAs. Some of Jinnah's prior work has examined, for example, differences between US and EU approaches to environmental protection through trade agreements (Jinnah and Morgera 2013); US approaches to strategically linking trade agreements to MEAs (Jinnah 2011); and the ways in which trade agreements serve as mechanisms for norm diffusion in Latin America (a topic developed in more detail in chapter 5 of this book; Jinnah and Lindsay 2016). Jean-Frédéric Morin's prior work has analyzed the drivers for the inclusion of environmental provisions in PTAs (Morin, Dür, and Lechner 2018); the introduction of new environmental provisions in the trade governance system (Morin, Pauwelyn, and Hollway 2017); and the transatlantic convergence between the US and the European approach (Morin and Rochette 2017). Most recently, together we have analyzed how linkages to climate change could be better leveraged to offer similar benefits (Morin and Jinnah 2018).

Paul Steinberg, Dale Colyer, Ida Bastiaens, and Evgeny Postnikov are some notable exceptions. Steinberg provided an early assessment of how major regional trade organizations have handled environmental issues (2002). Building on this and a 2007 analysis from the Organization for Economic Cooperation and Development (OECD), Colyer provides a largely descriptive first account of PTA environmental provisions in global trade agreements (2011). Bastiaens and Postnikov (2017) provide one of the few interventions that analytically unpacks PTA environmental politics. Bastiaens and Postnikov (2017) nicely draw together Jinnah and Lindsay's (2016) process-tracing analysis of environmental norms and policy diffusion through PTAs and Baccini and Urpelainen's (2014) statistical analysis of the timing of domestic implementation of North-South PTA standards. Specifically, they argue that the nature of enforcement mechanisms directly affects the timing of trading partner implementation of environmental provisions in North-South PTAs. They show that while both US and EU enforcement approaches can be effective in facilitating environmental policy change in trading partner nations, the United States' sanction-based enforcement mechanisms have catalyzed implementation of environmental provisions earlier than the European Union's softer, more cooperative approach.

Despite these important interventions, the pace of trade-environment politics scholarship lags far behind the empirical developments in this area. In short, PTAs now engage deeply and directly in environmental governance, yet we know very little about how and why they do so and with what effects. In asking *how environmental provisions in US PTAs impact environmental policy abroad,* this book uncovers how the United States pursues environmental objectives through trade agreements, the factors that enable and constrain its decisions about which environmental provisions are included in PTAs, the impacts of these provisions on trading partner nations' environmental policy and law, the extent to which these provisions enhance the effectiveness of environmental governance, and their diffusion in PTAs concluded by other countries.

Methods and Approach

This book is a broad intervention into the largely unchartered territory of environmental governance through PTAs. As such, we have identified a series of theoretically derived questions that aim to contribute to several core strands of the global governance literature. That is, rather than diving deeply into a narrow case of a single PTA, we look broadly at all US PTAs and seek to understand the diverse ways these agreements are shaping global environmental governance. Centrally, the book looks at how PTAs impact the global diffusion of environmental norms and policies through changes in domestic environmental law and international trade law, as well as through compliance with international environmental treaties.

We examine the United States for many of the reasons detailed above. The United States is a front-runner in terms of the innovation and reach of environmental provisions in its PTAs. Further, the extensive US PTA network (figure 1.5), coupled with the US practice of largely replicating (and extending) its environmental provisions from one PTA to the next, means that the capacity of US PTAs to influence environmental politics globally is substantial. Finally, as the largest economy in the world, the United States is a powerful actor in global trade politics. This imbalance of power between the United States and the majority of its trading partners (who are primarily developing countries), suggests that the United States likely dictates which environmental provisions make it into PTAs and which do not.[15] This latter point is particularly important, because it provides us more confidence in tracing the direction of causality when, for example, examining norms and policy diffusion. Therefore, if PTAs do have any impacts on global environmental politics, the United States is a good case through which to observe them. In other words, we intentionally select on the dependent variable because we are *not* interested in, for example, the conditions under which PTAs influence environmental politics, but rather in *if* they influence environmental politics *at all*, and if so, what this looks like empirically. We peer into a black box.

Our core approach is based on a qualitative case study analysis that is deeply enriched by quantitative data derived from a large-scale dataset of global PTAs. We triangulate all findings to the greatest extent possible using a mixed-method approach that includes document analysis, interviews with key informants, and quantitative data from the most comprehensive coding analysis of environmental provisions in global PTAs to date. Specifically, we use the Trade and Environment Database (TREND; Morin, Dür, and Lechner 2018). This dataset covers a large number of PTAs, using the full texts of 688 PTAs signed between 1947 and 2016.[16] TREND also stands out because of its fine-grained, content-based coding of 286 different types of environmental provisions, some of which are very common, while others are found in only one or two agreements. As these provisions were coded using software designed for qualitative analysis, TREND enables researchers to easily retrieve the full text of any environmental provision from any trade agreement. The dataset can also be used for quantitative analysis to compare groups of PTAs and critically map the impact of US provisions globally.

This comprehensive coding analysis is then used to enrich qualitative case studies that dive into the gritty politics of environmental provisions in US PTAs. We examine related but distinct theoretically derived questions

Introduction

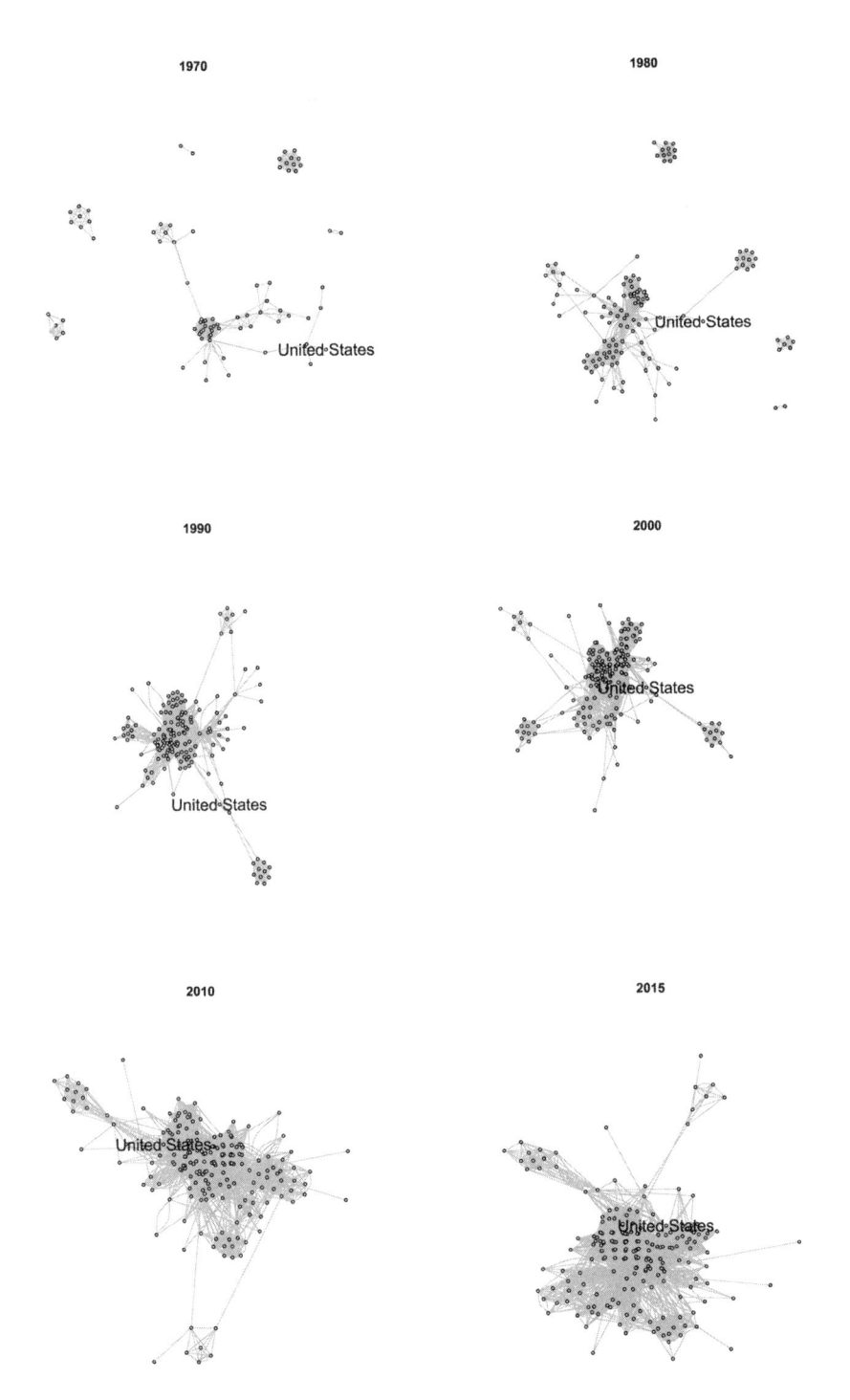

Figure 1.6
Growth of US-PTA network over time (1970–2015)

in each of the analytical chapters (chapters 4–6). These questions and the data-collection methods used to explore them are unpacked in great detail in each of the individual chapters. Core to our qualitative cases studies in all chapters are detailed process-tracing analyses. We rely heavily on government documents and reports of international and nongovernmental organizations (NGOs) to trace, for example, how norms and policies have diffused across countries through PTAs. We complement this document analysis with interview data. We conducted 14 interviews with government officials who negotiated the PTAs under examination and/or oversaw their implementation, as well as with NGO representatives who were active in lobbying the US government on environmental aspects of its PTAs. Finally, when possible, we also interviewed trading-partner nations about their perspectives on how and why environmental provisions are included in US PTAs and the impacts of those provisions in their home countries.

This rich combination of quantitative coding through TREND, with qualitative process tracing through documents and interviews, allows us to paint the most detailed picture of US trade-environment politics available in the literature to date, and centrally, to compare the US practice to that of other countries.

Roadmap of the Book

Chapter 2 details the political and legal history of environmental provisions in US PTAs. Using the TREND database, it identifies all environmental provisions in US agreements beginning in 1985 with the US-Israel agreement, up to the signature of USMCA. Drawing on interview data and document analysis, this chapter explains the evolution of these provisions against the backdrop of concurrent US politics and legal developments. In so doing, chapter 2 lays the empirical foundation for the analytical chapters that follow. Chapter 3 explores the empirical and theoretical explanations for linking trade and environmental issues in PTAs. It first reviews the linkage politics literature to help us understand the structural functions that regime linkages provide. It then dives into the literature on *why* states choose to link issues, with a focus on explanations from trade-environment politics specifically. Finally, chapter 3 draws on interview data with key informants on US trade policy development to empirically reflect on the factors that enable and constrain the process by which the United States selects specific environmental provisions to include in its PTAs. On this point, we highlight that these provisions are largely defined by established US laws, such as the 2002 Trade Act and Trade Promotion Authority ("fast-track" authority).

Chapters 4 through 6 explore in depth the various ways that PTAs can impact environmental governance. Chapter 4 asks if linkages between PTAs and environmental treaties can impact MEA effectiveness. As will be explained in chapter 2, many US PTAs require, for example, that efforts to implement obligations under specific environmental treaties shall not be seen as in violation of trade law. Some recent cases go even deeper, requiring overhaul of domestic institutions in order to implement specific provisions of specific environmental treaties. Chapter 4 analyzes the extent to which these linkages actually impact the effectiveness of these environmental treaties. Looking through the lens of the US-Peru PTA and its linkages to CITES, the chapter argues that these MEA linkages can in fact enhance MEA effectiveness in important ways.

Chapter 5 turns to the impacts of PTA environmental provisions on domestic environmental policy in trading-partner nations. Specifically, through a detailed process tracing exercise, it examines the ways PTAs serve to diffuse environmental norms and policies from US domestic law into the domestic law of trading-partner nations. It does so by looking at how two characteristically US environmental norms (effective enforcement and public participation) diffuse through three US PTAs—NAFTA; the Central American Free Trade Agreement (CAFTA-DR),[17] and the US-Peru PTA—into the domestic law of several Central and South American trading partners.

Chapter 6 goes one step further in the study of diffusion by tracking the replication of environmental provisions within the global trade governance system. It asks whether environmental provisions that had first appeared in US PTAs were subsequently incorporated in other countries' PTAs. Chapter 6 also asks whether provisions that were initially introduced in other countries' PTAs were replicated by the US government in its own PTAs. This chapter argues that this cross-fertilization between US and foreign PTAs is one of the driving forces behind the evolution of the global trade governance system.

Finally, chapter 7 summarizes our findings, reflects on the potential negative impacts of PTA environment linkages, and provides recommendations for how trade-environment linkages should be considered going forward.

Table 1.2
Summary of Research Questions and Findings

Chapter	Core Question	Central Finding
2	How has the US approach to trade-environment linkages evolved over time?	Environmental provisions in US PTAs have gotten progressively stronger and more far-reaching over time.
3	What factors enable and constrain the US government's decisions to select environmental provisions for incorporation into PTAs?	Rationales are diverse and overlapping. They include concerns about compliance costs, protectionist interests, domestic pressures from NGOs and others, contextual/situational factors, and trading-partner interests. Centrally, however, US decisions are circumscribed by domestic law and policy, which prescribe the specific provisions that may be included.
4	How do environmental provisions in US PTAs impact the effectiveness of MEAs?	Recent environmental provisions have enhanced the procedural effectiveness of certain MEAs by catalyzing implementation.
5	Do PTAs serve as mechanisms of environmental norm and policy diffusion from the United States to trading-partner nations?	Yes. Trading-partner nations replicate US domestic environmental provisions into their own domestic law via similar and/or verbatim PTA provisions.
6	Are US PTA's environmental provisions becoming a global standard?	Yes. Some US PTAs' environmental provisions were replicated by other countries, but significant differences remain between US agreements and agreements that do not involve the United States.

2 The Evolution of Environmental Provisions in US Trade Agreements

Environmental provisions in US trade agreements have gotten progressively stronger over time. Scholars have sliced this evolution in several ways. Some see only two phases, differing primarily in terms of how dispute settlement is treated (Bourgeois, Dawar, and Evenett 2007).[1] Others identify four phases (Gresser 2010). Although our own assessment is closely in line with Gresser's, we slice the history slightly differently. Gresser groups the US-Jordan Preferential Trade Agreement (PTA), opened for signature in 2000, with the seven that followed it (until 2006) because those subsequent agreements largely replicate the environmental provisions found in the Jordan agreement. However, we separate out, into a distinct phase, those agreements opened for signature after the renewal of "fast-track" authority in 2002, because with that renewal came a strengthening of environmental provisions over what we saw in the US-Jordan PTA.

More specifically, during the first phase (1985–1999), the United States recognized connections between trade and environmental goals, but positioned the latter as a secondary priority. This was done by incorporating highly circumscribed environmental exceptions to trade rules, rather than pursuing specific environmental objectives directly. During the second phase (1992–1999), US trade policy began to flesh out environmental provisions in trade agreements by identifying environmental objectives and developing norms to navigate potential synergies and conflicts between environmental protection and trade liberalization. Centrally, this was done by creating environmental cooperation mechanisms and by leveling the playing field to ensure that Mexico and other developing countries did not benefit economically from lower environmental standards and lax enforcement.

During phase three (2000–2001), the US executive branch began to integrate accountability mechanisms for environmental issues into its PTA review process. In phase four (2002–2005), the US Congress came on board by reinforcing and further strengthening those environmental provisions identified by the executive branch. Finally, during phase five (2006-present), the United States has greatly expanded its reach in using trade agreements to achieve environmental goals, especially those that it has already committed to under multilateral environmental agreements (MEAs) or otherwise through domestic legal instruments by, for example, greatly strengthening dispute-settlement provisions for environmental issues.

Rather than representing a departure from the previous phase, each phase has built on the last, incorporating and extending the reach of the environmental provisions contained therein. Importantly, this has been an issue that has historically enjoyed strong bipartisan support. Indeed, once an environmental provision is included in one US PTA, that provision often serves as a template for subsequent agreements irrespective of who was in the White House at the time of negotiations, signature, and/or entry into force (see table 2.1). Indeed, more often than not, environmental provisions are replicated verbatim from one US PTA to the next.

Finally, it should be noted that although the Trump administration has pulled the United States back from multilateral processes, including those related to trade negotiations, the policies developed during the third phase continue to influence ongoing bilateral and regional trade negotiations. As explained in the pages that follow, US negotiating objectives are defined by law and thus cannot easily be changed by presidential whim. This suggests that the third phase will continue into the foreseeable future, even if the pace of new negotiations has slowed under the Trump administration. We discuss this in more detail below in the context of the recent signature of United States, Mexico, and Canada Trade Agreement (USMCA), including as related to the 2018 renewal of US Trade Promotion Authority on June 30, 2018.

The next section provides an overview of the types of environmental provisions we find in US PTAs. This is followed by a narrative history that traces the evolution of environmental provisions in US trade agreements over time. That history is organized along the five phases of US trade-environment politics identified above, and it is explained against the political and legal backdrop that shapes and defines US negotiating objectives

Table 2.1
US Preferential Trade Agreements, 1985–2018

PTA[a]	Phase	Year Negotiations Began	Administration When Negotiations Began	Year of Signature	Administration at Time of Signature	Entry into Force for US	Administration at Time of Entry into Force
Israel	1	1984	Reagan	1985	Reagan	1985	Reagan
NAFTA	2	1991	H.W. Bush	1992	Clinton	1994	Clinton
Jordan	3	2000	Clinton	2000	Clinton	2001	G. W. Bush
Vietnam	3	~1995	Clinton	2000	Clinton	2001	G. W. Bush
Singapore	4	2000	Clinton	2003	G. W. Bush	2004	G. W. Bush
Chile	4	2000	Clinton	2003	G. W. Bush	2004	G. W. Bush
Australia	4	2003	G. W. Bush	2004	G. W. Bush	2005	G. W. Bush
CAFTA-DR	4	2004	G. W. Bush	2004	G. W. Bush	2006	G. W. Bush
Morocco	4	2003	G. W. Bush	2004	G. W. Bush	2006	G. W. Bush
Bahrain	4	2004	G. W. Bush	2004	G. W. Bush	2006	G. W. Bush
Peru	5	2004	G. W. Bush	2006	G. W. Bush	2009	Obama
Colombia	5	2004	G. W. Bush	2006	G. W. Bush	2012	Obama
Oman	5	2005	G. W. Bush	2006	G. W. Bush	2009	G. W. Bush
Korea[b]	5	2006	G. W. Bush	2007	G. W. Bush	2012	Obama
Panama	5	2004	G. W. Bush	2007	G. W. Bush	2012	Obama
TPP[c]	5	2008	G. W. Bush	2016	Obama	NA	NA
USMCA	5	2018	Trump	2018	Trump	NA	NA

[a] The agreements also include the content of their associated environmental cooperation agreement, if applicable.
[b] Currently under renegotiation by the Trump administration.
[c] The Trump administration withdrew from this agreement in 2017.

and strategies in trade-environment politics. The concluding section briefly compares the United States to other countries and suggests areas where the United States could integrate environmental provisions into future PTAs.

Overview of Environmental Provisions in US Preferential Trade Agreements

Based on a coding analysis of all US PTAs using the Trade and Environment Database (TREND),[2] we identify 130 distinct environmental provisions in US PTAs. These provisions are diverse, but can be grouped into the following 17 categories: preamble, affirmation of state sovereignty, domestic levels of protection, enforcement of domestic measures, public participation, transparency, improvement of environmental governance, implementation of the agreement, cooperation, technical assistance, coherence with non-environmental issues, specific environmental issues, limits to environmental measures, environmental exceptions, dispute settlement, joint institutions, and relationship with MEAs.

Table 2.2 below briefly explains each of the 17 categories; a more detailed description of each category can be found in the TREND codebook, which is contained in the appendix at the end of this chapter.

As noted above, TREND identifies 130 specific environmental provisions across these 17 categories. The appendix at the end of this chapter summarizes where each of these 130 environmental provisions can be found in individual US PTAs. First, however, we provide a narrative history of how these provisions found their way into US PTAs.

Phase One: 1985–1991

The first phase of trade-environment linkages in US trade policy was quite circumscribed, including only the 1985 US-Israel PTA. While the Israel PTA does not mention environmental issues or objectives explicitly, it adopts the general exceptions contained in the 1947 General Agreement on Tariffs and Trade (GATT). Those exceptions, which are replicated in all subsequent US PTAs, allow for countries to adopt environmental policies that would otherwise conflict with PTA obligations under certain conditions. Specifically, GATT Article XX(b) and (g) articulate that countries may implement environmental policies that:

Table 2.2
Categories of Environmental Provisions in US Preferential Trade Agreements

Categories	Description
Preamble	References to the need to protect the environment in the preamble of the trade agreement.
State sovereignty	Recognitions of state sovereignty over natural resources, including the regulatory, administrative, and judiciary sovereignty to govern environmental protection.
Domestic levels of protection	Commitments to maintain or to improve the level of environmental protection and condemnations of efforts to lower environmental protection for economic reasons.
Enforcement of domestic measures	Commitments to enforce domestic environmental law and mechanisms to improve domestic enforcement.
Public participation	Provisions related to the participation of stakeholders in domestic and international environmental law making.
Transparency	Provisions related to transparency of governmental or intergovernmental actions and decisions related to environmental protection.
Improvement of environmental governance	Promotion of specific policy instruments, such as green taxes, public-private partnerships, and certification schemes.
Implementation of the agreement	Mechanisms to facilitate the implementation of the agreement's environmental provisions, including monitoring, assessment, and funding mechanisms.
Cooperation	Commitments to cooperate in the field of the environment, including between scientists, regulatory agencies, and custom officers of all parties.
Technical assistance	Commitments from one party to provide assistance, capacity building, or funding to another party in the field of environmental protection.
Coherence with non-environmental issues	Provisions related to coherence between environmental policies and some other issue areas, including energy tourism, urban planning, health, and agriculture.
Specific environmental issues	Measures related to specific environmental issues, such as ground water, wetland, fisheries, invasive species, air pollution, oil spills, pesticides, or hazardous waste.

Table 2.2 (continued)

Categories	Description
Limits to environmental measures	Commitments that environmental measures should not be used for protectionist purposes.
Environmental exceptions	Exceptions to trade commitments on environmental grounds, including for trade services, investment protection, and the liberalization of public procurement.
Dispute settlement	Environmental measures related to dispute settlement, including for disputes between private parties, in investor-state disputes, or in state-state trade disputes.
Joint institutions	Creation of institutions to facilitate environmental cooperation.
Relationship with MEAs	Measures related to the ratification, implementation, or prevalence of some environmental agreements.

(b) [are] necessary to protect human, animal or plant life or health; [or]

(g) [relate] to the conservation of exhaustible natural resources if such measures are made effective in conjunction with restrictions on domestic production or consumption.

Although on the surface these provisions seem broadly permissive, they have been interpreted quite narrowly under the (1947) GATT and subsequently under the WTO (Jinnah 2003; Moran 2017). Centrally, the chapeau to GATT Article XX requires that such exceptions are applied in a way that does not constitute "arbitrary or unjustifiable discrimination" between countries, which along with the so-called "necessity test," have been the sticking points in granting these exemptions.[3]

It should be noted that until the early 1990s, the United States was ahead of the global curve in the field of environmental protection. On several accounts, it had more stringent, risk-adverse, and comprehensive domestic environmental regulations than any other country (Vogel 2012). Therefore, the United States included environmental exemptions in its PTAs as way of protecting US regulatory sovereignty on environmental matters (Morin and Rochette 2017). As indicated by table 2.3 below, several domestic US environmental measures have been challenged by other countries under the GATT and WTO on the grounds that they violated GATT/WTO trade rules. That the United States was most often a defendant/respondent

Table 2.3
GATT/WTO Disputes Related to the Environment and Involving the United States as Respondent

Year	Plaintiff	Resp.	Facts and issues	Articles	Decision
1980	Canada	US	US prohibits tuna products from Canada to protect dolphins	XI, XX(g) of GATT	Inconsistent with Art. XI; does not comply with Art. XX
1987	Mexico, Canada, EC[a]	US	US program to clean up hazardous waste included tax for imported oil	III of GATT	Inconsistent with Art. III
1991	Mexico	US	US prohibits imports of tuna from Mexico to protect dolphins	XI, XIII, III, XX of GATT	Inconsistent with Art. XI; not justified by Art. XX
1992	EC, Netherlands	US	US restricts imports of tuna to protect dolphins	XI, XIII, III, XX(b)(g) of GATT	Inconsistent with Art. XI; not justified by Art. XX
1993	EC	US	Taxes and standards on fuel economy for passenger cars	III XX(g) Of GATT	Inconsistent with III(4); not justified by XX(g)
1995	Venezuela, Brazil	US	Measures to reduce vehicle emissions of pollutants	III, XX(b)(d)(g) of GATT	Inconsistent with Art. III; not justified by XX
1997	Indonesia and others	US	US prohibits imports of shrimp unless "turtle excluder devices" are used	XI and XX(g) of GATT	Inconsistent with Art. XI; not justified by Art. XX
2009	Mexico	US	Conditions under which tuna sold in the United States may be labeled "dolphin-safe"	2 of the Agreement on Technical Barriers to Trade	Inconsistent with Art. 2.1

[a] EC refers to European Communities.

reflects its progressive environmental regulations during this time. However, the United States did not prevail in any of these cases, largely because the dispute-settlement body found that US domestic regulations were not applied in GATT/WTO-compliant ways (Jinnah 2003).

The US-Israel PTA also contains a clause that clarifies the legal relationship between the PTA and other multilateral agreements, including environmental ones. It states:

> The Parties affirm their respective rights and obligations with respect to each other under existing bilateral and multilateral agreements. . . . In the event of an inconsistency between provisions of this Agreement and such existing agreements, the provisions of this Agreement shall prevail. (Art. 3)

This clause makes clear that the PTA shall prevail in the event of conflict with the provisions of any MEA.

Phase Two: 1992–1998

After the US-Israel agreement, the United States didn't enter into any additional PTAs until the early 1990s, when it signed NAFTA with Mexico and Canada. The signature of NAFTA in 1992 marked the beginning of the second phase in US trade-environment politics. This phase not only replicated the environmental exceptions contained in Article XX of the GATT, but also added a slew of new innovations, which articulated normative relationships between trade and environmental governance and established rules to guide implementation of those norms and principles. Most of these innovations have their origins with NAFTA, but have been replicated widely across US PTAs.

It is important to note that NAFTA was negotiated and signed by US President George H.W. Bush in December 1992, after Bush lost to Bill Clinton in the November 1992 US presidential election. When Clinton took office in January 1993, he refused to take NAFTA to the Senate for ratification until environmental and labor standards were negotiated. Since the agreement was already signed, Clinton pushed for the inclusion of these provisions through so-called "side agreements." Side agreements are executive agreements that, unlike treaties, do not require US Congressional ratification, nor Senate advice and consent. Although side agreements can thus make it easier to attach environmental provisions to trade agreements, they have

The Evolution of Environmental Provisions in US Trade Agreements

been criticized as weak by many environmental groups, and considered a lost opportunity by some scholarly experts (Charnovitz 1994).

NAFTA's side agreement, called the North American Agreement on Environmental Cooperation (NAAEC), was designed to facilitate environmental cooperation between NAFTA parties and to encourage implementation of domestic environmental policies. It creates and is implemented by the Commission on Environmental Cooperation (CEC), whose primary governing body is the CEC Council. There are many environmental innovations contained in the NAAEC, several of which are a result of the broad mandate given to the CEC Council to examine a wide range of environmental issues, including transboundary pollution, invasive species, eco-labeling, and "other matters as it may decide" (Art. 10(2)). In fact, the NAFTA regime, including the NAAEC, is by far the most innovative trade agreement package ever concluded with respect to environmental protection. Figure 2.1 below builds on the TREND database and presents the most innovative trade agreements based on their number of unprecedented environmental provisions. NAFTA and NAAEC lead the ranking, with a combined number of 46 legal innovations (Morin, Pauwelyn, and Hollway 2017).

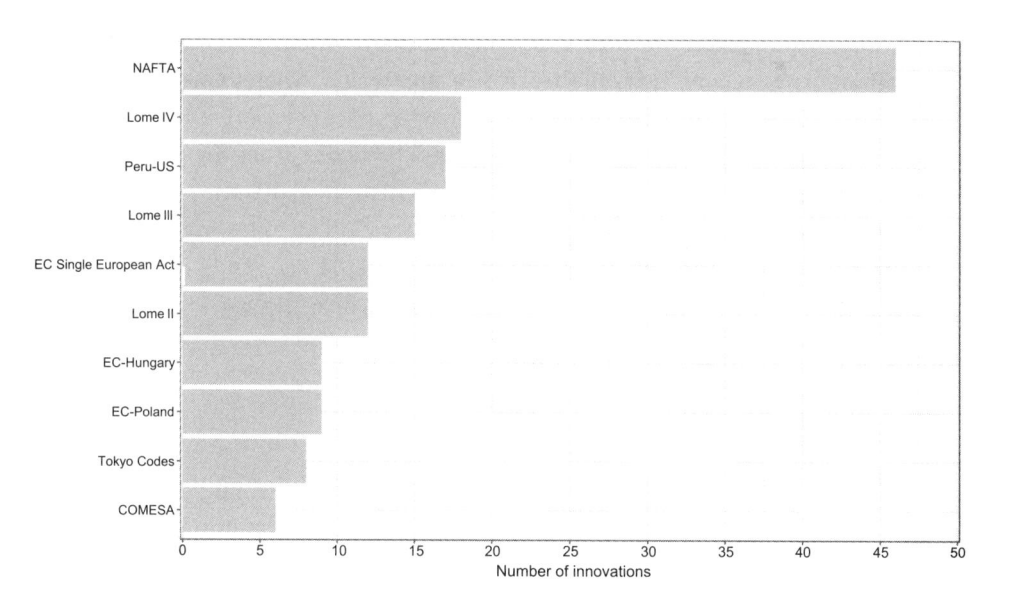

Figure 2.1
The most innovative trade agreements based on number of unprecedented environmental provisions

The NAAEC also contains several broad innovations that have been widely replicated, even in the absence of a similar overseeing commission under other PTAs. Most notably, the NAAEC contains provisions that allow for citizens to play a role in ensuring that their governments enforce existing environmental laws; broad public participation in environmental decision making; cooperation on environmental issues between countries; and environmental consultations to settle disputes. With the exception of the 2000 US-Vietnam agreement, which was sparse on environmental provisions, NAFTA's environmental provisions were largely replicated, in whole or in part, in all subsequent US PTAs to date. Importantly, following NAFTA, these provisions were brought into the main text of the PTAs, in either articles or full chapters on the environment, rather than relegated to weaker side agreements.

Although the main text of NAFTA itself is relatively thin on environmental provisions, it does lay out a list of three MEAs that would prevail in the event of any inconsistency with NAFTA. These are the Convention on International Trade in Endangered Species of Wild Fauna and Flora (CITES), the Basel Convention on the Transboundary Movement of Hazardous Wastes and their Disposal, and the Montreal Protocol on Substances that Deplete the Ozone Layer. All three of these MEAs use trade restrictions to secure their objectives, measures which, when implemented domestically, could be seen to violate PTA rules. The inclusion of these so-called "covered agreements" marks a distinct departure from the position taken in the 1985 US-Israel PTA, which implicitly articulated the opposite. Interestingly, this provision disappeared from US PTAs following NAFTA until 2006, when it reappeared in a new form in the Peru and Colombia agreements, which took a much more proactive stance on the relationship between PTAs and MEAs.

Phase Three: 1999–2001

The next political catalyst in the development of environmental provisions in US PTAs came in November 1999, when President Bill Clinton issued Executive Order (EO) 13141, which was complemented a year later by a set of implementing guidelines (Clinton 1999). The EO required, for the first time, that the US Trade Representative (USTR) and Council on Environmental Quality conduct environmental reviews of all new US trade agreements. The overarching goal of the reviews is to ensure that "environmental considerations are integrated into the development of US trade negotiating objectives and positions" (USTR and CEQ 2000, Art. IIIA(1)). To this end, the EO required that environmental reviews of environmental impacts be conducted "sufficiently early in the process to inform the development of negotiating positions" (Section 5(iii)). Although the reviews are to focus on environmental impacts in the United States, the EO indicated that "as appropriate and prudent, reviews may also examine global and transboundary impacts" (Section 5(iv)(b)). The guidelines clarified the factors that should be considered in evaluating if such a transboundary assessment is appropriate and prudent, including the scope and magnitude of any reasonably foreseeable impacts in trading-partner nations.

Importantly, and reflective of broader US environmental norms in trade agreements (see chapter 5), the EO also contained provisions for public participation in the process. These provisions were a major departure from US practice in this area, with trade negotiating positions being largely conducted behind closed doors through an interagency committee (Salzman 2001). The environmental reviews are required to meaningfully engage the public from an early stage. They begin with an invitation to the public to submit comments on the scope of the review, on the methods that should be used, and on the potential positive and negative environmental impacts of the trade agreement (USTR 2018). Importantly, the guidelines required that information collected through this process inform US negotiating objectives and positions. These new requirements opened the door for a wide swath of environmental issues and provisions to be considered in negotiating US PTAs into the future.

The first environmental review was undertaken for the US-Jordan PTA, which was also the first US PTA to contain a specific article related to the environment (Art. 5). One important development in the Jordan PTA's environment article (Art. 5) was that it not only discouraged parties from weakening environmental laws, as we saw in the NAAEC, but also encouraged them to strengthen these laws. Simultaneously, it made clear that this provision would not infringe on parties' sovereign rights to decide how exactly this should be done.[4]

Phase Four: 2002–2005

The next major development in US trade-environment politics came when the US Congress passed the Trade Act of 2002. This law renewed "fast-track" authority to then President George W. Bush, which had lapsed in 1994. Fast-track authority makes it much easier for the president to negotiate trade agreements, because it allows her/him to submit any trade deals to Congress for a vote, without the possibility of amendments or filibusters. In return, the president must follow a set of negotiation guidelines, including as related to the environment. The set of guidelines established in the Trade Act of 2002 ramped up the environmental governance provisions of EO 13141. Not only did it reinforce the EO's requirements to conduct environmental reviews, but it also institutionalized several concrete environmental negotiating objectives. These included ensuring that US trade partners enforce environmental laws, strengthening the capacity of US trading partners to protect the environment, and promoting the consideration of MEAs.

Negotiated in tandem with the Trade Act of 2002, the Chile (2003) and Singapore (2003) PTAs reflect these strengthened environmental standards, and they would largely serve as a template for four US PTAs that were finalized before fast-track authority expired in July 2007 (Smith 2011). This included US PTAs with Australia (2004), Morocco (2004), Bahrain (2004), and Oman (2006),[5] as well as the negotiations of the Central American Free Trade Agreement (2004). Notably, these PTAs expanded the US-Jordan PTA's environment article into full scale environment chapters, which provided for various innovative environmental provisions, including enhanced cooperation, additional environmental exceptions, strengthened provisions for public participation and transparency, and stronger dispute-settlement provisions.

A particularly important innovation during this phase was the emergence of enforcement mechanisms for violation of non-derogation provisions—that is, those that require parties to enforce their domestic environmental laws. Beginning with the 2004 Chile PTA, US PTAs contain stipulations on dispute settlement, which provide for monetary penalties and possibly tariff suspensions in disputes surrounding parties' failure to enforce environmental laws. These penalties are explicitly limited in both the amount of monetary remedy available and how the reward must be used. In addition,

The Evolution of Environmental Provisions in US Trade Agreements 35

such penalties were only available for non-derogation, and could not be used to enforce any other PTA environmental provisions.

Phase Five: 2006–Present

On May 10, 2007, another important document, the Bipartisan Agreement on Trade Policy, was released that would shape the development of US trade policy surrounding environmental issues. This agreement, often referred to as simply the "May 10 Agreement," was signed between the George W. Bush administration and the Democrats in Congress. It required the Bush administration to renegotiate the not-yet-ratified PTAs with Peru and Panama (and to a lesser extent Korea) to reflect a set of principles laid out in the agreement.[6] In doing so, the May 10 Agreement signals the beginning of the fifth phase of US trade-environment politics. Centrally, the May 10 agreement required countries to adopt, implement, and effectively enforce laws and regulations related to a list of seven MEAs to which they are party. This went much further than the covered agreements list under NAFTA, in that these provisions weren't about protecting from conflict, but rather required implementation and enforcement. The list also expanded NAFTA's list of covered agreements, which included CITES and the Montreal Protocol, to now also include the International Convention for the Prevention of Pollution from Ships, the Inter-American Tropical Tuna Convention, the Ramsar Convention on Wetlands, the International Convention for the Regulation of Whaling, and the Convention on Conservation of Antarctic Marine Living Resources. Notably, the Basel Convention was removed from the list.

Although this change was important, what really differentiates this phase from the others are two additional requirements of the May 10 agreement that position PTAs to secure environmental objectives. First, it requires, for the first time, that *all* PTA environment obligations be subject to the same dispute settlement and enforcement mechanisms as all other FTA obligations. Unlike previous provisions for dispute settlement of environmental provisions, these are now uncircumcised in terms of remedy and apply to all environmental provisions, not just effective enforcement/non-derogation provisions. This marks an important policy shift in US trade politics. As articulated by the USTR:

> We have agreed that all of our [P]TA environmental obligations will be enforced on the same basis as the commercial provisions of our agreements—same remedies, procedures, and sanctions. Previously, our environmental settlement procedures focused on the use of fines, as opposed to trade sanctions, and were limited to the obligation to effectively enforce environmental laws. (USTR 2007a)

Second, the May 10 agreement outlined highly specific provisions for inclusion of an annex on forest sector governance in the Peru PTA. These provisions included requirements to provide for capacity building in Peru, cooperation between law enforcement officials, and steps to strengthen Peru's domestic forest governance laws and regulations. This level of specificity was a massive departure from any prior guidelines for negotiating environmental provisions in US trade agreements.

Indeed, the strengthened dispute-settlement procedures and extended list of seven "covered agreements" appeared in these renegotiated PTAs. In addition, a new innovation appeared related to biodiversity in the agreements with Peru and Colombia, and the annex on forest sector governance in the Peru agreement shattered ceilings with respect to the degree of specificity and level of prescription for domestic environmental policy change it required of Peru. Particularly in the context of the strengthened dispute-settlement provisions, these changes mark a massive strengthening of environmental governance through trade agreements.

The new biodiversity article contained in agreements with both Peru and Colombia underscores the importance of conservation and sustainable use of biodiversity in achieving sustainable development, as well as the need to respect and preserve traditional knowledge. Importantly, it also notes the importance of public participation and consultation on these issues. None of this language requires specific action, but it is significant in that it implicitly speaks to controversial issues that combine trade, environment, and intellectual property concerns such as the role of traditional knowledge and ownership of biological diversity. As discussed in chapter 4, it is further notable in that it reflects the objectives of the Convention on Biological Diversity, to which the United States is not even party.

The Peru agreement's Annex on Forest Sector Governance provides for the most specific and prescriptive provisions in any PTA to date (US or otherwise). Rationalized by the recognition that "good forest sector governance is critical to promoting the economic value and sustainable management of forest resources" (para. 1), the annex's eight pages are packed full of provisions that require Peru to make substantial changes to its domestic environmental policies. For example, the annex requires Peru to increase the resources it devotes to enforcement of forestry regulation, increase the weight of penalties brought against those who participate in illegal timber operations, and improve its existing monitoring programs to be more aligned with timber-relevant provisions of CITES. Importantly, all of these provisions are fully enforceable under the PTA's dispute-settlement mechanism. (The annex provisions as related to CITES as well as public participation and effective enforcement are unpacked in more detail in chapters 4 and 5, respectively.)

US bilateral trade negotiations slowed after Trade Promotion Authority (i.e., fast-track authority) lapsed in 2007. It was not restored until 2015 under the Obama administration, with the Bipartisan Congressional Trade Priorities and Accountability Act (TPA-2015). The TPA-2015 largely replicated the environmental guidelines articulated in EO 13141, the Trade Act of 2002 (TPA-2002), and the May 10, 2007, agreement as related to, for example, environmental reviews, effective enforcement/non-derogation, promotion of MEAs, dispute settlement, and covered agreements. However, it also contained an important amendment in the Trade Facilitation and Trade Enforcement Act of 2015 (Public Law 114–125), which did two important things. First, it added new provisions related to the elimination of fisheries subsidies and addressing illegal, unreported, and unregulated (IUU) fishing (Sect. 914 para. (c)). Perhaps more importantly, for the first time in US trade policy, we see a TPA requirement to keep an environmental issue *out* of US trade policy as a condition of "fast-track" authority. Specifically, the amendment prohibits the president from addressing critical aspects of climate change through its trade agreements. The text reads:

> ensure that trade agreements do not establish obligations for the United States regarding greenhouse gas emissions measures, including obligations that require changes to United States laws or regulations or that would affect the implementation of such laws or regulations, other than those fulfilling the other negotiating objectives in this section. (Sect 914 para. (b))

Although it doesn't prohibit the United States from addressing all aspects of climate change through trade agreements, such as adaptation or renewable energy cooperation, this drastically circumscribes the potential of trade agreements to address what many believe is the most important environmental issue of our time.

Only one PTA, the Trans-Pacific Partnership (TPP), was agreed by the time the Obama administration left office in January 2017. Opened for signature on February 4, 2016, the TPP was agreed with 11 other countries: Australia, Brunei, Canada, Chile, Japan, Malaysia, Mexico, New Zealand, Peru, Singapore, and Vietnam. It was never ratified by the United States, however, and President Donald Trump signed an executive order withdrawing the United States from the TPP on his first day in office on January 20, 2017. Although many expected the TPP to die out with the US withdrawal, the remaining 11 countries continued to negotiate the agreement, changing the name to the Comprehensive and Progressive Trans-Pacific Partnership (CPTPP). Leaders of all 11 countries met in Santiago, Chile, to sign the agreement on March 8, 2018.

Although the United States is not a party to the CPTPP and did not participate in the negotiations of that agreement, the 2018 CPTPP text is largely drawn from the 2016 TPP, which the United States did negotiate. As such, it is interesting to note the environmental provisions contained therein as a window into the US trade-environment politics. Using this case as an instructive example, chapter 5 picks up this thread to examine how US environmental norms can continue to influence trade agreements to which the United States is not even a party.

The TPP is quite progressive on environmental provisions in terms of both number of provisions and their specificity. It replicates verbatim in many cases environmental provisions contained in previous US PTAs, including as related to effective enforcement, requirements to implement MEAs such as CITES, public participation, environmental cooperation, and fully enforceable dispute settlement. The last is something that several CPTPP countries adopted for the first time in any PTA. In total, 90 percent of the TPP's (and by extension the CPTPP's) environmental provisions can be found in prior US trade agreements (Morin and Beaumier 2016).

It is worth noting that the CPTPP contains far-reaching and innovative provisions as compared to marine capture fisheries in any PTA to date. These provisions reflect the ongoing WTO discussions on subsidies and IUU fishing. These ongoing WTO negotiations have been fraught and characterized by deep divisions between CPTPP countries, with the United States, New Zealand, Chile, and Peru on the one hand, who have advocated for top-down bans on fish subsidies, and Japan on the other hand, who has long resisted disciplining of fish subsidies at all within the WTO, and more recently has advocated for limited bans on such subsidies only when subsidies can be linked to overfishing and overcapacity (Campling and Havice 2017). It is surprising, therefore, that these countries were able to reach agreement on these issues through regional trade negotiations. Nonetheless, some experts have characterized the final text as reflecting "minimal convergence" on these issues, suggesting the United States wasn't able to meaningfully secure its environmental preferences in this case (Campling and Havice 2017).

On July 17, 2017, the USTR released a set of objectives to guide the renegotiation of NAFTA, including as related to environmental issues (USTR 2017a). These guidelines, and the text that was finally adopted, are very much in line with the most recently agreed US PTAs. For example, USMCA brings environmental provisions into the main text instead of solely as a side agreement, makes all environmental provisions fully enforceable under the PTA's dispute-resolution mechanism, establishes rules to ensure effective enforcement of environmental laws, requires parties to implement MEA obligations, and strengthens mechanisms for public participation. It also incorporates several of the TPP provisions related to fishery subsidies and IUU fishing.

This signals that, despite the Trump administration's paltry reputation on environmental politics, it does not intend to weaken environmental provisions in trade agreements. This can, at least in part, be explained by US laws (e.g., TPA-2015, under which NAFTA was renegotiated), which require many of these environmental provisions as a condition of granting fast-track authority to the president. Although President Trump could attempt to push a trade agreement through Congress in the absence of fast-track authority, it would be a very politically risky move as the agreement would be open to debate and amendment by a starkly divided Congress. Likewise, the movement to incorporate environmental provisions on fish subsides and IUU fishing, which are not required by TPA-2015, are very much in line with US negotiating positions within the WTO on these issues. The TPA-2015 issues must be included in order for Congress to approve the renegotiated agreement in the future.

As summarized in the appendix below, environmental provisions in US trade agreements have gotten stronger over time. Beginning as simple exceptions to trade obligations under specific circumstances, they have evolved into highly prescriptive and fully enforceable provisions that, in some cases, rival the reach of parallel MEAs (see chapter 4). Further, as reflected in the USMCA's environmental provisions and Trump's March 2018 request that Congress extend his fast-track authority, this trend will likely continue until at least 2021, when Trump's renewed fast-track authority will be due to expire.

Conclusions

The United States is clearly a global innovator in linking trade and environmental policies. The environmental provisions in its PTAs have evolved significantly over the years. In 1985, the United States merely restated the environmental exemptions allowed under the GATT; in the 1990s, it began requiring trading partners to implement existing environmental laws and began conducting environmental reviews of all PTAs; and in the 2000s, it began requiring that specific environmental provisions be included in all PTAs, incorporated highly prescriptive forest provisions, and made all environmental provisions fully enforceable through sanction- and penalty-based dispute settlement. The latter was replicated in the more recent agreements (alongside additional innovations, including on fishing issues, plastic pollution, and wildlife trafficking), and reflects an important departure from practice in other countries.

Indeed, US innovations are quite distinct from innovations that have emerged in other countries. Notably, the US brand of trade-environment politics is quite different, and continues to diverge, from the approach taken by the European Union, for example. In addition to their diverging policies as related to dispute settlement, the European Union has been more open to demands from some Latin American countries to include provisions related to the intersection of biodiversity and intellectual property rights. The European Free Trade Association's 2008 agreement with Colombia is the first PTA to include a section within an intellectual property rights chapter on issues related to biodiversity (Vivas-Eugui 2009). These provisions make important inroads toward aligning the intellectual property rights provisions in a PTA with the requirements of the Convention on Biological Diversity and its Nagoya Protocol, by, for example, recognizing sovereign rights over genetic resources and requiring the fulfillment of prior informed consent procedures and its application to traditional knowledge.[7]

Despite important US innovations in this area, there is also ample room for improvement in US trade policy surrounding the environment. For example, in some instances, environmental linkages have been pursued without adequate foresight to potential on-the-ground implications in trading-partner nations. This oversight has been linked to social unrest in at least one case, pointing to a need for more attention to the implications of templating highly prescriptive provisions from one PTA to the next, as well as providing for short implementation periods, as was the case with the US-Peru PTA.

The United States has also missed opportunities to use trade agreements to address low-hanging fruit in areas such as climate change (Morin and Jinnah 2018). Clear linkages exist between climate change and various trade issues, including border tax adjustments on carbon, emissions trading, and fossil-fuel subsidies. Although some countries, such as the European Union, have been highly innovative in including climate provisions in their agreements (Jinnah and Morgera 2013), their contribution to climate governance has been limited because they remain weakly "legalized," fail to replicate broadly in the global trade system, and have not been adopted by the largest greenhouse gas emitters (Morin and Jinnah 2018). These linkages are minimal, however many opportunities remain both globally and in the United States in particular. Given the ambitious targets included in the 2015 Paris Agreement on climate change, this is an important area where trade policy could make a critical contribution to the public good and is therefore an area that the United States (and other countries) should move into.

Appendix: Environmental Provisions in US Preferential Trade Agreements

Distribution of Environmental Provisions in US Agreements (1985–2018)

Agreement[a]	Year of signature	Preamble	Affirmation of state sovereignty						Domestic levels of protection			Enforcement of domestic measures			Public participation				Transparency					Improvement of environmental performance			
		1	2	3	4	5	6	7	8	9	10	11	12	13	14	15	16	17	18	19	20	21	22	23	24	25	26
Israel	1985	•																									
NAFTA	1992	•	•						•	•	•	•		•	•	•		•	•		•			•	•		•
Jordan	2000		•		•			•	•	•	•	•	•		•	•		•						•			
Vietnam	2000								•	•	•	•	•		•	•											
Singapore	2003	•	•						•	•	•	•			•	•			•	•	•			•			•
Chile	2003	•	•			•		•	•	•	•	•			•	•	•	•	•	•	•	•	•	•	•	•	•
Australia	2004	•			•	•		•	•	•	•	•		•	•	•	•	•	•	•	•	•		•	•	•	•
CAFTA-DR	2004	•			•				•	•	•	•		•	•	•	•	•	•	•	•	•	•	•	•	•	•
Morocco	2004	•			•				•	•	•	•			•	•	•	•	•	•	•	•		•	•	•	•
Bahrain	2004	•			•				•	•	•	•			•	•	•	•	•	•	•	•		•	•	•	•
Peru	2006	•		•	•			•	•	•	•	•	•	•	•	•	•	•	•	•	•	•	•	•	•	•	•
Colombia	2006	•		•	•			•	•	•	•	•	•	•	•	•	•	•	•	•	•	•	•	•	•	•	•
Oman	2006	•			•				•	•	•	•			•	•	•	•	•	•	•	•		•	•	•	•
Korea	2007	•			•			•	•	•	•	•	•	•	•	•	•	•	•	•	•	•	•	•	•	•	•
Panama	2007	•			•			•	•	•	•	•	•	•	•	•	•	•	•	•	•	•	•	•	•	•	•
TPP	2016	•			•				•	•	•	•	•	•	•	•	•	•	•	•	•	•	•	•	•	•	•
USMCA	2018	•			•				•	•	•	•	•	•	•	•	•	•	•	•	•	•	•	•	•	•	•

1. Preamble
2. Sovereignty over natural resources
3. Regulatory sovereignty
4. Sovereignty or independence of national tribunals in application of environmental measures
5. No extraterritorial enforcement activities
6. No right of action under a party's domestic law
7. Recognition of a development gap or different capabilities
8. Inappropriate to encourage trade or investment by relaxing environmental measures
9. Strengthen levels of protection
10. Definition of environmental law
11. Enforcement of domestic measures (binding or nonbinding)
12. Cooperation on enforcement
13. Factual report on enforcement
14. Public participation in the adoption of environmental measures
15. Public participation in the implementation of the agreement
16. Direct contact between non-state actors of both parties
17. Education and public awareness
18. Publication of environmental laws
19. Communication with public on actions taken under the agreement
20. Communicate decisions of joint institutions
21. Make available communications received from the public
22. Public sessions of joint institutions
23. Promotion of voluntary measures
24. Promotion of economic instruments
25. Encourage production of environmental goods or services
26. Encourage trade in environmental goods or services

		Implementation of the agreement					Cooperation								Technical assistance					Coherence with non-environmental issues									
Agreement	Year of signature	27	28	29	30	31	32	33	34	35	36	37	38	39	40	41	42	43	44	45	46	47	48	49	50	51	52	53	54
Israel	1985																												
NAFTA	1992	•	•																										
Jordan	2000					•					•						•												
Vietnam	2000					•					•						•												
Singapore	2003			•			•		•			•	•	•	•														
Chile	2003			•			•	•	•	•	•		•	•	•	•				•	•	•			•	•			
Australia	2004				•		•	•	•	•	•		•	•	•						•	•			•	•			
CAFTA-DR	2004			•			•	•	•	•	•	•	•	•	•	•	•			•	•	•						•	
Morocco	2004			•			•	•	•	•	•	•	•	•	•	•	•												
Bahrain	2004			•			•	•	•	•	•	•	•	•	•														
Peru	2006			•		•	•	•	•	•	•	•	•	•	•	•	•				•	•					•		
Colombia	2006			•	•		•	•	•	•	•	•	•	•	•	•	•				•	•					•		
Oman	2006			•	•	•	•	•	•	•	•	•	•	•	•	•	•							•					
Korea	2007			•		•	•	•	•	•	•	•	•	•	•	•	•		•	•	•	•	•		•	•	•	•	•
Panama	2007			•	•		•	•	•	•	•	•	•	•	•	•	•		•	•	•	•			•	•	•	•	•
TPP	2016			•			•	•	•	•	•	•	•	•	•	•	•		•	•	•	•			•	•	•	•	•
USMCA	2018		•				•	•	•	•	•	•	•	•	•	•	•		•	•	•	•	•		•	•	•	•	•

27. Individual monitoring of the environment
28. Individual environmental assessment
29. Funding of cooperation activities
30. Each party must fund its own implementation of the agreement
31. Environmental impact assessment of the agreement
32. Joint scientific research
33. Joint environment assessments and studies
34. Exchange of information
35. Communication when taking environmental protection measures
36. Communication between customs authorities
37. Harmonization of environmental measures
38. Cooperation in negotiation of future agreements
39. Vague commitment to cooperate
40. Technical assistance to a party
41. Technical assistance to non-state actors
42. Technology transfer
43. Funding of technical assistance
44. Emergency assistance in case of natural disaster
45. Mutual supportiveness between environment, trade, and development
46. Coherence with domestic trade or investment policies
47. Interaction with energy policies
48. Interaction with mining policies
49. Interaction with tourism policies
50. Interaction with social policies
51. Interaction with urban development policies
52. Interaction with agriculture policies
53. Interaction with traditional knowledge policies
54. Interaction with human health policies

		Specific environmental issues																										
Agreement	Year of signature	55	56	57	58	59	60	61	62	63	64	65	66	67	68	69	70	71	72	73	74	75	76	77	78	79	80	81
Israel	1985	•																										
NAFTA	1992		•				•																					
Jordan	2000	•				•																					•	
Vietnam	2000																											
Singapore	2003										•																	
Chile	2003									•	•																	
Australia	2004		•					•			•	•					•	•			•	•		•			•	•
CAFTA-DR	2004			•			•					•	•				•	•			•						•	
Morocco	2004						•		•						•	•	•									•		
Bahrain	2004		•		•				•		•			•	•			•	•				•					
Peru	2006					•		•		•	•			•		•	•	•		•								
Colombia	2006			•					•		•		•	•	•		•	•	•	•			•	•			•	•
Oman	2006				•						•	•	•		•		•	•	•	•	•						•	•
Korea	2007			•				•			•		•	•	•		•	•		•			•	•	•	•	•	•
Panama	2007										•		•	•	•		•	•		•							•	•
TPP	2016		•						•	•	•	•			•		•	•		•				•	•	•	•	•
USMCA	2018		•				•		•	•	•	•			•		•	•	•	•		•		•	•	•	•	•

55. Coral reefs
56. Seas and oceans
57. Coastal areas
58. Aquifers, ground water
59. Water efficiency
60. Water pollution and other water issues
61. Wetlands
62. Fisheries
63. Forests
64. Endangered species and their illegal trade
65. Whales and seals
66. Migratory species
67. Invasive species
68. Shared species
69. Genetic resources
70. Protected areas
71. Biodiversity (general)
72. Renewable energy
73. Energy efficiency
74. Climate change
75. Ozone layer
76. Air pollution
77. Vehicle emission standards
78. Oil spills
79. Other natural disasters
80. Hazardous waste
81. Pesticides and chemicals

Agreement	Year of signature	Limits to environmental measures	Environmental exceptions											Dispute settlement													
		82	83	84	85	86	87	88	89	90	91	92	93	94	95	96	97	98	99	100	101	102	103	104	105	106
Israel	1985		•																							
NAFTA	1992		•	•	•			•			•			•	•		•		•	•	•	•	•	•		
Jordan	2000		•	•	•																					
Vietnam	2000		•	•	•			•						•												
Singapore	2003		•	•	•			•	•	•	•			•	•		•		•	•	•	•	•			
Chile	2003	•	•	•	•			•	•	•	•			•	•		•	•	•	•	•	•	•	•		
Australia	2004		•	•	•			•	•	•	•			•	•				•	•	•	•	•	•		
CAFTA-DR	2004		•	•	•			•	•	•	•			•	•		•		•	•	•	•	•	•		
Morocco	2004		•	•	•			•	•	•	•			•	•		•	•	•	•	•	•	•	•		
Bahrain	2004		•	•	•			•	•	•	•			•	•				•	•	•	•	•	•		
Peru	2006		•	•	•			•	•	•	•	•		•	•	•	•		•	•	•	•	•	•	•	
Colombia	2006		•	•	•	•	•	•	•	•	•	•		•	•	•	•		•	•	•	•	•	•	•	
Oman	2006		•	•	•			•	•	•	•			•	•				•	•	•	•	•	•		
Korea	2007	•	•	•	•			•	•	•	•			•	•		•		•	•	•	•	•	•	•	
Panama	2007		•	•	•			•	•	•	•			•	•		•		•	•	•	•	•	•	•	
TPP	2016	•	•	•	•			•	•	•	•			•	•		•		•	•	•	•	•	•	•	•
USMCA	2018	•	•	•	•			•	•	•	•			•	•		•		•	•	•	•	•	•	•	•

82. Environmental measures not to be used for protectionist purposes
83. Trade in goods: necessary to protect animal, human or plant life or health
84. Trade in goods: conservation of natural resources
85. Trade in services: measures to protect animal, human, or plant life or health
86. Trade in services: conservation of natural resources
87. Trade in services: environmental protection
88. Technical Barriers to Trade (TBT): all exceptions for environmental purposes
89. Sanitary and Phytosanitary (SPS): all exceptions for environmental purposes
90. Investment: general exception
91. Investment: specific on establishment
92. Investment: specific on performance requirements
93. Investment: specific on expropriation
94. Intellectual property: all exceptions for environmental purposes
95. Procurement: all exceptions for environmental purposes
96. Subsidies: all exception for environmental purposes
97. Private access to remedies, procedural guarantees, and appropriate sanctions
98. Commitment to consider alleged violation brought by citizen of a party
99. Commitment to consider alleged violation brought by foreigner
100. Environmental experts as panelists
101. Environmental experts to be consulted by panel
102. Failure to enforce domestic laws: non-jurisdictional mechanism
103. Failure to enforce domestic laws: suspension of benefits
104. Non-compliance with environmental provisions: non-jurisdictional mechanism
105. Non-compliance with environmental provisions: general dispute-settlement mechanism (DSM) procedures applicable
106. Non-compliance with environmental provisions: suspension of benefits

50 Chapter 2

		Joint institutions			Relationship with environmental agreements																			
Agreement	Year of signature	107	108	109	110	111	112	113	114	115	116	117	118	119	120	121	122	123	124	125	126	127	128	129	130
Israel	1985																					•			
NAFTA	1992		•					•			•			•							•	•	•		•
Jordan	2000		•																						
Vietnam	2000																								
Singapore	2003		•		•	•															•		•		•
Chile	2003		•		•	•				•											•		•		•
Australia	2004		•																						
CAFTA-DR	2004		•	•	•	•																	•		•
Morocco	2004		•		•	•																	•		•
Bahrain	2004		•		•	•																	•		•
Peru	2006		•		•	•	•	•	•	•	•	•	•	•	•	•	•	•	•	•	•	•	•	•	•
Colombia	2006		•		•	•	•	•	•	•	•	•	•	•	•	•	•	•	•	•	•	•	•	•	•
Oman	2006		•		•	•																	•		•
Korea	2007		•		•	•	•	•	•	•	•	•	•		•	•	•	•	•		•	•	•	•	•
Panama	2007		•		•	•	•	•	•	•	•	•	•	•	•	•	•	•	•	•	•	•	•	•	•
TPP	2016		•		•	•	•	•		•		•									•		•		•
USMCA	2018		•		•	•	•	•	•	•	•	•	•								•		•		•

107. National contact point
108. Intergovernmental committee or similar structure
109. International secretariat or similar structure
110. Use of MEA DSM
111. Defer to or consult relevant MEA entity in DSM
112. International standards presumed to be in conformity with free trade agreement obligations
113. CITES: implementation
114. CITES: prevalence
115. Montreal Protocol: implementation
116. Montreal Protocol: prevalence
117. Convention for the Prevention of Pollution from Ships (MARPOL): implementation
118. Convention for the Prevention of Pollution from Ships (MARPOL): prevalence
119. Basel Convention: prevalence
120. Ramsar Convention on Wetlands: implementation
121. Ramsar Convention on Wetlands: prevalence
122. Convention for the Conservation of Antarctic Marine Living Resources (CCAMLR): implementation
123. Ramsar Convention on Wetlands: prevalence
124. Whaling Convention: implementation
125. Whaling Convention: prevalence
126. Stockholm Declaration: implementation
127. Rio Declaration: implementation
128. Implementation of international agreements to which they are party (general)
129. Prevalence of international agreements to which they are party (general)
130. Other reference to international agreements to which they are party (general)

[a] The agreements also include the content of their associated environmental cooperation agreement, if applicable.

3 Why Link Trade and Environmental Politics?

The Politics of Institutional Linkages

The incorporation of environmental provisions into trade agreements is a classic example of linkage politics. At its core, the politics of institution linkages seeks to understand how, why, and with what implications different areas of international law and politics intersect and interact with one another. Linkage politics explores such questions as: under what conditions does cooperation among biodiversity treaties on species of common concern yield better conservation outcomes? How do the chemicals treaties streamline their workflow to more efficiently manage resources? How are human rights norms folded into climate change law? Who defines these linkages, and with what implications? How transferable are these lessons between regimes and across policy areas? This book is centrally concerned with how, why, and with what implications states link trade and environmental politics by incorporating environmental provisions into preferential trade agreements (PTAs).

Studying the politics of institutional linkages can help us to better understand myriad dynamics in global governance. This includes how connections between international institutions can enhance regime effectiveness, divert funding in new directions, transfer authority from one site to another, and impact issues of equity and accountability in global politics. There are many examples of this in the literature. In our own previous work, for example, we have argued that despite a plethora of institutional linkages, trade agreements fall short of making any meaningful contribution to climate politics, largely because climate provisions in trade agreements are weakly legalized (Morin and Jinnah 2018). Jinnah has also argued that linkage politics between trade and environmental issues at the WTO have, in some instances, entrenched existing power dynamics in ways that disadvantage developing-country interests (Jinnah 2014). Morin has shown that developing countries have strategically linked environmental issues to intellectual property in order to create broader coalitions at the World Intellectual Property Organization (Morin 2008, 2014).

Many others have navigated the politics of institutional linkages as well. Tana Johnson (2015), for example, has explored how specific types of trade-environment linkages at the WTO emerged in the first place, arguing that some can be traced back to political pressures faced by governments in the late 1980s and early 1990s. Kati Kulovesi (2011) has explored how environmental issues have challenged the legitimacy of the WTO's dispute-settlement process, and Dan Esty (2002) has proposed solutions to the WTO's "legitimacy crisis" through more links with broader publics and more sensitivity to environmental issues.

Scholars of international law have made many other important contributions to our understanding of linkage politics within the trade-environment realm. Riccardo Pavoni (2010), for example, has demonstrated how the international legal principle of "mutual supportiveness" has been used to address tensions between the WTO and many other linked issues, including health, cultural diversity, and environment. Mark Axelrod (2011a) has made similar arguments related to the use of "savings clauses" in international law, and Steve Charnovitz (2002b) has outlined an analytical framework for considering which issues should be linked to the WTO at all.

Linkage politics is by no means limited to the trade-environment realm, however. Environmental politics is rich with examples of states creating mechanisms to link different treaty regimes in order to pursue specific objectives. Henrik Selin (2010), for example, has illuminated how linkages between multilateral chemicals treaties have created opportunities to diffuse policies and build coalitions across treaty regimes. Michele Betsill and colleagues (2015) have argued for developing more productive linkages across the global climate regime in order to enhance outcomes, such as increased emissions reductions and finance. Mark Axelrod (2011b) has demonstrated how regional fisheries management organizations use linkages to climate change to distract from other regime priorities. Similarly, in previous work, Jinnah (2014) has analyzed how secretariats of international biodiversity treaties have created institutional linkages to climate change in order to open up additional funding streams for biodiversity governance. There are countless more examples. The field is rich.

Linkage politics also extends beyond the environmental arena. Vinod Aggarwal and Kristi Govella (2013), for example, have showcased the politics of linkages between the various trade and security regimes. Unni Gopinathan and colleagues (2018) have uncovered contrasting rationales for why multilateral development and trade organizations choose to link their agendas to global health. Christina Davis (2004) has shown that institutional linkages between trade and agriculture have counteracted domestic obstacles to policy reforms, while Morin (2008; 2014) has argued that similar linkages between patent law and public health have created new obstacles for domestic reforms.

Linkage politics, therefore, provides a rich theoretical backdrop to help us better understand this book's empirical analyses of trade-environment linkages in US trade agreements. Centrally, this theoretical literature can help to illuminate not only how, but, importantly, *why* states might choose to link environmental and trade issues in the first place. This question of why states would do this is of central interest to this book. We therefore spend some time here exploring how the literature answers the question: why link trade and environmental issues? We then evaluate these rationales alongside our own new empirical interview data, wherein we asked key informants in the design of US trade policy why they chose the specific environmental linkages that we currently see in US trade agreements, how those decisions were made and by whom, and with what lessons going forward.

The remainder of the chapter is organized as follows. The next section surveys the literature on linkage politics. We briefly outline high-level typologies that have built a foundation for subsequent analyses of linkage politics before detailing some key contributions from the more specific literature on "why link?" in the first place. The second half of the chapter turns to the empirical question of how and why the US government selected certain issues for inclusion in its PTA. We conclude with an assessment of how the "why link?" literature comports with and diverges from our own empirical data on the topic in the US case.

Typologies of Linkage in Environmental Politics

Scholars use the terms "linkage," "overlap," "interplay," and "interaction" in slightly different ways to analyze and explain how different areas of international law and politics intersect and interact with one another. In differentiating between overlap and linkage, Oran Young defines linkage as resulting from "self-conscious" decision making, whereas overlap results from "unreflective" decisions (2002). He underscores, however, that even if overlap between regimes is incidental, it can also lead to interaction, or interplay, between them. He adds that "conscious efforts to make use of interplay to promote both cooperative and competitive ends constitute a domain of activities that can be thought of as the 'politics of institutional linkages'" (Young, 2002). Kristin Rosendal offers a complementary explanation, which inserts linkage as a necessary step between overlap and interplay (2001b). This book is interested in how and why the US government consciously creates such linkages between trade and environmental policies in order to promote particular environmental outcomes.

In his classic intervention, which catalyzed discussion of this topic, Ernst Haas (1980) outlines three rationales for linking issues in international regimes. He identifies tactical linkages, which are used to obtain bargaining leverage; linkages that are developed to maintain the cohesion of coalitions; and substantive linkages, which are based on consensual knowledge linked to an agreed social goal. Importantly, Haas stresses that power relations underlie all decisions to link issues within regimes.

The early 2000s saw an explosion of literature that typologizes institutional linkages, overlap, and interplay, with no fewer than 16 separate categories identified by core contributors to this discussion (e.g., Young 1996, 2002; Stokke 2000, 2001; Rosendal 2001a, 2001b; Selin and VanDeveer 2003). The typological landscape is dense and not worth navigating in detail here. Rather, this section briefly reviews those categories of "self-conscious" linkages, which characterize the majority of trade-environment linkages we explore in this book.

Young defines two forms of temporal linkages: formative and operational (2002). Formative links are those that occur during the formation, or reformation, of a regime. Operational links are involved in the day-to-day operation of a regime (Young 2002). Both are at play in this book. For example, provisions built directly into PTAs are formative, whereas environmental cooperation activities developed on the basis of PTAs' environmental cooperation agreements are operational in nature.

Olav Stokke's (2001) differentiation between utilitarian and ideational linkages is also relevant here. Whereas the former are largely aimed at cost reductions, the latter aim to draw political attention to the problems addressed in another regime. Ideational links are most visible in US PTAs within the Forest Annex to the US-Peru PTA, which draws significant attention to the Convention on International Trade in Endangered Species of Wild Fauna and Flora (CITES). Stokke's category of normative interplay refers to the "extent to which the legality or legitimacy of rules and institutions is confirmed or lessened by their level of coherence with other rules" (2000, 227). We see this in, for example, NAFTA's list of "covered [environmental] agreements," which are protected from challenge in the event of legal conflict with the trade agreement. Finally, Stokke's categories of diffusion and political spillover linkages are central to the various processes we discuss in chapters 4–6. Diffusion linkages occur when a regime emulates the substantive or operational solutions and principles contained in other regimes. We see these most prominently in the discussions in chapters 4 and 6 about how US environmental provisions diffuse into trading-partner domestic law and third-party PTAs, respectively. Political spillover linkages, wherein "actor interests and capabilities associated with one regime significantly shape the operation or impacts of another" (Stokke 2000, 226), are most visible in chapter 4's analysis of how the CITES provisions were deeply entrenched within the US-Peru PTA.

Henrik Selin and Stacy VanDeveer (2003) offer some additional analytical leverage in their designation of functional linkages (following Young and others) as well as political ones, wherein "content and design of one regime . . . affect the formation of or operation of another" (19). Again, we see these political linkages most clearly in the CITES linkages in the US-Peru PTA, which build CITES implementation directly into the agreement. Importantly, Selin and VanDeveer (2003) argue that actor linkages—those that are agent-based—can play a critical role in driving the outcomes of political linkages. In other words, who is doing the linking matters to what the linkages look like. We illuminate this in the second half of this chapter, wherein we discuss how nongovernmental organizations (NGOs) and US interests in multilateral environmental agreements (MEAs) shaped the development of critical environmental linkages in US trade policy.

Another important contribution from Oberthür and Ghering (2006) outlines an analytical framework for analyzing interactions between regimes. They identify several causal mechanisms that allow us to better assess the cause-and-effect relationships between "source" and "target" regimes. Specifically, they argue that all cases of institutional interaction can be understood as either influencing the decision-making process of a target regime (via cognitive or commitment interaction), or by affecting the target's implementation and effectiveness (via behavioral/outcome interaction and impact-level interaction).

Finally, much more recently, Betsill and colleagues (2015) outlined a very useful typology of motivations for creating institutional linkages. They propose two basic rationales: those related to division of labor, and those related to catalyzing action. These overlay well onto Young's prior, more static formative and operational linkages, but go further in assigning agency to understand motivations for creating these connections in the first place. Division of labor linkages, which have been the primary focus of the institutional interplay/interaction literature, are largely related to questions of efficiency or competition avoidance. These linkages are akin to Stokke's (2001) utilitarian linkages described above. Such linkages that aim to divide labor more efficiently might, for example, assign specific functions to specific institutions so as to avoid duplication of effort on overlapping areas of interest, or to decrease incentives for forum shopping. This might be the case when PTAs give preference to MEAs in the case of legal conflict. Such linkages are uncommon among environmental provisions in US PTAs. Similar to the division of labor argument, some scholars argue that trade-environment linkages are meant to "harmonize" issue areas by eliminating competing policies (Arda 2000).

Betsill and colleagues' (2015) second rationale is to catalyze action. These linkages aim to enable specific actions to achieve specific regime goals. For Betsill and colleagues (2015), these are things like coordination between carbon markets and private actors to enhance greenhouse gas reductions. In US trade agreements, environmental linkages that seek to catalyze action in trading-partner nations are prolific. These aim to enforce domestic environmental laws, implement MEAs, create mechanisms for public participation in environmental decision making, and more.

Table 3.1
Types of Trade-Environment Linkages in US Preferential Trade Agreements

Linkage Type	Explanation	Examples from US trade agreements
Formative	Occurs in the formation or reformation of a regime.	Decision to complement NAFTA with a side agreement on the environment
Operational	Related to the day-to-day operations of a regime.	Citizen submissions process under NAFTA
Utilitarian/Division of Labor	Reduces costs	Selected MEAs should prevail over the PTA in case of legal incompatibility
Ideational	Draws political attention to problems addressed in another regime	Reference to the moratorium on whaling
Diffusion	Occurs when a regime emulates solutions or principles from another regime	Third-party nations incorporating US PTA environmental provisions
Political Spillover	Occurs when activities in one regime affect those of another	Specific measures related to CITES implementation in US-Peru PTA
Normative	Addresses coherency with other regimes to affect legitimacy	Requirement to implement a list of MEAs
Actor	Agent-based linkages across institutions	CITES secretariat participation in implementation of Peru FTA and CITES
Catalytic	Enables actions to achieve regime goals	Requirements to enforce domestic environmental laws under several US PTAs

Why Link Trade and Environmental Issues?

Several authors have explored the question of why governments choose to link environmental issues to trade agreements. As Morin, Dür, and Lechner (2018) have previously distilled, three explanations are particularly prolific in the literature: domestic pressure from environmental groups, protectionist interests, and low compliance costs for environmental provisions.

On the former, domestic pressures from environmental groups are thought to be important because, in most countries—developed and developing—a large proportion of citizens consider the benefits of environmental protection to be well worth the costs (Bättig and Bernauer 2009; Bernauer and Nguyen 2015). Several scholars have highlighted the role played by NGOs, trade unions, and businesses in lobbying governments for particular types of linkages and for shifts from past practice in such linkages (e.g., Johnson 2015; Lechner 2016). This role is well established empirically in the case of NAFTA, wherein the National Wildlife Federation, the Natural Resources Defense Council, and the World Wildlife Fund were instrumental in shaping NAFTA's environmental side agreement (Gallagher 2004; Strange 2015).

Figure 3.1 makes this point clear. Each point represents a different country. The countries are distributed on the x-axis based on their level of democracy according to the Polity IV database of 2016. They range from the most autocratic on the left-hand side to the more democratic on the right-hand side. Countries are also distributed on the y-axis based on the

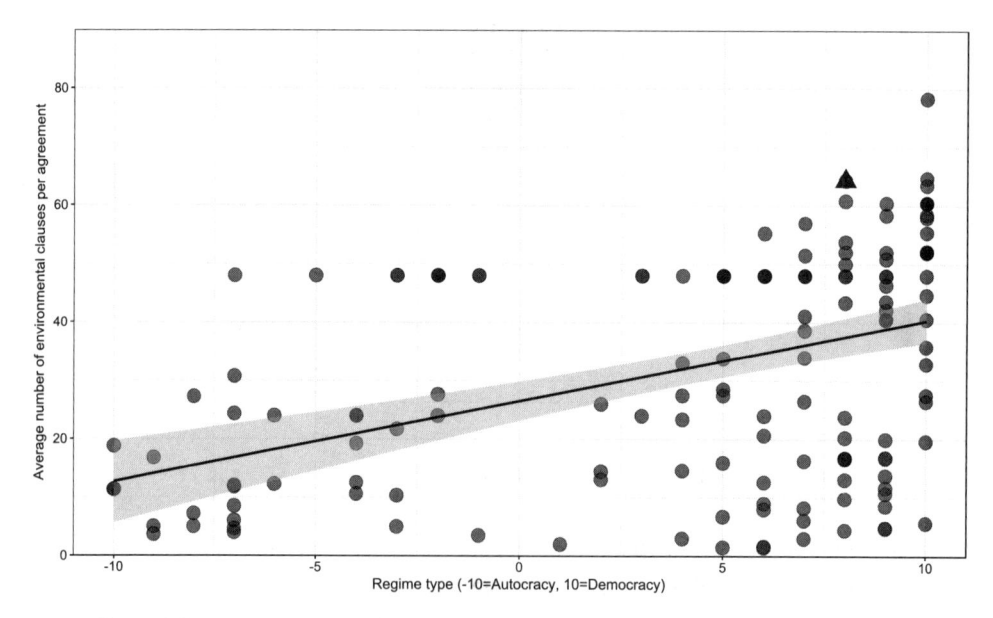

Figure 3.1
Relation between level of democracy and average number of environmental clauses in PTAs concluded since 2000

average number of environmental provisions in the PTAs concluded since 2000, as documented by the TREND database. The correlation between these two variables is 0.435. The United States, represented as a triangle, appears as one of the most democratic countries, and one with the highest average number of environmental provisions per PTA.

Protectionist interests or, put more generously, a desire to level the playing field, are also commonly lodged as an explanation for the inclusion of environmental provisions in trade agreements (Bhagwati 1995b; Subramanian 1992; Lechner 2016). The basic argument is that firms based in countries with higher levels of environmental protection bear higher costs of production than do firms based in countries with lower levels of environmental protection. In requiring trading partners to raise their levels of environmental protection, costs associated with this disparity are reduced. This disparity, and thus the desire to ameliorate it, is higher between developed and developing countries where trade has more significant distributional effects between trading partners. For example, in an analysis of WTO, NAFTA, and EU environmental negotiations, Steinberg (1997) argues that rich "green" states drive trade-environment linkages in order to force developing countries to accept higher environmental standards and greener rules. The premise of the latter has been challenged recently by scholars who highlight that developing countries also have strong interests in incorporating environmental provisions into trade agreements, though their priorities may be quite different (Bernauer and Nguyen 2015).

Compliance costs are an important theme in the literature for explaining why states incorporate environmental provisions into trade agreements. For example, pre-existing environmental provisions in trade agreements can greatly decrease the cost of incorporating such linkages in future agreements (Milewicz et al. 2016). Unsurprisingly, perhaps, once a country has implemented an environmental provision, the cost of replicating that provision in future agreements is low. Similarly, it is less costly for countries with stringent domestic environmental laws to incorporate such provisions in their trade agreements, perhaps in part with the intention of diffusing such environmental commitments to other countries (Jinnah and Lindsay 2016). This latter motivation may overlap with protectionist explanations as well, depending on the nature of the environmental provision being included. Several scholars have also highlighted the reputational, or "audience costs," of diverging from environmental provisions in trade agreements once a country has included such provisions in previous agreements (Lechner 2016; Milewicz et al. 2016). Pulling these three core explanations together, Morin, Dür, and Lechner (2018) have demonstrated, using the TREND database, that democracies, countries that face import competition, and those that care most about the environment have been more likely to incorporate environmental provisions into their trade agreements. Complementing these central explanatory threads in the trade-environment literature are several important case studies that also offer instructive explanations for why states link policies across institutions. Jinnah's (2011) prior analysis of the US-Peru PTA has argued that states may choose to link institutions as a way to transfer regulatory authority from an agreement with weaker enforcement mechanisms (environmental) to one with stronger enforcement mechanisms (trade). Furthermore, Poletti and Sicurelli's (2015) analysis of the inclusion of provisions relating to biofuels in the EU-Malaysia PTA argues that states may choose to export environmental standards as a means to achieve immunity from legal challenges.

The broader literature on environmental linkages offers several additional insights that might be relevant to trade-environment linkages specifically. Axelrod's (2011b) examination of regional fisheries management organizations, for example, argues that countries create linkages to high-profile issues, such as climate change, as a way to divert attention from more contentious regime priorities. In their assessment of why states choose to integrate policy areas, Johnson and Urpelainen (2012) provide a somewhat different perspective. Looking across policy fields within environmental governance (e.g., ozone-climate, forest-climate), they theorize that linkages that enhance positive spillovers are less likely to be pursued than those that mitigate negative ones. In other words, they argue that states are more likely to link policy areas, such as trade and environment, not to capitalize on synergies, but rather when cooperation in one area undermines cooperation in another area.

Finally, although these contributions are far more scarce, there are also some important insights into how states choose to link one type of environmental policy over another within trade agreements. Morin and Rochette (2017) have demonstrated, for example, how countries' policy linkages converge over time as they learn from one another. Lechner (2016) has shown how particular domestic characteristics can trigger lobbying for specific environmental provisions, and Blümer and colleagues (n.d.) argue that states choose provisions that preserve regulatory sovereignty and, to a lesser extent, to level the playing field to pursue other interests. There is far more theoretical work to be done in this area. The next section begins to unpack some possible hypotheses on this question by looking empirically at why the United States chose certain environmental issues to link to its own trade agreements.

How and Why Does the United States Link Trade and Environmental Issues?

Many environmental provisions contained in US PTAs are defined by existing law and policy. For example, the 2002 Trade Act required the United States to include specific environmental policies in its PTAs (e.g., as related to effective enforcement). However, there are also many provisions that go beyond what is mandated through law, and domestic law only provides a general framework for provisions that are framed and fleshed out in far more detail in US PTAs. In order to better understand the processes that shape how the United States selects and frames particular environmental policies in its trade agreements, we conducted 14 interviews with key informants who have been active in the design, negotiation, and/or implementation of the environmental provisions in US trade agreements. Depending on where interviewees were based, interviews were either conducted over the phone or in person in Washington, DC, between October 2017 and June 2018. All interviews were conducted on the condition of anonymity, with various members of the US government, representatives from environmental NGOs, and government representatives from trading-partner nations. Centrally, interviewees were asked to explain the process by which specific environmental provisions were selected for inclusion in US trade agreements.

Importantly, all of the US government officials we interviewed highlighted the interagency process through which environmental provisions are internally identified and developed in US trade agreements. Specifically, the US Trade Representative (USTR) facilitates two interagency processes, the Trade Policy Review Group and the Trade Policy Staff Committee, both of which were established under the 1962 Trade Expansion Act. Through these two groups, 20 US government agencies must consult and agree on all policy papers and negotiating documents related to US trade agreements, including those related to environmental provisions. A recent example of a policy document that was agreed by this group is the official negotiating objectives for the United States, Mexico, and Canada Trade Agreement (USMCA), including its environmental provisions (USTR 2017a). Given the inclusion of environmental issues in these documents, the Trade Policy Review Group and Staff Committee include several executive agencies that work actively on environmental issues, including the Council on Environmental Quality, the State Department, the Department of the Interior, the Department of Energy, and the EPA.

Several interviewees highlighted that, although USTR leads the process and typically plays a more central role identifying specific issues for inclusion, interviewees generally felt well consulted on environmental issues that were of relevance to their respective agencies. One interviewee noted that the interagency process works on the basis of "effective consensus," with economic departments driving the conversation and big decisions, but with input from specialized agencies on environmental issues. Another said that the interagency process is "both formal and informal. The informal process queues up the issues before taking it into the formal process" in order to make consensus more likely. In describing the consultative role, one interviewee highlighted concerns in his/her agency about including CITES in US trade agreements, fearing that USTR was not the right agency to play such a central role in CITES implementation. Although these concerns were not heeded—CITES features prominently in several US trade agreements—this interviewee did report that USTR has taken its implementation role quite seriously and has consulted heavily with those agencies that are better positioned to guide CITES implementation.

Figure 3.2 shows that countries link trade negotiations to different environmental issues. Based on the TREND database, this radar chart indicates the percentage of PTAs signed since 1990 that included provisions on nine different environmental issues. All US trade agreements address endangered species and other biodiversity issues, in contrast to less than 50 percent for US partners and less than 25 percent for other countries. However, US agreements rarely address climate change, the ozone layer, and desertification. As detailed below, this is due to a range of factors, including pressure from domestic interest groups; which MEAs the United States has long

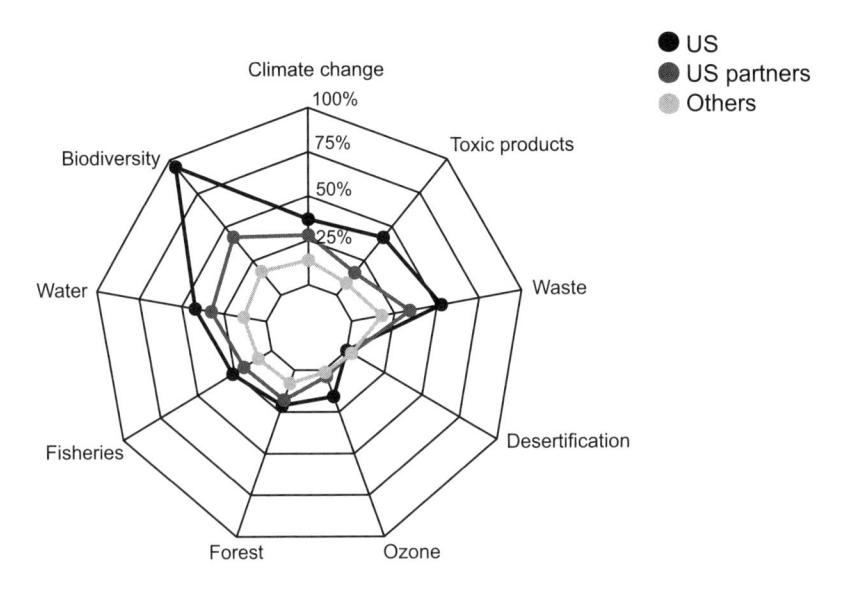

Figure 3.2
Linkages with specific issue areas in PTAs signed since 1990

been party to; the structure of domestic environmental legislation; and the constraints of domestic trade policy, especially trade promotion authority, which has explicitly prohibited the United States from addressing greenhouse gas emissions in trade agreements since 2015.

Complementing this interagency process is a patchwork of ad hoc and more formalized mechanisms for consultation with NGOs and other nonstate actors. These consultations reflect what Morin, Dür, and Lechner (2018) identify in the literature as domestic pressures on linkage politics. Central to the formalized NGO process is the Trade and Environment Policy Advisory Committee (TEPAC). TEPAC is an advisory body to USTR on environmental issues. It consists of no more than 35 members (currently only 13) from environmental interest groups, industry, agriculture, academia, NGOs, and others with expertise in trade and environment matters. The current 13 TEPAC members hail primarily from environmental groups: the Environmental Investigation Agency; Humane Society International; University of California Santa Barbara; the Nature Conservancy; the Peterson Institute for International Economics; the National Foreign Trade Council; the Environmental Defense Fund; Conservation International; the International Fund for Animal Welfare; Venable, Baetjer, Howard, and Civiletti (a law firm); World Animal Protection; Oceana; and the International Woods Products Association.

In describing how TEPAC is consulted, one US government representative highlighted TEPAC's role in providing feedback on draft agendas for Environmental Affairs Council meetings under various PTAs, as well as on a timber-shipment verification mission to Peru. While many interviewees stressed the critical role of TEPAC in incorporating diverse stakeholders into, for example, agenda formation, one NGO representative stressed that the constitution of TEPAC needs to be rethought to ensure the right constellation of voices with the most relevant expertise are included.

NGO involvement is also informal and ad hoc. Interviewees highlighted that key NGOs with known expertise in specific environmental issues are consulted in a similar way to TEPAC, but more informally. Perhaps most importantly, several interviewees noted that some NGOs, such as the Natural Resources Defense Council (NRDC), the Sierra Club, Friends of the Earth, and the Environmental Investigation Agency (EIA) have "had the ear" of key staffers on the US Congress House Ways and Means Committee at important points in time, which has been instrumental in driving forward some specific environmental provisions. For example, several US government representatives highlighted the key role of the EIA in drafting the Forest Annex of the US-Peru PTA, which remains the most far-reaching environmental provision in any trade agreement globally.[1]

Similarly, one NGO representative reported that in the process of consulting NGOs on the Forest Annex, Hill staffers asked NRDC what they should do to make the PTA more "environmentally friendly." According to this interviewee, NRDC had an established program working on forest issues, and it was NRDC that secured the central place at the table for these issues, including as related to the Forest Annex's CITES provisions. As one NGO interviewee put it, "NGOs are consulted, but ultimately who and how was all about contacts."

In addition to these types of domestic pressures, compliance costs also appear to be a key driver in determining which environmental issues appear in US trade agreements. In other words, when the United States is already implementing and complying with specific environmental policies, it is more likely to include those policies in its trade agreements because the cost of doing so is low. This is unsurprising and essentially supports DeSombre's (2000) theory of "internationalization," which asserts that the

US government is more likely to include existing domestic laws and policies in their international environmental agreements.

For example, as we argue in chapter 5, several environmental norms and policies (e.g., public participation and effective enforcement) that we find in US trade agreements are drawn directly from US domestic environmental law. Several interviewees further confirmed that the list of seven MEAs whose implementation is required in all post-2007 US PTAs were agreed upon because they were both trade-related, and because the United States was already party to all of those agreements. Interview data also confirm our assertion in chapter 6 that such replication is also common among US trading partners. That is, once US PTAs have been implemented in trading-partner nations, they often replicate those provisions in their future PTAs with third-party nations. Interviews pointed to public participation provisions in several Latin American country PTAs as evidence of this. The TREND database supports this finding as well.

Existing institutions are also critical (albeit unsurprisingly) to ensuring low compliance costs. Such institutions can ensure predictable replication of environmental provisions in future trade agreements. Central in the US trade-environment case are the "May 10 agreement" and US Trade Promotion Authority (TPA), also called "fast-track authority." Both are explained in more detail in chapter 2. In brief, however, these two legal instruments delineate a baseline for environmental (and many other) provisions in US trade agreements. As explained in chapter 2, through TPA, Congress grants the US president broad authority to negotiate trade agreements and subject them to an up-or-down congressional vote (no amendments or filibuster) on the condition that specific provisions are included in those PTAs. This includes environmental provisions that US trading partners *must* accept if they want to enter into a PTA with the United States. TPA authority has been renewed by Congress five times since it was first enacted in 1974, with the most recent renewal on July 1, 2018, extending authority to June 30, 2021 (Nascimento 2018).

The 2007 Bipartisan Trade Deal, commonly known as the "May 10 agreement," serves a similar role. It was agreed by Congress after the Democrats took control with four PTAs (Peru, Panama, Columbia, South Korea), negotiated by Republican President George W. Bush, still awaiting Congressional approval. The Democrats refused to approve the PTAs unless they were amended to include several provisions, including environmental ones. The

May 10 agreement is, for example, the origin of the MEA list noted above, as well as of the requirement that environmental provisions be subject to full dispute-settlement procedures, as we detail in chapter 4. Although the May 10 agreement only applied to the four PTAs on the table in 2007, its provisions were subsequently adopted in the Trade Act of 2015, which renewed TPA and established these requirements for all US PTAs negotiated under TPA going forward.

Protectionist interests may also play a role in explaining why the United States links trade and environmental policies, along with which environmental policies get pursued and which ones do not. Although interviewees were understandably hesitant to attribute specific environmental policies to protectionist interests per se, some did note that "leveling the playing field" for domestic industry is an important consideration for many involved in constructing US trade policy. At least one interviewee said that s/he talks about "leveling the playing field" in some groups and "environmental protection" in others; the framing depends on who s/he is trying to sell the issue to. Further, one NGO representative said that although it was not the only rationale, one reason domestic interest groups were able to get the US-Peru Forest Annex was because of protectionist motivations to protect domestic industry. S/he underscored that this was "at least a part of the picture, but it is difficult to say how large a part."

The exclusion of climate change from US PTAs is another important example of protectionist interests driving environment-trade linkages. Core to the US argument for never joining the United Nations Framework Convention on Climate Change (UNFCCC) are competitiveness concerns; the cost of reducing greenhouse gases is high, and the United States does not want to disadvantage itself in relation to other countries, especially emerging economies (Jinnah 2017). TPA requires that the United States be a full party to any listed MEAs in its PTAs, and the 2015 amendment to TPA explicitly prohibits the United States from taking on any greenhouse gas reduction commitments through its PTAs. The implication of this is that the UNFCCC will not be substantively linked to any US PTA in the foreseeable future.

Additional US motivations for linking trade and environmental issues that came up in interviews, but are less well addressed in the literature, include trading-partner interests and situational characteristics. As Morin and Gauquelin (2016) have highlighted elsewhere, Latin American countries have been successful in including biodiversity provisions in their PTAs with the United States. The US-Peru PTA, for example, includes a biodiversity article that—without explicitly referencing the Convention on Biological Diversity, to which the United States is not a party—essentially mirrors its objectives. Interview data suggest that they were able to do this because the United States generally supports biodiversity conservation, but was unable to ratify the Convention on Biological Diversity due to concerns about intellectual property issues. As one Peruvian government official noted in underscoring the importance of the biodiversity article in that PTA, "the annex was the bargain. The broader environmental chapter took up our interests." As such, it is likely that the biodiversity article was a small concession the United States made for Peru's acceptance of the Forest Annex, which one US government official noted was "shoved down their throat."[2]

Finally, some interviewees also stressed the importance of situational factors in determining which environmental issues get included in PTAs and which do not. Centrally, there is broad agreement that environmental issues should be as trade-related as possible. For example, all TPA-listed MEAs have clear trade relevance. The Montreal Protocol, for example, controls trade in ozone-depleting chemicals. Others stressed more temporal elements of this relationship, such as: for which issues do we have data to support trade relevance; what is politically important now; and which issues might gain support from the president? Illegal timber trade from Peru was well documented in the late 2000s, making it ripe, according to one interviewee, for inclusion in the Peru PTA. As one interviewee noted, referring to the Forest Annex:

> It was the product of contingent circumstance, for sure. It was directly related to the fact that the issue was a high-profile trade issue at the time and that data existed to demonstrate that it was a problem. I recall conversations that probably the same thing was happening in Colombia and Panama, but we didn't have the data [to support inclusion in those PTAs]. If you were to negotiate this agreement now, it would come out very differently.

Other interviewees stressed the Trump administration's continued support for cracking down on transnational crime, including wildlife trafficking. This is evidenced, for example, in President Trump's 2017 Executive Order 13773 on "Enforcing Federal Law with Respect to Transnational Criminal Organizations and Preventing International Trafficking," which explicitly includes wildlife-related crime (para. 2(a)(1)). "We were all surprised by that," s/he noted.

Conclusions

The literature and our interview data with key informants support a host of political factors and processes that shape how the United States frames and extends trade and environmental linkages in its trade agreements, which move beyond the minimum requirements as laid out in domestic trade law. Domestic pressures from NGOs and other interest groups have helped shape key environmental features of some US PTAs. Compliance costs, especially in the form of existing institutions, laws that ensure predictability, and low (if any) implementation hurdles are also important. Protectionist interests are also likely at play, especially when it comes to excluding issues, notably climate change, from all US PTAs. Trading-partner interests, especially biodiversity interests from Latin American trading partners, also help explain why the United States chooses specific environmental issues to link to its trade agreements. Finally, situational or contextual variables are also important. Things like having data to support the need for environmental action and having political support from the administration are also key in shaping US trade-environment linkages.

It should also be noted that not all decisions about which environmental issues to pursue are made in the text of the PTA itself. Many US PTAs are also negotiated in parallel with environmental cooperation agreements (ECAs). These ECAs outline specific areas where the United States and its trading partners can cooperate on environmental issues. Importantly, there is no expectation that these issues be trade-related. Countries develop work plans to cooperate on everything from increased transparency and public participation in environmental decision making (USTR 2014a) to support for environmental education activities (USTR 2014b). These negotiations are led by the State Department, rather than USTR, and decisions are made on a case-by-case basis in consultation with trading partners. These cooperative arrangements are often overlooked in the trade-environment literature. They shouldn't be, however. ECAs are an important mechanism of environmental capacity building in developing countries. From 2005 to 2015, the United States spent more than $177 million on activities like helping developing countries implement legislation for MEAs, training national scientific authorities, conducting public awareness campaigns, and developing cooperative projects to, for example, promote sustainable fisheries, protect migratory species, improve air quality, promote sustainable tourism, and more (USTR 2015a). As one interviewee put it, "developing countries view environmental cooperation agreements as a benefit. They are a huge priority for them. They see the cooperation as the carrot and the environment chapters as the stick." Further, US government officials interviewed for this study highlighted the flexible nature of cooperation agreements precisely because they are outside the official PTA. One noted that they are used to identify common priorities, such as fisheries or water management. Another noted, "you can be liberal on your cooperation without a precedent that anything and everything is trade-related." This perspective widens the scope of possibilities for environmental issues that can be pursued through PTAs. In evaluating how and why environmental provisions are incorporated into PTAs, ECAs hold much potential for on-the-ground progress and are a place for further research, inquiry, and practice.

4 Can Trade Agreements Enhance the Effectiveness of Multilateral Environmental Agreements?

Linkages between preferential trade agreements (PTAs) and multilateral environmental agreements (MEAs) are prolific and increasing globally over time. In this chapter, we explore the impacts of these MEA-PTA linkages on MEA effectiveness. Specifically, we look at how trade agreements can enhance implementation of MEAs to which they are linked. In short, we argue that, intentionally or not, trade agreements can enhance MEA effectiveness by serving as vectors to catalyze MEA implementation and by strengthening MEA compliance mechanisms.

At first, our argument might appear as a counterintuitive claim, with trade liberalization and environmental protection long portrayed as two conflicting objectives (Conca 2000; Morin and Bialais 2018). This objection has valid grounds. First, trade agreements can increase pollution levels by stimulating production, consumption, and long-distance transportation of goods.[1] Second, trade agreements can limit the regulatory capacity of political leaders to enact environmental regulations that frustrate the interest of exporters and investors.[2] Third, bilateralism is often considered to undermine multilateral governance by creating a complex web of inconsistent rules and exacerbating power imbalances (e.g., Bhagwati 2008). This chapter does not directly address these claims on trade/environment and bilateralism/multilateralism antagonisms. More modestly, it looks at one specific case and argues that among the many possible impacts of MEA linkages in PTAs is an increase in MEA procedural effectiveness.

Specifically, this chapter examines the linkages between the US-Peru agreement and the Convention on International Trade in Endangered Species of Wild Fauna and Flora (CITES). We focus on this linkage because the CITES-related provisions in the US-Peru agreement are groundbreaking. As such, if PTAs can or do contribute to MEA effectiveness, this case is one in which we are likely to see such effects. Although this limits our ability to theorize about the conditions under which PTAs might enhance MEA effectiveness, we are more interested in the preliminary question of *if* they can do so at all, which has yet to be answered despite an increase globally in efforts to pursue such linkages.

It would be easy to confuse CITES effectiveness with the broader systemic problem of illegal logging in Peru. To be clear, we focus here only on the CITES-specific provisions contained in the US-Peru PTA's Annex on Forest Sector Governance. The annex contains many provisions related to forest sector governance broadly, including as related to CITES. However, the CITES-related provisions are only a small portion of the annex and largely relate to procedural elements of CITES implementation. We do not look at the broader goals of the annex, which are largely related to illegal logging in Peru. As such, although our central argument is that the PTA has enhanced CITES effectiveness, Peru's forest sector still suffers from immense problems, mainly related to *illegal* logging (Urrunaga, Johnson, and Dhayneé Orbegozo Sánchez 2018). These issues are critically important, but outside the scope of CITES, which only regulates *legal* trade in endangered species. The PTA has not solved all forest sector governance problems in Peru, and has possibly even exacerbated some of them. However, our attention here is focused on how the PTA has catalyzed implementation of and compliance with CITES alone. As we discuss in the conclusion, despite the potential MEA-enhancing functions that PTAs can provide, the complexity of this case highlights the need to carefully consider PTA environmental provisions in place-specific ways.

The next section presents an overview of MEA-PTA linkages and argues that the United States is one of the key architects of theses linkages, particularly on matters related to CITES. The following section, "Measuring Effectiveness," explains how we understand and measure the contribution of PTAs to MEA effectiveness. In "CITES and Its Linkages in the US-Peru Agreement," we then present the empirics, briefly introducing CITES and detailing how CITES linkages appear in US agreements with a focus on the US-Peru agreement. In the following sections, "Compliance Mechanisms: Precision, Delegation, Obligation" and "Implementation: Evidence of Domestic Policy Change," we analyze whether the US-Peru agreement improves the effectiveness of CITES, in looking at the implications of

Can Trade Agreements Enhance Multilateral Environmental Agreements? 75

CITES-PTA linkages for CITES compliance capacity and implementation, respectively. We conclude by considering what these linkages mean for themes picked up in previous chapters, such as norm diffusion, and we distill a new argument from the data related to increased MEA ambition and "back-door" environmental governance via trade agreements.

Overview of Preferential Trade Agreement–Multilateral Environmental Agreement Linkages

Exploring the Trade and Environment Database (TREND) reveals that the practice of introducing references to MEAs in trade agreements emerged within the last three decades (Morin and Bialais 2018). Figure 4.1 below illustrates the increasing number of PTAs concluded around the world that include at least one reference to an MEA. As the number of PTAs rose rapidly from the mid-1990s, it is unsurprising that the absolute number of PTAs with at least one reference to an MEA also increased sharply. Figure 4.1 shows that beyond this growth in absolute numbers, it is the relative share of PTAs with at least one reference to an MEA that is also increasing

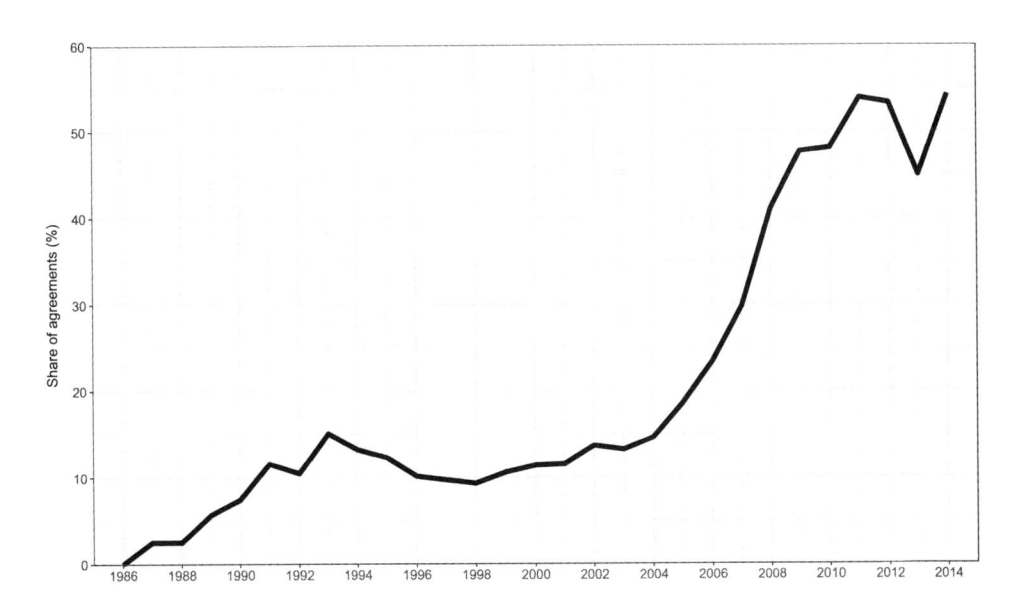

Figure 4.1
Share of PTAs with at least one reference to an MEA (moving average ± 2 years)

over time. From 10 percent of PTAs referring to MEAs in the early 1990s, this share now exceeds 50 percent of PTAs.

Some MEAs are referenced in PTAs more frequently than others. Figure 4.2 shows that CITES is, by far, the most frequently cited MEA. In total, 63 PTAs explicitly refer to CITES. In contrast, only 15 PTAs refer to the 1997 Kyoto Protocol to the United Nations Framework Convention on Climate Change.

Several factors explain this sharp difference in the number of references to these MEAs. First, CITES is a relatively old MEA. It was concluded nearly 25 years prior to the Kyoto Protocol and, therefore, has had more time to be incorporated into trade agreements. However, this factor alone is not sufficient to explain the popularity of CITES in trade agreements. Although 10 percent of PTAs concluded after 1973 include a reference to CITES, less than 5 percent of PTAs signed after 1997 include a reference to the Kyoto Protocol.

More significant than MEA longevity in explaining their number of references in PTAs is their content and their parties. *Ceteris paribus*, MEAs that include several trade-related provisions are more frequently referenced in PTAs than MEAs that are not trade-related. Also, MEAs that are strongly promoted by the United States are more frequently referenced in the global PTA universe than those that the United States has not ratified (Morin, Michaud, and Bialais 2016; Morin and Gauquelin 2016).[3] The 2000 Cartagena Protocol on Biosafety regulates trade of genetically modified organisms but is not supported by the United States and is rarely cited in PTAs. Conversely, although the United States is a strong advocate of the International Convention for the Regulation of Whaling, it is not directly trade-related and is rarely mentioned in PTAs. CITES, and to a lesser extent the Montreal Protocol on Substances that Deplete the Ozone Layer, are both trade-related and actively supported by the United States. They are also among the most widely referenced MEAs, as illustrated by figure 4.2.

US leadership in driving PTA-MEA linkages appears clearly when distinguishing three different types of PTA references to MEAs. Although not as important in terms of US leadership in this area, the first and most superficial type of reference aims to provide contextual information for interpretative purposes. They include recitals recalling the importance of an MEA in the preamble of a PTA or general statements inviting parties to the PTA to consider the ratification of an MEA. In contrast to these superficial recitals,

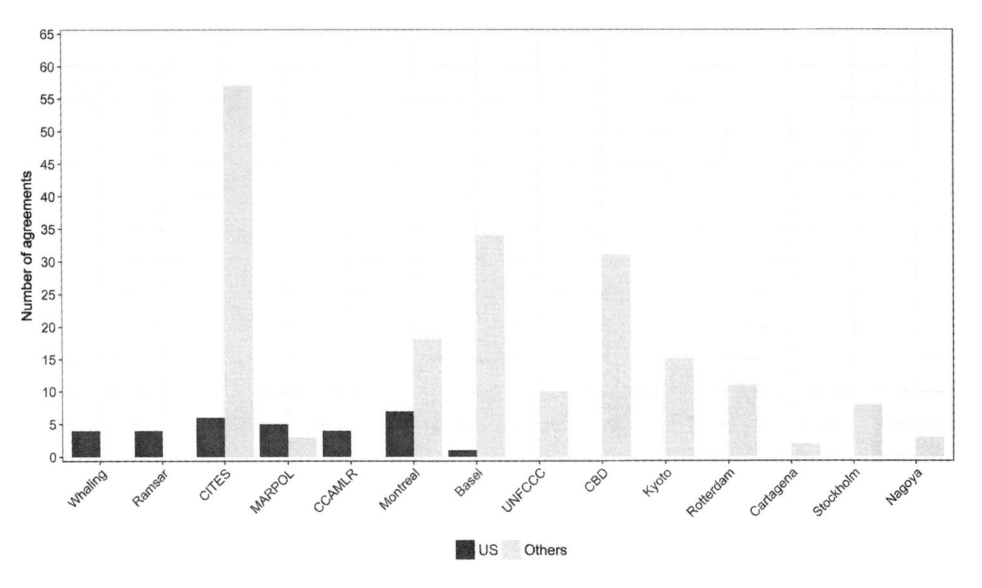

Figure 4.2
Cumulative number of PTAs referring to selected MEAs (1947–2016)

US leadership appears with higher degrees of commitment in the second type of reference. Indeed, the United States and its partners from NAFTA were the first to include in a PTA a conflict-settling clause that favors MEAs. NAFTA Article 104 innovated by providing clearly that "in the event of any inconsistency between this agreement and the specific trade obligations set out in . . . [CITES, the Montreal Protocol, the Basel Convention, and other agreements set out in Annex 104.1], such obligations shall prevail." Several agreements subsequently negotiated by the United States and its trade partners reproduce this ground-breaking provision verbatim.

The third type of reference reflects a commitment within a PTA to implement provisions of an MEA. The United States began including such references with the US-Peru agreement. Recent US PTAs call for the implementation of CITES, the Montreal Protocol, and the International Convention for the Prevention of Pollution from Ships. At time of writing, only US PTAs subject this requirement to implement an MEA to the PTA's full dispute-settlement mechanism, although some other countries are considering duplicating this US model in their future PTAs (Morin and Rochette 2017).

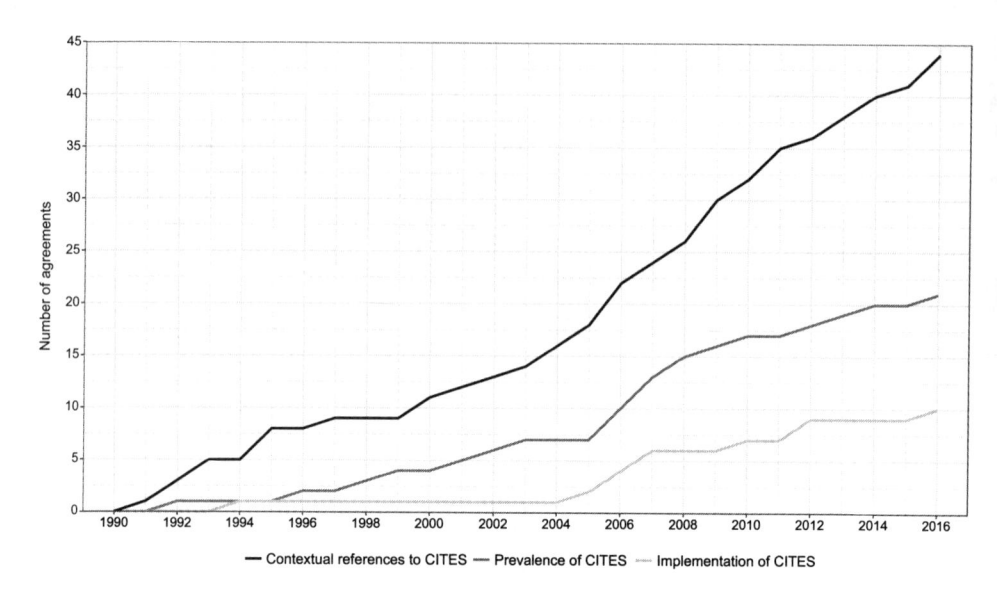

Figure 4.3
Number of PTAs referring to CITES by type of references (1990–2016)

Figure 4.3 illustrates the diffusion of these three types of PTA-MEA linkages with the example of CITES, the most frequently cited MEA in the global PTA universe. Although the most superficial type of references to CITES are mainly found in non-US PTAs, the United States initiated the second type of reference with NAFTA, and it is party to most PTAs requiring the implementation of CITES.

The United States is clearly a pioneer in inserting meaningful references to CITES in its PTAs, a practice that has been replicated by US trading partners in their own PTAs with third parties. The next sections investigate the consequences of these references in terms of CITES effectiveness. A case study approach is used, focusing on the US-Peru PTA contribution to CITES effectiveness in Peru. We begin by clarifying what we mean by MEA effectiveness.

Measuring Effectiveness

Much of the MEA effectiveness literature has focused on the role of compliance and how to improve it (Mitchell 1994; Jacobson and Weiss 1998). Although noncompliance can certainly undermine effectiveness (Susskind and Ali 2015), it does not necessarily guarantee effectiveness either. Rather, other factors can also contribute to a multifaceted understanding of MEA effectiveness. Oran Young's (1994) typology of regime effectiveness suggests six dimensions through which effectiveness can be considered and measured: problem solving, goal attainment, behavioral, procedural, constitutive, and evaluative (table 4.1).

We focus here on procedural effectiveness not because we necessarily privilege this dimension over others, but merely because data are most readily available to assess this dimension. Further, the centrality of

Table 4.1
Dimensions of Regime Effectiveness

Dimension of Effectiveness	Description	Example(s)
Problem Solving	Solves the problems that motivated parties to create them in the first place	Slows climate change; stops ozone depletion
Goal Attainment	Extent to which a regime's stated goals are attained over time	Maintains temperature increase below 2 degrees C; phases of ozone-depleting substances
Behavioral	Regime causes one or more of its members to alter their behavior	US reduces emissions by 26–28% below 2005 levels; EU phases out use of CFCs
Procedural	Provisions are implemented in the domestic legal and political systems and complied with by member states	US domestic legislation calls for economy-wide emission reductions of 26–28%; developed countries meet the incremental cost of CFC phase out for developing countries
Constitutive	Parties dedicate time, energy, and resources to regime implementation	Congress funds EPA to implement greenhouse gas reduction policies and earmarks funds for the Multilateral Fund
Evaluative	Regime produces results that are efficient, equitable, sustainable, or robust	Developed countries pay the incremental costs transition to renewables for Least Developed Countries and Small Island Developing States; developing countries are given longer transition times to phase out CFCs

Source: Young (1994)

implementation and compliance to procedural effectiveness is important in considering effectiveness of MEAs specifically, because several MEAs are comparatively long on ambition relative to these factors. As such, in assessing procedural effectiveness, we consider independently each of its two central elements: implementation and compliance.

Implementation in its most straightforward sense is the way that states incorporate the requirements of international treaties into domestic law (Brandi, Blümer, and Morin, forthcoming). In order to asses implementation, we look at the MEA-specific provisions in the US-Peru PTA and analyze the extent to which trading partners adopted domestic laws or policies that incorporate those MEA obligations after the PTA was agreed between its parties.[4] Given their innovative character and their extensive treatment in the US-Peru PTA, Peru's implementation of the CITES-relevant provisions in the US-Peru PTA is extremely well documented. We are therefore able to look at Secretariat, state, and NGO reports on implementation and formal Secretariat-produced quantitative measurements of the levels of MEA implementation among parties. As is detailed below, many of these official reports directly identify causal links between CITES provisions in the PTA and Peru's enhanced implementation of CITES.[5]

Empirically, measuring compliance is more difficult because observing adherence with implemented policies can take a long time, and the US-Peru PTA is relatively recent. We therefore analyze compliance theoretically, based on the rationalist assumption that stronger mechanisms of compliance are more likely to yield higher levels of compliance in practice. Although this measurement is imperfect, in that strong institutional mechanisms don't necessarily guarantee compliance, when viewed in a comparative perspective—that is, relative to existing MEA compliance mechanisms—this measurement can provide a compelling rationale for the *likelihood* of enhanced compliance in future.

We engage theories of international law to evaluate compliance mechanisms within the US-Peru PTA that are relevant to CITES provisions. We broadly categorize compliance mechanisms here as either managerial or legalistic.[6] The managerial model relies primarily on cooperative, problem-solving approaches to incentivize countries to comply. It assumes non-compliance results from a lack of capacity, which can be addressed through measures such as technical support, financial assistance, and trainings (Guzman 2002).

In contrast, legalistic models better capture non-compliance rooted in cost calculus. They are designed to achieve compliance through coercive mechanisms such as sanctions or penalties, which increase costs of non-compliance. They are highly prescriptive in nature and typically require countries to relegate some sovereignty under the agreement. As demonstrated in table 4.2, US PTAs use a mixture of managerial and more legalistic compliance mechanisms.

We measure the degree of legalization along three metrics: precision, delegation, and obligation (Abbot et al. 2000, 17–18). Precision narrows the scope for interpretation of a given commitment. More specific or detailed commitments are more precise, and thus more strongly legalized than commitments that are vague and open to interpretation in varied domestic contexts. For example, a PTA requirement that a party designate a specific domestic agency as lead in implementing an MEA is more precise than one that simply requires parties to implement the MEA. Delegation is a reflection of the type and extent to which external actors are involved in monitoring and enforcing compliance. For example, delegation that involves adjudicators with the power to impose penalties for non-compliance exhibits high delegation in comparison to delegation that relies on nonbinding arbitration, delegation of enforcement to nongovernmental organizations (NGOs), or is delinked from dispute settlement entirely. Finally, obligation reflects the strength of the commitment made by PTA parties to a particular policy. For example, a normative obligation to consider implementing CITES provisions (i.e., states "should" implement the CITES) is weaker than an obligation that requires states to do so (i.e., states "shall" implement the CITES). When precision, obligation, and delegation are all strong, we categorize compliance as highly legalized.

It should be noted that although obligation can be very important in evaluating legalization, weak precision and/or delegation temper the importance of obligation in evaluating compliance strength. For example, when precision is weak, obligation becomes less important, because state discretion to interpret what they "shall" do is quite wide. Similarly, a strong obligation to allow for third-party inspections of exports, for example, is more indicative of strong compliance mechanisms than is, for example, a strong obligation to merely self-report on the content of those exports (Morin and Jinnah 2018).

Table 4.2

Compliance Measures in US Preferential Trade Agreements (PTAs)

		Legalized approach			
		Suspension of benefits if failure to enforce domestic law	Non-jurisdictional mechanism if non-compliance with environmental provisions	Dispute Settlement Mechanism (DSM applicable if non-compliance with PTA environmental provisions	Suspension of benefits if noncompliance with PTA environmental provisions
NAFTA	1992	•	•	•	•
Vietnam	2000				
Jordan	2000				
Singapore	2003	•	•		
Chile	2003	•	•		
Australia	2004	•	•		
Morocco	2004	•	•		
CAFTA	2004	•	•		
Bahrain	2004	•	•	•	
Oman	2006	•	•		
Peru	2006		•	•	•
Colombia	2006		•	•	•
Panama	2007		•	•	•
Korea	2007		•	•	•
TPP	2016		•	•	•
USMCA	2018		•	•	•

In general, MEAs deploy managerial approaches to compliance, wherein precision and delegation are typically weak. States are generally reluctant to sacrifice sovereignty over control of their natural resources, and MEAs are often developed by consensus, resulting in relatively weak approaches to environmental problem-solving (Susskind and Ali 2015). As such, MEAs generally secure compliance by relying on a suite of managerial approaches. These include leveraging reputational and normative force (Weiss and

Managerial approach				
Intergovernmental committee	Technical assistance provided to another party	Technology transfer in the field of environment	Commitment to consider alleged violation	Public participation in the implementation of agreement
•	•	•	•	•
				•
•	•	•		•
•	•		•	•
•	•		•	•
•	•		•	•
•	•		•	•
•	•	•	•	•
•	•		•	•
•	•		•	•
•	•	•	•	•
•			•	•
•	•		•	•
•			•	•
•	•	•	•	•
•	•	•	•	•

Jacobson 2000), establishing mechanisms for capacity building and information sharing, and relying heavily on NGOs for monitoring and "naming and shaming" (Betsill and Correll 2008; Raustiala 1997; Yamin 2001). Dispute resolutions are typically handled through mediation or other soft, often nonbinding mechanisms, with little available remedy beyond reputational incentives.

In contrast, trade agreements typically use a combination of managerial *and* legalistic approaches to secure compliance (Jinnah and Lindsay 2016). Although strong dispute-resolution systems capable of delivering sanctions and fines for non-compliance are central features of most trade agreements (i.e., legalistic), many also include provisions that promote cooperation between countries on environmental issues and support capacity building and other mechanisms for improving implementation (i.e., managerial; Morin, Dür, and Lechner 2018). Until recently, these managerial approaches have typically been reserved for environmental provisions contained in trade agreements, whereas legalistic mechanisms have historically been reserved for provisions more centrally related to trade liberalization (Jinnah and Morgera 2013).[7]

It is frequently assumed that more legalistic environmental commitments, which are more mandatory and enforceable, are "stronger" and more likely to secure compliance with environmental provisions (Matisoff 2010; Jinnah and Lindsay 2016). However, there is evidence suggesting that more managerial provisions can also lead to increased environmental cooperation, which can in turn favor domestic environmental protection (Yoo and Kim 2016; Bastiaens and Postnikov 2017). Moreover, whereas a strictly managerial compliance model may be too weak to secure wide compliance, a strictly legalistic model might be counterproductive because it is less likely to catalyze changes in underlying beliefs, can backfire if seen as unfair, and because diplomatic considerations make formal inter-state disputes unlikely (Matisoff 2010).

Both approaches have benefits and drawbacks, since both approaches address different sources of non-compliance. Whereas managerial models capture non-compliance rooted in lack of capacity, more legalistic models capture non-compliance rooted in cost calculus. Therefore, we argue here that a combination of legalistic and managerial models is most likely to yield higher levels of compliance than either model can secure in isolation. Empirically speaking, this means that whether linking to additional legalistic or managerial mechanisms will strengthen compliance in any given case depends on the landscape of existing compliance mechanism available in the absence of the linkage. In other words, if an MEA has strong managerial and weak legalistic compliance mechanisms, then linkages that allow for stronger legalistic compliance approaches to MEA provisions can strengthen MEA compliance mechanisms and, in turn, enhance overall MEA effectiveness.

In order to evaluate potential impacts of MEA-PTA linkages on MEA compliance, we analyze the degree of legalization of the specific compliance mechanisms within the US-Peru PTA that are applicable to the CITES provisions therein. The more strongly legalized the compliance mechanisms, the stronger CITES compliance is likely to be. Because we are primarily interested in how PTAs can contribute to MEA effectiveness, we measure the relative degree of legalization—that is, in comparison to what is available under MEAs themselves. That is, we evaluate whether the US-Peru PTA's compliance measures are strongly or weakly legalized in comparison to those available under CITES.[8] Secondarily, we also look to new managerial compliance mechanisms under the PTA, which may further enhance the existing CITES managerial model. In order words, we are interested in whether the PTA provides stronger compliance measures for its CITES provisions than is available under CITES itself for the same or similar provisions. If so, we argue it contributes to enhanced CITES effectiveness.

In summary, we consider two factors as particularly important in evaluating PTA contributions to improvements in MEA procedural effectiveness: implementation and compliance. In order to evaluate PTA contribution to MEA implementation, we first look for PTA provisions that require improvements in trading partners' implementation of CITES provisions. We also look for new domestic policies and laws in trading-partner nations that reflect CITES-relevant obligations made under the PTA. When CITES-specific policies or laws are observed that can be traced back to PTA implementation through document analysis and/or interview data, we find that PTA provisions have enhanced CITES implementation. Second, we look for evidence of more legalistic compliance mechanisms as indicators of enhanced future CITES compliance. That is, if the PTA-MEA linkage provides for more legalistic compliance approaches to complement existing managerial approaches available under CITES, we find that CITES compliance is either stronger or likely to strengthen in the future. If improvements in either variable are observed and can be causally linked to the PTA provisions, we argue that the PTA has indeed enhanced MEA effectiveness.

CITES and Its Linkages in the US-Peru Agreement

CITES aims to "ensure that international trade in specimens of wild animals and plants does not threaten their survival" (CITES Secretariat 2007c). It does this by tracking species trade through a managerial system of trade permits and certificates, and by identifying species to be tracked through a listing system. CITES currently lists over 35,000 species in three appendices. Each CITES appendix affords a different level of protection, ranging from a complete ban on commercial trade, to allowing trade under certain levels when supported by scientific evidence, to requesting support from other countries in controlling trade in certain species. Importantly for our discussion here, CITES parties are encouraged, but not required, to develop scientifically based export quotas to control trade in Appendix-II–listed species, such that trade does not threaten species survival.

CITES manages compliance issues in three ways: through the Convention itself, through Conference of the Parties (COP) decisions, which are regularly updated and retired at each successive COP, and through COP resolutions, which have a longer life than decisions. The Convention itself calls for dispute settlement, first, through negotiation between the parties involved, and subsequently through binding arbitration. Although the latter reflects relatively strong delegation in comparison to many other MEAs, as we discuss below, it reflects far weaker delegation than what is available under the US-Peru PTA. The Convention also allows the CITES Secretariat to communicate directly with parties whom it suspects are failing to implement the Convention (Art. XIII). Upon receiving such communication, the party must provide information about the implementation failure and may choose to conduct an inquiry. All information arising from this process must be communicated to the COP, who can "make whatever recommendations it deems appropriate" on the matter (Art. XIII.3). Again, although there is some degree of precision in requiring response and communication, the nature of the obligation is quite weak compared to what we find under the US-Peru PTA.

At time of writing, the most recent CITES COP decisions on "compliance matters" merely require parties to engage in information sharing regarding compliance approaches (Decision 17.65), reflecting a strongly managerial approach. In its most recent resolution on compliance, CITES parties lay out draft guidelines on compliance, which explicitly call for a "supportive and non-adversarial approach" (CITES Resolution Conference 14.3). Centrally, the guidelines provide for compliance matters to be handled by the CITES Standing Committee, which can request information regarding possible compliance matters. In cases of violations, the Standing Committee's remedy is highly circumscribed, however, with options including in-country assistance, public notification, requesting special reporting from the violating country, and provision of advice to that country (CITES Resolution Conference 14.3). In cases of persistent non-compliance, the Standing Committee may suspend trade in CITES-listed species with the non-complying country. Although the latter reflects some legalistic characteristics, delegation is quite weak in comparison to what is available under the US-Peru PTA, and the vast majority of these mechanisms are strongly managerial, focused on capacity building and transparency.

The US-Peru agreement includes detailed provisions related to CITES, especially in its Annex on Forest Sector Governance. The annex not only promotes environmental norms and principles, but also establishes rules for implementing them. Notably, it contains numerous provisions related *explicitly* to the implementation and enforcement of CITES in Peru. It is further notable that the provisions contained in the annex directly reflect the CITES Secretariat's recommendations to Peru regarding implementation of the mahogany trade controls (CITES Standing Committee 55).[9]

The annex requires Peru to adopt a wide range of policies related to implementing CITES, many of which relate directly to compliance mechanisms as well. These commitments include requiring Peru to increase criminal penalties to deter illegal timber trade; inventory and conduct population analyses of CITES-listed species; calculate "accurate" conversion factors[10] to inform decisions on CITES export quotas;[11] adopt a strategic plan of action to implement the CITES Appendix-II listing of bigleaf mahogany; establish an annual export quota for bigleaf mahogany; and develop systems to verify the legal origin and chain of custody of CITES-listed tree species. These provisions mirror and even target CITES requirements that Peru had previously habitually resisted implementing (Jinnah 2011). Importantly, the PTA provided an explicit timeline requiring Peru to implement many of these CITES-relevant Forest Annex provisions within 18 months of entry into force of the PTA (Annex 18.3.4, para. 3).

The annex also contains provisions requiring Peru to establish an auditing system to track producers and exporters of timber products to the

United States; verify their compliance with relevant laws; allow US officials to participate in those verifications; and provide verification of such information to the United States upon request. The United States may deny entry of shipments subject to verification, or even to a specific enterprise that knowingly provides false information. Further, if Peru fails to submit a verification report as requested, the United States may take "any other such actions with respect to the exporter's timber products that it considers appropriate" (paragraph 14).

Notably, the annex does not limit its applicability to mahogany. Rather, its requirements apply to *all* CITES-listed timber species irrespective of which appendix the species is listed in. This is important because, while mahogany is the only Appendix-II–listed timber species in Peru, the country is also a range state for Appendix-III–listed cedar (*cedrella oradata*). Therefore, TPA timber management requirements apply more stringent controls to cedar than are applicable under CITES itself.

Finally, unlike its predecessors, the US-Peru PTA opens compliance with the entire environmental chapter, including the provisions in the Forest Annex, to the PTA's full dispute-resolution system. Whereas previous agreements severely restricted the scope of access to non-derogation violations, and/or circumscribed available remedy, under the US-Peru PTA, violations could be subject to sanctions just like any other provision of the agreement (Jinnah 2011). This means that Peru's failure to implement the CITES-relevant provisions of the Forest Annex is now subject to sanction-based enforcement (see table 4.2 above). Violations do not automatically trigger dispute settlement—this is, of course, a matter of diplomatic calculus.

Compliance Mechanisms: Precision, Delegation, Obligation

In this section, we analyze the strength of the compliance mechanisms contained in the US-Peru PTA (presented in the previous section) that would apply to CITES provisions. We measure compliance mechanism strength by evaluating the degree of legalization (precision, delegation, obligation) of these provisions, which is presumed to be positively correlated with compliance strength. We are interested in the strength of compliance mechanisms in a *relative* sense—that is, are CITES-relevant compliance mechanisms stronger under the US-Peru PTA than under CITES alone? Therefore, we evaluate the PTA's compliance approach for CITES-relevant provisions in comparison to what is available via CITES own compliance approach, which was presented above. We argue the PTA has indeed enhanced CITES compliance capacity, and thus contributed to CITES procedural effectiveness.

The US-Peru Forest Annex contains several CITES-relevant compliance mechanisms that are not only far more legalistic than what is available under CITES alone, but that move far beyond anything we have seen in any other US PTAs in terms of not only their nature, but also their degrees of precision, delegation, and obligation. For example, the annex's requirement that Peru inventory and conduct population analyses of CITES-listed species is unparalleled in its degree of precision. Whereas other PTAs that reference CITES (or any other MEA) typically stop short of prescriptive provisions related to how an MEA should be implemented and/or enforced domestically, the Forest Annex is quite aggressive and precise in doing the opposite. As summarized above, other examples of strongly precise CITES compliance provisions include that Peru adopt a strategic plan of action to implement the CITES Appendix II listing of bigleaf mahogany; establish an annual export quota for bigleaf mahogany; and develop systems to verify the legal origin and chain of custody of CITES-listed tree species. These provisions mirror CITES requirements that Peru had previously habitually resisted implementing under CITES alone and are remarkable—indeed, unparalleled in their depth of intervention with domestic environmental policy in a trading-partner nation (Jinnah 2011).

In addition, the annex requires Peru to do several things that have not been publicly discussed in the CITES context. These include, for example, identifying which specific domestic agencies should oversee physical inspections of any proposed extractions of CITES-listed tree species in Peru, and requiring Peru to increase criminal penalties to deter illegal timber trade. The latter is especially important in pushing Peru toward a strongly coercive domestic enforcement regime. This level of precision is again unprecedented in any PTA-MEA linkage.

The US-Peru PTA is also strong on delegation vis-à-vis the CITES-relevant compliance provisions. Two provisions are particularly notable. First, in order to facilitate verification that Peruvian exporters or producers have complied with domestic laws, the annex requires Peru to allow US officials to participate in inspections of any "exporter or producer, or of any other enterprise in the territory of Peru in the chain of production or transportation for the product concerned." As with the highly precise CITES provisions described above, allowing a trading partner this level of enforcement capacity, especially as related to compliance with an *environmental* provision, is unprecedented. Second, and more importantly, the US-Peru PTA is the first PTA globally to open its full environment chapter, including the highly precise Forest Annex, to unrestricted remedy under the dispute-settlement procedures. Although previous US agreements contained dispute-settlement procedures, such procedures were highly circumscribed, limiting the amount of remedy available and/or the purposes for which such remedy could be used. Importantly, making these highly precise CITES provisions enforceable via this type of dispute settlement is far stronger than any available remedy for non-compliance available under CITES itself.

Finally, the level of obligation related to CITES-provisions is also strong in the US-Peru PTA. In short, all of the commitments described in this section are things that Peru "shall" do. There is no suggestion that Peru should consider these measures, or attempt to implement them only if funding permits. Peru "shall" do all of these things: the strongest form of mandate in international law. Further, the PTA not only required Peru to do these things, but provided an explicit timeline requiring Peru to implement many of these CITES-relevant Forest Annex provisions within 18 months of entry into force of the PTA (Annex 18.3.4, para. 3). This level of obligation is again unprecedented in any US PTA, and as discussed in more detail in chapter 6, globally as well.

These important compliance improvements can likely be explained, at least in part, by the strong degree of delegation within the US-Peru PTA, which directly linked these elements of CITES compliance and the PTA's dispute-settlement system. In subjecting the full environment chapter, including the CITES provisions in the annex, to this sanction-based enforcement mechanism, the PTA endowed CITES with much stronger delegation-based compliance than we had seen in any previous trade agreement in the United States or globally. CITES compliance mechanisms have historically been characterized by low levels of delegation, utilizing instead managerial approaches, such as confiscation of illegal specimens and information sharing about compliance approaches. Although violations do not automatically trigger dispute settlement, they open the door for coercion-based compliance procedures for failure to implement CITES provisions.

The PTA also makes CITES's existing managerial approach stronger. For example, by linking CITES provisions to PTA implementation, the United

States was able to siphon approximately $90 million to environmental cooperation programs in Peru since 2009, which has largely been dedicated to implementation of the environment chapter and Forest Annex in Peru through capacity building and training programs (USTR 2013; Inside US Trade 2015; Urrunaga, Johnson, and Orbegozo Sánchez 2018). Further, when Peru failed to meet the 18-month implementation deadline noted above, the US Trade Representative (USTR) declined to trigger dispute settlement, but instead pursued a managerial approach by engaging Peru in a joint action plan (2013) to help Peru fully implement these provisions.[12] As such, even if formal dispute settlement is unlikely for violation of environmental provisions, the threat of this possibility can catalyze important diplomatic approaches to dispute resolution that may not have otherwise been possible. This is clearly visible in the December 2012 US decision to engage Peru in a managerial-based joint action plan to facilitate Peru's implementation of the Forest Annex following a petition from the US-based Environmental Investigation Agency (EIA) requesting official action (e.g., audits) under the annex to investigate illegal logging in Peru.[13]

Implementation: Evidence of Domestic Policy Change

In this section and the following one, we evaluate if and how the far-reaching CITES provisions contained in the US-Peru PTA have an impact on CITES effectiveness. As described above, we evaluate procedural effectiveness by looking at changes in implementation and compliance. On implementation, we look for any evidence that the PTA catalyzed CITES implementation in Peru. We focus on implementation improvements in Peru (not the United States) because Peru had long failed to implement key provisions of CITES (Jinnah 2011), and the PTA's CITES-related provisions are nearly exclusively explicitly directed at Peru (i.e., Peru shall . . .).

Although Peru's implementation of the Forest Annex remains incomplete and highly controversial (EIA 2015), there is much evidence to suggest that the trade pressure surrounding the TPA has catalyzed Peru to enact regulatory and participatory reform that it would otherwise have little incentive to pursue. The USTR reports that PTA pushed Peru to establish key forest institutions, including an independent forest oversight body; amend its criminal code to penalize illegal logging and wildlife trafficking; adopt laws and policies to comply with CITES; and enact a new Forest and Wildlife law. In its official assessments of Peru's implementation of the US-Peru PTA, the USTR has made clear that the PTA is directly responsible for important improvements in Peru's implementation of its CITES obligations (USTR 2013). Although far more critical of Peru's efforts, especially, as it relates to controlling illegal trade (not covered by CITES), the EIA[14] has also attributed many of Peru's post-2006 law/policy changes to its implementation of the PTA provisions (EIA 2015). Official reports to the 2009 CITES Plants Committee from scientific authorities further support this linkage:

> In Peru, a national legislative reform is in process. New Law Decrees and Resolutions include the creation of the Ministry of Environment for the conservation and sustainable use of natural resources, biological diversity and protected areas; and Decree No 1090 (28 June 2008) which created a Forestry and Wildlife Law establishing new definitions for forestry resources and use. *Changes in laws and regulations are related to compliance with the Peru-USA Free Trade Agreement*, and will affect forest conservation and sustainable use. (Mejía et al. 2008, 32; emphasis added)

Some of these legislative reforms implement CITES in ways that were previously intractable under CITES alone. For example, in June 2007, the CITES secretariat highlighted key barriers to Peru's implementation of its existing Strategic Action Plan for Mahogany, or PAEC, citing this as a major problem for CITES implementation in the country:

> The lack of political will at the highest governmental level to implement the PAEC are major issues that could seriously impede an effective implementation of the Convention. (SC55 Doc.12)

It is striking therefore that immediately following the 2007 US Congressional approval of the PTA, which *requires* the action plan be implemented, Peru approved the plan (Mejía et al. 2008, 33).

Peru has also increased implementation of policies that directly enhance compliance with CITES, which have been catalyzed by this linkage. For example, prior to agreement of the PTA in 2007, Peru's process for developing quotas for mahogany exports was heavily criticized by NGOs and others as being insufficiently based on science, including in ignoring Peru's own Scientific Authority's advice on the matter (Mejía et al. 2008, 25; Del Gatto et al. 2009). The PTA required that Peru's procedures for developing export quotas be revised to better reflect scientific advice, including in being based on technical studies that re-evaluate procedures for stock inventory and conversion factors. Immediately following agreement of the PTA, Peru revised its post-2006 export-quota procedures in line with requirements in the Forest Annex, and issued a 2007 export quota that was for the first time established in accordance with Peru's Scientific Authority's advice.[15] Not only was this an achievement in implementation of policy, but it also resulted in real compliance improvements. For example, Peru's 2007 export quota for mahogany represented a decrease of almost 79 percent from the 2006 quota. In 2008, the export quota would drop even further, to an 86 percent drop from 2006. Although the quota began to increase in 2007, it still remained well below pre-PTA quotas,[16] and overall exports of mahogany continued to remain well-below pre-PTA levels as well, although some observers have argued that this was due to a decimation of the stock rather than a change in policies.

The PTA's role in catalyzing Peru's implementing of CITES is perhaps most clear, however, with respect to its official recognition under the convention's National Legislation Project. The project was established at COP8 in 1992 (CITES Resolution Conference 8.4, Rev. COP 15) "to promote and facilitate the enactment of adequate legislation" to implement the convention (COP 14, Doc. 24, 1). Although countries are given quite a bit of leeway

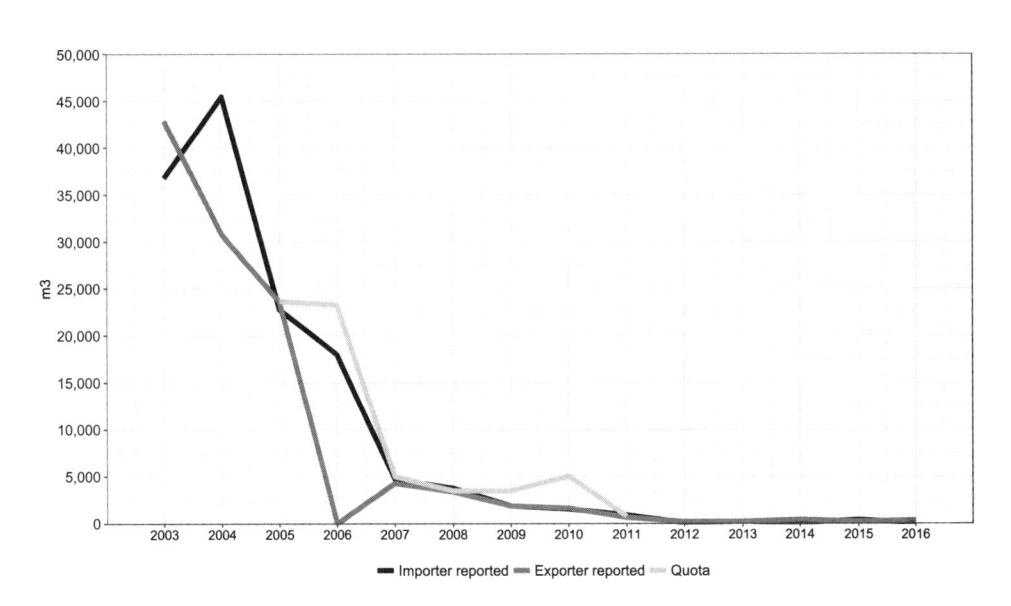

Figure 4.4
Mahogany exports from Peru (2003–2016)[17]

to implement CITES as they see fit, the Secretariat provides general guidance indicating that minimum requirements for "adequate legislation" are the designation of national CITES authorities; prohibition of trade in violation of the convention; penalization of illegal trade; and authorization to confiscate specimens illegally traded or processed (COP 12, Doc. 28, 2). At COP11 in 2000, CITES parties were evaluated and placed in one of three categories corresponding to their level of implementation.

Although Peru had draft legislation in place from at least March 2004 (SC50 Doc. 29:8), it failed to enact this legislation until June 2008 and thus remained in Category 2 for *nine years*. The CITES Secretariat reports that at the request of both Peru and the United States "in connection with the [PTA] the Secretariat undertook a legislative assistance mission to Peru in May 2008 to finalize the legislation before the expiry of US 'fast-track' authority" (SC57 Doc. 18). Subsequently, at the next meeting of the CITES Standing Committee in July 2009, Peru was for the first time moved from Category 2 to Category 1—reflecting its full implementation of CITES by this metric. Again, in its formal assessment of Peru's implementation of the PTA, USTR directly attributes these changes to Peru's efforts at implementing the PTA.

Interview data strongly support the causal link between the PTA and this measurement of CITES effectiveness. Several US government officials interviewed for this study, across agencies, underscored that the United States made clear that in order for Peru to be seen as in compliance with its CITES-relevant obligations in the Forest Annex, it must implement legislations that moved it from Category 2 to Category 1 under CITES. This was critically important, because compliance with such provisions was a prerequisite for the PTA to enter into force. One interviewee noted that for these reasons, the entry into force period "is the most powerful period to get countries to implement MEAs."

Several interviewees further noted that this approach was taken with other trading partners as well, such as Morocco and Chile. Although those agreements do not have the same prescriptive CITES provisions as the Peru PTA, they do have general requirements to implement CITES. As such, the United States required those countries also to move from Category 2 to Category 1 to be in compliance with that obligation under their respective PTAs. Importantly, as another US government interviewee explains, the United States provided support through the PTA to those countries to "get their implementing legislation up to snuff and helped with training their national scientific authorities as well."

In summary, there is strong evidence to suggest that the US-Peru PTA has increased CITES procedural effectiveness by catalyzing Peru's implementation of key CITES provisions related to protected tree species, such as bigleaf mahogany. Centrally, following the entry into force of the PTA, Peru implemented CITES-relevant PTA provisions that resulted in Peru being recategorized from Category 2 ("generally do not meet all requirements of CITES") to Category 1 ("generally meets all requirements of CITES"). This is remarkable, as Peru has been resistant to implementing such policies for years despite political pressure to do so within the CITES context (Jinnah 2011). Indeed, Peru had been stuck in Category 2 for nine years prior to the US-Peru PTA being agreed. The US-Peru PTA also enhances the compliance mechanisms of CITES by applying the PTA's more legalistic compliance mechanisms to CITES provisions. Centrally, it provides for uncircumscribed remedy under the PTA's dispute-settlement system for any violations of the CITES-relevant provisions.

Conclusions

Our analysis demonstrates how environmental provisions in trade agreements can be used to improve the effectiveness of MEAs. Specifically, we argue that procedural effectiveness, as measured through improvements in MEA implementation and compliance, is already being enhanced in biodiversity MEAs. Not only do many US trade agreements already incorporate provisions that require implementation of MEAs (at varying levels of specificity), but in some cases they link compliance with those MEA-relevant provisions to the trade agreement's full dispute-resolution mechanism. Indeed, some recent studies show that agreements with detailed environmental provisions are associated with reduced emissions of CO_2 and suspended particulate matter (Martínez-Zarzoso and Oueslati 2016; Baghdadi, Martínez-Zarzoso, and Zitouna 2013; Zhou, Tian, and Zhou 2017). In complementing MEAs' historically managerial mechanisms with more legalistic ones by linking MEA to PTAs in this way, trade agreements can strengthen MEA compliance capacity. As demonstrated most clearly in the case of CITES-relevant provisions in the US-Peru PTA, these managerial and legalistic mechanisms can together catalyze important implementation improvements.

It should be noted that PTAs can also enhance MEA effectiveness by significantly enhancing the managerial mechanisms available under the MEA alone. Notably, including MEAs provisions in PTAs can open up new sources of funding for capacity building for environmental enforcement. As noted above, the United States dedicated $90 million to capacity building and training programs related to the Forest Annex and environment chapter (USTR 2013; Inside US Trade 2015; Urrunaga, Johnson, and Orbegozo Sánchez 2018). Resource allocation at this level for capacity building far outstrips CITES's triennial budget for these activities from all of its parties combined. As noted by one US government official interviewed for this study: "It is fair to say that linking MEAs to [P]TAs increases MEA effectiveness, primarily because Congress appropriates funds for MEA implementation [through PTAs]." This official underscored that this doesn't necessarily mean problem-solving effectiveness is enhanced, noting that although Peru has received "the lion's share" of such funding, illegal timber trade still remains a major problem there.

Although this chapter demonstrates how the addition of new legalistic and enhanced managerial compliance tools can contribute to MEA implementation and compliance, there remains much work to be done in exploring the conditions under which legalistic tools can have positive effects for implementation of environmental provisions more broadly. That is, there is mixed evidence surrounding the impacts of the legalistic tools in catalyzing implementation of environmental provisions that are not explicitly tied to an MEA, such as CITES. For example, illegal timber exports from Peru have continued to be a major problem following the entry into force of the agreement despite the procedural effectiveness improvements we note above. These increases may actually be the result of increased compliance capacity. That is, it may be that illegal ships have stayed at the same level or even decreased, but Peru's capacity to enforce and therefore identify and document illegal shipments has increased. It is also possible that there is a shift in species that are being targeted. As CITES provisions make it more difficult to export bigleaf mahogany and cedar, illegal export may have shifted to other species not protected under CITES.

It should be noted that some environmental groups have strongly criticized Peru's implementation of the PTA's environmental provisions (EIA

2015). Most notably, the EIA has produced a series of reports calling for US government action in the face of Peru's failure to implement various provisions of the US-Peru PTA, including for example Article 18.3.2., which requires that parties not weaken existing environmental laws. EIA has argued that the Peruvian government has weakened such laws, by for example, reducing penalties for violation of environmental laws and taking certain powers away from Peru's environment ministry (Inside US Trade 2015). Although their critiques are extremely germane to the overarching motivation for this book (i.e., what role can PTAs play in environmental protection?), they are less relevant for the arguments we make here about MEA effectiveness. The critiques are leveled at the PTA broadly, including the Forest Annex. They are not targeted at the CITES-relevant provisions per se. The critiques that do address forest governance, while important for conservation, are targeted at illegal logging and trade. In contrast, CITES only addresses *legal* trade. It does not have mechanisms or provisions to tackle illegal trade and its effectiveness cannot be evaluated by looking at trends in *illegal* trade.

Therefore, although these critiques are less critical to our precise analysis here of how PTA-MEA linkages might impact implementation of and developing compliance mechanisms for CITES (i.e., procedural effectiveness), there are important broader lessons for how PTAs should/could be leveraged to contribute to environmental protection (i.e., problem-solving effectiveness). Importantly, EIA's report that illegal trade in CITES-listed species continued following the entry into force of the PTA, points to the possibility that stricter controls on legal logging, as required under the PTA, can have the unintended impact of driving illegal trade, or causing increased logging of species not protected by the included MEAs. It is unclear, however, if illegal logging of CITES-listed species increased under the PTA. If it did, this has substantial implications for the problem-solving effectiveness of MEAs. Further, if an increase is observed, these critiques also draw into question findings in the recent literature (cited above) that more detailed environmental provisions in PTAs enhance problem-solving effectiveness, as the US-Peru PTA contains *the* most detailed environmental provisions of any PTAs globally. Regardless, these critiques demand a very careful approach to linking such issues in the future.

Our analysis also uncovers how trade agreements are being used to improve MEA effectiveness in unexpected ways. In the CITES case, we see trade agreements being used to enhance the ambition of specific MEA provisions. For example, the US-Peru PTA regulates trade in cedar (an Appendix-III–listed species under CITES) more strongly than does CITES itself by requiring the same timber management practices for cedar as it does for mahogany (an Appendix-II–listed species). Indeed, Peru is already beginning to take action on cedar protection that moves beyond the requirements of an Appendix-III listing under CITES. Whereas CITES only requires that Peru provide proof of legal origin for its cedar exports, the country is involved in scientific assessments and studies that reflect what would be required for conducting non-detriment findings for Appendix-II–listed species. Upon returning from a recent site visit to Peru to assess implementation of the Convention, one CITES veteran expert noted:

> [Peru is] already starting to implement cedar as if it were in Appendix-II. They are doing a lot of research on cedar not requested by the Convention, which only requires certification of legal origin. The provisions in the Annex regarding any Appendix species are very demanding—this is now [Peruvian] law so they are doing this. . . . They have many species that are outside the [CITES] treaty and deserve the same action but they are only doing these studies for cedar.[18]

MEA provisions in trade agreements may well yield additional effectiveness improvements along some of Young's other dimensions of effectiveness (see table 4.1). For example, in catalyzing implementation of specific new forest management practices, the US Peru-PTA also prompted improvements in constitutive effectiveness (i.e., dedication of resources to regime implementation), and in funding implementation efforts through Congressional appropriations for PTA implementation. For example, in helping Peru transition to science-based quotas for mahogany exports, the PTA also contributed to improvements in effectiveness as measured through goal attainment (i.e., extent to which regime goals are met over time). However, these linkages may also (unintentionally) erode regime effectiveness along other dimensions. For example, the highly prescriptive forest management provisions in the US-Peru PTA did not adequately account for existing land tenure issues and helped to stoke violent protests from indigenous communities in 2009 (Jinnah 2011). These aspects of the PTA are clearly not equitable nor robust, suggesting an erosion of evaluative effectiveness. Further, as one NGO interviewee noted, "the annex didn't cause the trade flows of illegal timber to stop, they just moved to China," which suggests the problem-solving effectiveness is also not necessarily significantly improving.

In addition to enhancing the ambition of MEAs, trade agreements are also being used to engage parties in "back-door" environmental governance. That is, some trade agreements commit parties to environmental goals that those countries were unable or unwilling to commit to through MEAs themselves. More specifically, trade agreements can contribute to back-door environmental governance in two circumstances. The first is when the multilateral route seems blocked. Multilateral negotiations, such as the decision to list another species under the CITES, bring together several countries around a relatively narrow issue area. In contrast, PTA negotiations involve a limited number of partners, but cover a multitude of different issues. This context fosters bargaining, trade-offs, and the conclusion of far-reaching commitments. As a result, some recent US trade agreements set out stricter and more precise environmental commitments than those found in MEAs. The other circumstance is when domestic constraints, such as pressure from interest groups or blockage from the Parliament or other lawmakers prevent negotiators from adopting their favored norms, leading to "involuntary defection" in two-level game parlance (Putnam 1988). Given the broad coverage of PTAs, it is easier for negotiators to bury environmental provisions in PTAs, as the US government did with benefit-sharing provisions under the Convention on Biological Diversity that were opposed by the biotechnology industry and some members of the US Congress (Blomquist 2002). Further, as detailed in chapter 2, three bilateral trade agreements, including the US-Peru PTA, commit the United States to the core provisions of the Convention on Biological Diversity, to which the United States is not a party. As an OECD study concludes, states use trade negotiations as a strategic vehicle to pursue their international environmental agenda and enhance the global enforcement of their favored environmental norms (OECD 2007).

The CITES case further illuminates some the ways trade agreements can serve as mechanisms of norm diffusion (as we discuss in greater detail in chapter 5). For example, the United States, Mexico, and Canada Trade Agreement contains several provisions related to CITES and replicates the unique provisions that subject environmental provisions in US trade agreements to strong, punitive, enforcement-based dispute settlement. Even with the US withdrawal from the TPP under the Trump administration, we may still see US environmental and governance norms diffusing globally through the TPP. As we detail in chapter 6, we see also see the Nagoya

Protocol's access and benefit-sharing norms diffusing from Latin American countries to others through trade agreement linkages.

MEA linkages in trade agreements are proliferating over time, with trade negotiations progressively becoming vectors for the implementation of MEA obligations and increasingly linking such provisions to enforcement-based dispute settlement. The nature of these provisions varies greatly, however, depending on the countries involved. While the United States incorporates a detailed provision on biodiversity in its most recent PTAs, the European Union increasingly includes climate-related provisions in its own PTAs, such as commitments to implement the United Nations Framework Convention on Climate Change and its Kyoto Protocol, or requirements to establish a domestic emission-trading scheme for greenhouse gas emissions. However, these strong standards are not yet widely replicated in agreements between third countries, perhaps because they remain little known, or because other countries are more wary of including such environmentally prescriptive provisions in their trade agreements.

Interview data further support some indirect benefits of the PTA's environmental provisions. For example, Peruvian government representatives stressed that one of the most important outcomes of the PTA was that it enhanced cooperation and dialogue with the United States, and underscored that the PTA was "foundational" in helping Peru to build up domestic institutions for the environment and beyond. They further noted that, although the Forest Annex was highly prescriptive, the annex was "the bargain" they accepted in exchange for the broader environmental chapter, which reflected their interests in issues such as biodiversity.

There is also a question of whether the Forest Annex in particular is too prescriptive, delving too deeply into the domestic policy of another country. Interviewees had mixed perspectives on this. Some argued that the PTA did not tell Peru how to implement the provisions or to take many of the most controversial measures that it did, such as redefining eminent domain. Others supported strongly prescriptive provisions to pursue US environmental interests through trade agreements. Others were far more cautionary, noting:

> The annex is a unique beast. I don't think we'll see something that was as detailed as that again. It's been a bear for us and for Peru to implement. Some would argue it's been a big bludgeon to get Peru to make progress. It goes quite deeply into Peru's domestic processes. As someone who cares about national sovereignty,

it horrifies me, in a sense, but it provided an interesting road map for how to improve forest governance in Peru. It has brought high-level attention [to these issues] on the Hill, they are focused on it, they want briefing notes on it all the time—NGOs like [EIA] are really interested in it, and they have the ear of staffers and Congress people; they keep the pressure on. Peru rues the day that they agreed to the Forest Sector Governance Annex. To me personally, it is an overreach, but EIA probably doesn't agree with that.

Finally, given the potential for unintended consequences (e.g., social unrest resulting from insufficient fit between prescribed policies and preexisting domestic structures or interests, driving illegal activities), great care should be exercised in creating such linkages. Moreover, this case demonstrates that although MEA provisions hold promise for improving procedural outputs, detailed environmental provisions should be considered for inclusion in PTAs in a way that accounts for the politics and potential unintended impacts on the ground in trading-partner nations. For example, Urrunaga and colleagues (2018) report that in June 2009, then Peruvian President Allan Garcia used the US-Peru PTA's annex as a pretext to pass a series of controversial legislative decrees that impacted indigenous people's lands without their consultation or consent. This resulted in widespread indigenous protests across the country that left 33 dead and 200 injured in a violent clash with police in Bagua, Peru (Urrunaga, Johnson, and Orbegozo Sánchez 2018). Indeed, the annex's precise and detailed provisions counter decades of normative practice in environmental governance, which has historically left MEA obligations in the form of overarching goals, leaving states to interpret and implement them in a domestically appropriate manner. This mix of interests and outcomes points to the need for increased attention to the conditions under which PTA-MEA linkages yield beneficial outcomes for the environment and the people who depend on it for their livelihoods.

5 Can Preferential Trade Agreements Diffuse Environmental Norms?

This chapter explores how preferential trade agreements (PTAs) can play a role in helping environmental norms and policies spread, or diffuse, from one country to another. We argue, through an empirical examination of three US PTAs, that PTAs have indeed served to diffuse environmental norms to trading-partner nations. We focus on two key norms in US environmental policy: effective enforcement (i.e., "bona fide decisions" to allocate resources to enforce compliance with environmental laws)[1] and public participation (i.e., the inclusion of opportunities for citizen engagement in governmental decision making). We examine these norms across three US PTAs: 1992's NAFTA, the 2004 Central American Free Trade Agreement (CAFTA-DR),[2] and the 2006 Peru Trade Promotion Agreement. Our central argument is that key norms from US domestic environmental law and policy (i.e., public participation and effective enforcement) have diffused through environmental linkages within US PTAs and have been incorporated into domestic policy and practice in trading-partner nations. In illuminating this new mechanism of environmental norm diffusion (i.e., PTAs), we further demonstrate the potential for PTAs to shape environmental policy and practice across borders.

This analysis is particularly timely, given the geographic reach of the PTAs globally that are currently under (re)negotiation, and thus the potential for far-reaching environmental norm diffusion through these agreements. Recent scholarship has demonstrated how countries are increasingly diffusing their various trade provisions by templating language from one trade agreement to the next (Allee and Lugg 2016). For example, although the United States officially withdrew from the Trans-Pacific Partnership (TPP) in 2017, the United States had influenced the TPP's language more than any other country, with approximately 45 percent of the text of US PTAs from 1995–2015 found verbatim in the TPP, and 73 percent of the US-Jordan PTA copied directly into the TPP's chapter on environment (Allee and Lugg 2016). Although remaining TPP countries have already removed some US-generated text on, for example, intellectual property from this PTA, the US thumbprint remains visible on the revised agreement as well.

This chapter examines how trade agreements between two or more countries can serve as mechanisms of environmental norm diffusion between the parties to these agreements. In other words, we examine how environmental norms can diffuse from one domestic system to another by way of trade agreements. We build on recent scholarship that suggests a strong *potential* for US trade agreements to influence environmental policies abroad through the increasingly far-reaching and prescriptive provisions contained in those agreements (Jinnah 2011).[3] Our argument further extends findings that NAFTA's implementation has resulted in environmental policy changes in Mexico (Baver 2011). We take the next step in this analysis by linking environmental policy change to *several* PTAs across *several* trading-partner nations. Further, we trace these changes in trading partners' domestic environmental law and policy back to their source in US domestic law. In doing so, we show how these changes reflect *new* environmental norms that are not "home grown" but rather are imported from abroad through PTAs.

The next section situates our analysis in the broader literature on norm diffusion. We then outline our methodological approach, explaining how we know norm diffusion when we see it. This is followed by the empirical analysis, which traces our two norms of interest from US domestic environmental policy, through US PTAs, and into environmental policies and practices in trading-partner nations. The chapter's conclusion discusses the implications of environmental norm diffusion for environmental performance and equity.

Norm and Policy Diffusion through Issue Linkage

Norms and policies are closely tethered. Norms set boundaries for political life by setting standards of behavior and defining expectations for what is or should be. In short, norms are collective ideas, principles, and/or expectations of behavior. International norms such as state sovereignty, abolition of slavery, human rights, and nonproliferation are strongly legalized[4] in international law. Environmental norms tend to be weaker, characterized largely by lower levels of precision, for example. Environmental norms include such ideas as the "polluter pays" principle and common but differentiated responsibilities, which, when included in international treaties, are often left for states to interpret and operationalize in particular contexts. Here we examine key US norms that define ideas and expectations for how policy should be made (i.e., public participation) and enforced (i.e., effectively). We further demonstrate how these norms were either weak or absent in selected countries prior to their requirement through US PTAs.

Whereas norms identify goals, policies delineate how those goals should be achieved. Policies "internalize" or formalize norms in ways that can define specific pathways for action, more easily assign accountability, and sometimes enable enforcement through law (Finnemore and Sikkink 1998). Policies reiterate and articulate norms, but also explain how norms should be achieved through, for example, targets and timetables, reporting requirements, and institutional arrangements.

Norms are thus deeply embedded within policies (and laws). In international treaties, norms are often articulated in preambular text. For example, the Convention on Biological Diversity's preamble establishes the need to "conserve biodiversity . . . for present and future generations," and the WTO's General Agreement on Tariffs and Trade preamble asserts that relations between countries "should be conducted with a view to . . . developing the full use of resources of the world." Norms are also found in operational treaty texts, which are often translated into domestic law and policy through ratification and implementation. The extent to which policies reiterate norms, therefore, is a proxy, albeit an imperfect one, for whether or not norms have been internalized within a particular political system.

In highlighting how the United States incorporates environmental norms into its PTAs, this chapter engages discussions on norm diffusion and policy transfer. These literatures diverge with respect to terminology, methodology, and case selection. However, they are essentially interested in the same processes—the movement of ideas across borders—and there is substantial conceptual overlap in how they treat the transnational movement of norms and policies (Marsh and Sharman 2009). We, therefore, treat their contributions holistically, drawing on the strands of each that are most relevant to the analysis undertaken here.

Norm diffusion is the movement and adoption of norms across political borders. In brief, the literature points to four main theories of norm diffusion: learning, competition, coercion, and social construction (Dobbin, Simmons, and Garrett 2007; Morin and Gold 2014). In the environmental policy context, learning is often identified as an important driver of norm and policy diffusion; for example, "front-runner" states model environmental policies that are emulated and adapted by others (Busch, Jörgens, and Tews 2005). Competition, too, has been identified as a driver of diffusion, as states harmonize environmental policies upward (Vogel 1995). Coercion is relatively understudied in the environmental context. Finally, constructivists have underscored the role of international organizations in spreading ideas among states (Finnemore 1993).

Scholars have also identified specific mechanisms of norm diffusion, such as persuasion, localization, and institutional translation (Keck and Sikkink 1998; Acharya 2004; Bettiza and Dionigi 2014). We are in close conversation with this previous work on mechanisms in identifying a new mechanism of environmental norm diffusion: issue linkage and, more specifically, environmental linkages in PTAs. That is, by incorporating environmental provisions into trade agreements, the United States has not only used issue linkage to change bargaining dynamics, as discussed by previous scholars, but it has also diffused key US environmental norms into trading-partner countries' *domestic* laws and policies.

Whereas "tactical linkages" are typically deployed to gain bargaining leverage by making one's behavior on an issue conditional on another's behavior on a separate issue (Haas 1980; Axelrod and Keohane 1985), the linkages examined here link separate issues within a single agreement. That is, trade agreements require specific environmental policy changes in trading-partner nations that are tangential to the core objectives of the trade agreement. In some cases, such linkages even aim to achieve the environmental objectives required by an entirely separate environmental treaty, as discussed in chapter 4 with the Convention on International Trade in Endangered Species of Wild Fauna and Flora (CITES) and the US-Peru PTA. Whereas "tactical linkages" are used to shift bargaining leverage across agreements, the trade-environment linkages examined here achieve the adoption of tangential policy objectives by incorporating them directly into PTAs. Further, whereas previous work has shown how environmental norms diffuse from domestic law to international trade law (Allee and

Can Preferential Trade Agreements Diffuse Environmental Norms?

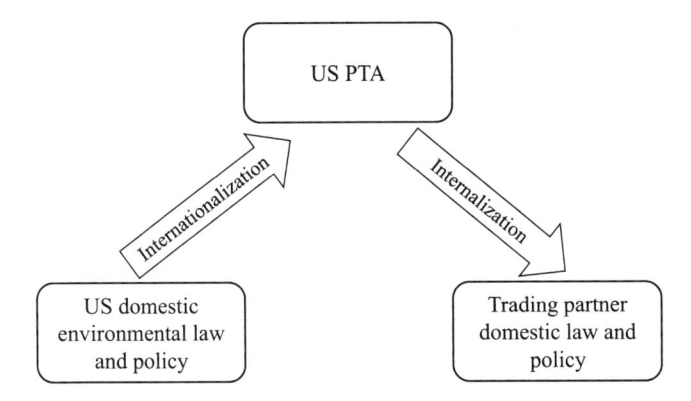

Figure 5.1
Diffusion of environmental norms through trade agreements

Lugg 2016), we go a step further in tracing the subsequent *incorporation* of those environmental norms into domestic law and policy in trading-partner nations.

In short, this chapter draws together the literatures on issue linkage and norm diffusion by demonstrating how environmental linkages in US PTAs serve as mechanisms to diffuse US environmental norms to trading-partner nations.

How Do We Know Norm Diffusion When We See It?

We use process tracing to demonstrate how environmental linkages within US PTAs serve as mechanisms to diffuse US environmental norms abroad. Specifically, we use documents, such as legal texts, US and Peruvian government reports, and NGO reports, to trace the movement of two US environmental norms—legalistic enforcement and public participation—from domestic US policy, through US PTAs, and ultimately into the domestic laws and policies in trading-partner nations.

We focus on these two specific norms because we find them consistently across most US PTAs, as well as in much US domestic law—both within and beyond the environment context. Public participation provisions include any language that requires the involvement of private actors and/or civil society in issues related to environmental governance. This might include provisions requiring the empowering of civil society, allowing for public comment, and/or requiring public notification of environmental decision making. Effective enforcement involves "bona fide decisions" to allocate resources to enforce compliance with environmental laws and, as discussed in chapter 4, can take a legalistic and/or managerial approach. Whereas managerial enforcement relies on cooperative mechanisms, such as capacity building, to incentivize compliance, legalistic mechanisms are designed to achieve compliance through coercive mechanisms, such as sanctions or penalties, which increase costs of non-compliance. The United States uses both types of mechanisms in its domestic and international environmental policies, and considers both to be central to effective enforcement. Further, at time of writing, the United States is the only country that utilizes strong legalistic mechanisms to enforce environmental provisions in its PTAs.

Figures 5.2 and 5.3 show the number of public participation and effective enforcement clauses in US PTAs, in comparison to those of its trading partners (in PTAs concluded after their agreement with the United States), as well as in the PTAs of other countries.[5] In both figures, NAFTA (the triangle on the 1992 value of the x-axis) appears as a highly innovative agreement, with a record number of clauses on public participation and on effective enforcement. US PTAs (represented by triangles) are among those with the most clauses on these two issues over the entire period. Most non-US agreements that also include a high number of clauses on public participation and effective enforcement are PTAs signed by US trading partners with third countries. This further suggests that the United States is a driving force at the center of the global diffusion of norms related to public participation in environmental governance and effective enforcement of domestic environmental law.

We want to show *how* (i.e., the mechanisms through which) these norms move across borders. To do so, we conducted our analysis in four steps. First, we showed the emergence of public participation and effective enforcement norms in US domestic environmental law and policy by examining key pieces of US environmental law and policy and explaining how these norms are central to those documents. Second, we showed how the United States has "internationalized" these norms (see DeSombre 2000) by replicating them in the three US PTAs examined in this study: NAFTA, CAFTA-DR, and the US-Peru PTA. We examined those PTAs for articulations of these norms to show how those PTA articulations are uniquely similar in

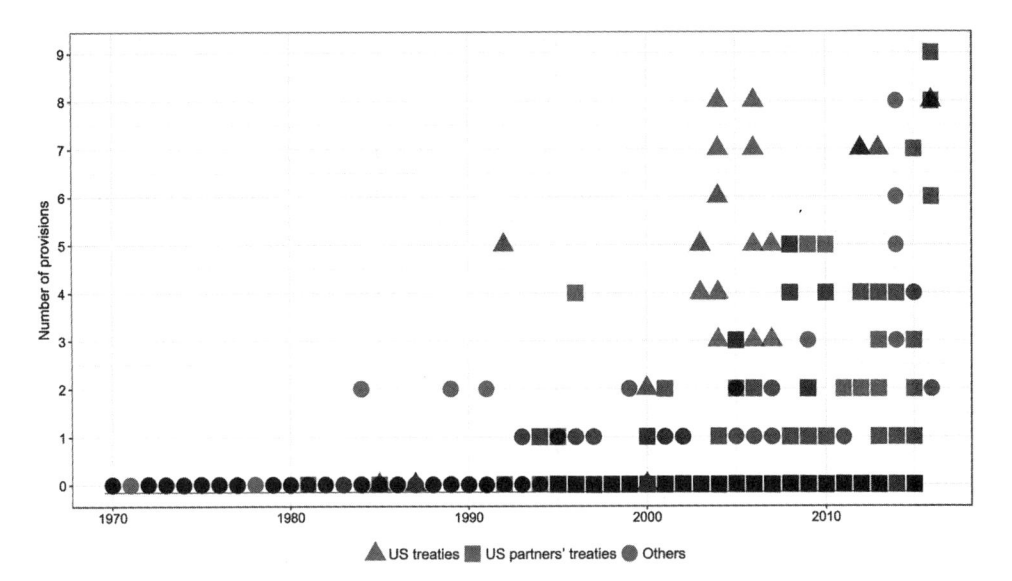

Can Preferential Trade Agreements Diffuse Environmental Norms? 109

Figure 5.2
Number of clauses on public participation in PTAs (1970–2016)

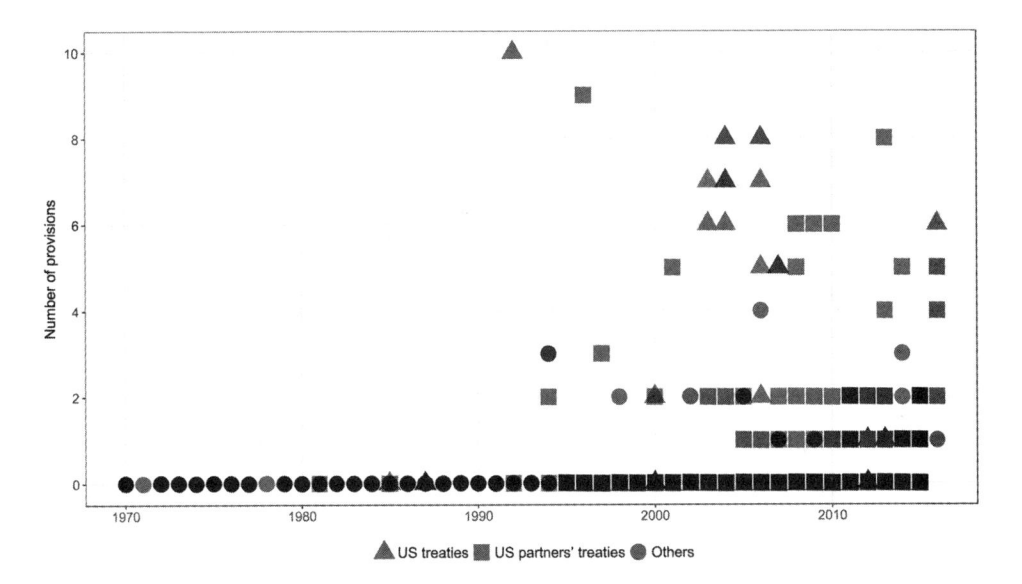

Figure 5.3
Number of provisions on enforcement of domestic measures in PTAs (1970–2016)

approach to, and in some cases replicated verbatim from, those found in US domestic environmental law and policy.

Third, and centrally, we looked for evidence of norm internalization into the domestic laws and policies of trading-partner nations. We argue that when norms have been internalized, they have begun to diffuse. Although we understand diffusion not as a binary concept but as existing along a continuum, we do not attempt to evaluate the degree of diffusion here. Rather, we analyzed whether effective enforcement and public participation have, at a minimum, begun to diffuse through issue linkage. Therefore, following Katzenstein (1996), we identified internalization by looking for the incorporation of these norms into domestic policy and practice. Like diffusion, internalization should be measured along a continuum, with deep behavioral change being an indicator of strong norm internalization, and policy change being a weaker indicator. The degree of internalization thus depends on the degree to which changes are internalized and also provides a preliminary indication of whether or not norms have diffused across borders.

Specifically, we looked at the policies that trading partners adopted to implement the effective enforcement and public participation provisions of their US PTAs. We analyzed documents from the US Trade Representative (USTR), the Commission for Environmental Cooperation, nongovernmental organizations (NGOs), and trading-partner governments that summarize the implementation activities in those nations. Using these secondary documents, as opposed to the laws and policies themselves, allowed us both to quickly narrow down the universe of relevant documents and to identify policies that were enacted specifically to implement the PTA.

Finally, we conducted a counterfactual analysis, reflecting on alternative explanations for the presence of public participation and effective enforcement in the domestic environmental policy and practices in trading-partner nations. We first looked for these norms in the PTAs that trading-partner nations had signed with other countries prior to their US PTAs. If these norms were important in domestic environmental policy prior to the US PTAs, we would expect to see them in those countries' prior PTAs with other trading partners as well. The absence of such provisions from these PTAs would be a strong indication of diffusion from the United States. We ruled out preexisting internalization of effective enforcement and public participation norms through secondary analyses of domestic environmental policies in trading-partner nations prior to the entry into force of the US PTAs.

Effective Enforcement and Public Participation in US Law and Policy

Effective enforcement and public participation have long been central norms in US environmental law. Legalistic mechanisms feature prominently in the US domestic approach to effective enforcement through, for example, fines and criminal sentences. Public participation is also central to the US domestic environmental policy process through, for example, opportunities for public comment on draft laws and public opportunities for legal remediation. This section details the origins of these two norms in US environmental law and policy.

The US approach to effective enforcement of environmental laws has relied heavily on legal recourse for noncompliance through civil and criminal penalties. Central US environmental laws, such as the 1970 Clean Air Act and the 1972 Clean Water Act (CWA) emphasize formal rules and procedures and the extensive use of prosecution and litigation (Raustiala 1995). Under the CWA, for example, any wastewater discharge from a point source without a permit is subject to a fine of US$25,000 per day (Hodas 1995). Conservation-oriented laws, such as the 1973 Endangered Species Act and the 1900 Lacey Act (amended 2008), similarly impose civil and criminal penalties for violations.

These laws are strongly enforced. In 2014 alone, the US EPA completed 15,600 inspections and evaluations, issuing approximately US$80 million in criminal fines and almost US$100 million for federal administrative and civil judicial penalties (US EPA 2014). This is quite different from the approach taken by many US trading partners, which tend to have weaker enforcement mechanisms (Harrison 1995; Husted and Logsdon 1997).

Public participation is also prolific in US environmental law and policy. Public (or citizen) participation refers to "purposeful activities in which citizens take part in relation to government" (Spyke 1999, 266). It often includes access to information, access to justice, and participation in environmental decision making.

Public participation is incorporated into several parts of the US policy process. Policy development provisions often call for transparency and access to information. The 1969 National Environmental Policy Act, for example, incorporated public participation by allowing for public comment on all federal environmental impact statements (Spyke 1999). Public comment periods, public hearings, and citizen review panels provide core avenues for citizen participation under the Environmental Policy Act and several other US environmental laws (Fiorino 1990).

Public participation provisions also dovetail with enforcement provisions. For example, the CWA extends the responsibility for enforcement to citizens, calling for their participation in "the enforcement of any regulation, standard, effluent limitation, plan, or program" (§101(e), 33 U.S.C. §1251(e), section 101(e)). Finally, citizen suit provisions, such as those in the CWA, Clean Air Act, and Endangered Species Act, provide a mechanism for citizen enforcement by challenging a government's failure to enforce its environmental laws.

Environmental Norms in US Preferential Trade Agreements

This section details how US norms of public participation and effective enforcement are replicated in three US PTAs, one from each phase of US trade policy described in chapter 3: NAFTA (1992), the CAFTA-DR (2004), and the Peru PTA (2006). Although NAFTA has received substantial attention in the environment literature on PTAs to date, CAFTA-DR and the Peru PTA have been largely understudied, demanding increased analytical attention.

North American Free Trade Agreement

NAFTA asserts that trade and investment should not compromise the environment, prohibits waiving or derogating from environmental measures to attract investment, and lists several MEAs whose trade provisions are effectively immune from challenge should they conflict with NAFTA's trade provisions. The majority of NAFTA's environmental provisions, however, are formally incorporated in the parallel North American Agreement on Environmental Cooperation (NAAEC). The NAAEC requires parties to strive for "high levels of environmental protection" and "to continue to improve [environmental] laws" (Art. 3). The NAAEC further established the Commission on Environmental Cooperation (CEC) to support implementation of its environmental provisions, including those related to effective enforcement and public participation.

NAFTA put significant pressure on Mexico to improve its environmental enforcement activities by using both legalistic and managerial enforcement methods that reflect those in US environmental policy. On the former, for example, it requires parties to "ensure that judicial, quasi-judicial or administrative enforcement proceedings are available" for environmental law enforcement, and to create processes for public participation in investigations of alleged violations (Arts. 5 and 6). Many of the managerial enforcement mechanisms to ensure effective enforcement of environmental law and policy can be found in the NAAEC. Now standard in US PTAs, these bilateral and regional activities are referred to as "cooperative activities" and include things such as joint trainings to increase government enforcement capacity and partnerships with nongovernment stakeholders to promote environmental protection and effective enforcement.

The NAAEC also promotes transparency and public participation as a main objective of the agreement (Art. 1(h)). It established a public submission process for enforcement matters, which allows citizens to request a review of a party's alleged failure to enforce its environmental laws. The NAAEC outlines procedures for this review and for making such information publicly available. The NAAEC also provides for a relatively weak consultation/arbitral process through which parties can resolve disputes related to their failure to enforce environmental laws. NAFTA further provides opportunities for the public to attend CEC meetings and be appointed to advisory committees, and it makes many CEC reports publicly available. The NAAEC also requires that many other documents be made publicly available and provides opportunities for public participation in procedural matters and cooperation activities (Art. 4.1).

Central American Free Trade Agreement

CAFTA-DR was negotiated under the 2002 fast-track authority, which, as discussed in chapter 3, required that specific environmental objectives be included in all US trade agreements. As such, CAFTA-DR's environmental provisions were directly incorporated into the PTA itself rather than included in a "side agreement," as was the case with NAFTA. CAFTA included a full chapter on environmental issues, which includes provisions on the effective enforcement of environmental laws and public participation in enforcement. The environment chapter also requires environmental cooperation between parties. To implement those provisions, the parties negotiated a parallel environmental cooperation agreement (ECA).[6] Similar to the NAAEC, the ECA is a separate executive agreement negotiated alongside the PTA, does not require US congressional approval, and focuses entirely on operationalizing the PTA's environmental cooperation activities.

Whereas trade ministries take the lead on PTA implementation, the ECA allowed the environment ministries in Latin American countries and the Department of State in the United States to define priorities and goals for environmental cooperation. The parties identified several goals, including effective enforcement of environmental laws. Similar to the concerns raised by civil society actors during NAFTA's negotiation, several concerns were raised regarding Central American countries' track records of environmental law enforcement during the CAFTA-DR negotiations (USTR 2003). While all of the Central American countries had passed a general framework law on the environment, a lack of fiscal and human resources limited their ability to enforce those laws (USTR 2003). As such, the parties focused primarily on managerial approaches, such as strengthening enforcement capacity and fostering public participation in the ECA. However, they did identify legalistic approaches to complement these managerial ones, such as a priority to ensure that judicial, quasi-judicial, or administrative proceedings are available to sanction or remedy violations of environmental laws (US Department of State 2012).

The environment chapter also provides a weak consultation process to resolve environment-related disputes. The US emphasis on effective enforcement is also evident in the decision to restrict access to CAFTA-DR's much stronger, sanction-based dispute-settlement system to claims made under the effective enforcement clause alone. Yet remedy is still quite limited for all other environmental disputes, which must be handled through the weak consultation process. Also like NAFTA, CAFTA-DR's environment chapter sets up a process wherein members of the public can request review of a party's alleged failure to enforce its environmental laws.

The CAFTA-DR environment chapter also places a heavy emphasis on public participation. As we discussed above, the public submissions process allows individuals to request reviews of alleged violations of environmental laws. Parties further agreed to ensure the availability of "judicial, quasi-judicial, or administrative proceedings . . . to sanction or remedy violations of its environmental laws" (Art. 17.3.1). CAFTA-DR also provides for public involvement in environmental decision making. For example, individuals may be involved in advisory committees or submit comments and recommendations on environmental cooperation activities. Cooperation activities, too, have focused on enhancing public participation—for example, by supporting public involvement in environmental decision making through small grants to civil society organizations (OAS 2014).

US-Peru Preferential Trade Agreement

As with CAFTA-DR, the 2006 US-Peru PTA contains an environment chapter that mandates effective enforcement of domestic environmental laws and includes several new environmental provisions, such as one covering biodiversity conservation.[7] It also contains several environmental provisions typical of other US PTAs, including those related to the implementation of MEAs that may otherwise conflict with trade rules as well as environmental cooperation to enhance capacity to protect the environment. Following instructions contained in the 2007 Bipartisan Trade Deal, the US-Peru PTA also includes greatly strengthened legalistic enforcement provisions for environmental matters by allowing unrestricted recourse for noncompliance through the PTA's sanction-based dispute-settlement clause. Finally, the environment chapter contains an annex on forest sector governance, which addresses the economic and environmental impacts of illegal logging and wildlife trade and details how Peru should revise domestic forest policy to improve forest governance.[8] Like CAFTA-DR, the Peru PTA established an ECA to implement environmental cooperation provisions of the PTA's environment chapter, including through a strengthening of Peruvian national enforcement capacity. As with CAFTA-DR's ECA, a separate agreement allowed environmental cooperation to be led outside of trade ministries and did not require US congressional ratification.

The environment chapter of the Peru Agreement requires effective enforcement in several ways. Centrally, the PTA calls for legalistic effective enforcement through prosecutorial discretion. This is supported by provisions on procedural matters, which mandate that parties investigate alleged violations of environmental laws and make such violations punishable through sanctions, fines, imprisonment, and/or facility closures. The strongest legalistic enforcement provisions in the US-Peru PTA environment chapter are found in the article on environmental consultations. As we noted above, prior agreements such as NAFTA and CAFTA-DR had contained comparatively weak provisions for environmental consultations. The

US-Peru Agreement greatly strengthened these provisions, allowing parties to seek unrestricted remedy under the agreement's primary sanction-based dispute-settlement system for any dispute under the PTA's environment chapter.

The Forest Annex also contains several strong managerial and legalistic provisions on effective enforcement. On the former, these include requirements to increase the number of enforcement personnel, develop anticorruption plans, and strengthen existing institutions for enforcing forest laws. On the latter, these include provisions providing for strong civil and criminal liability and penalties and allowing the United States to directly engage in enforcement activities in Peru. Specifically, upon US request, Peru must audit specific producers or exporters, verify that such actors are in compliance with Peru's forest laws, and allow US officials to participate in site visits to conduct these verifications.

Public participation is also plentiful throughout the environment chapter, its Forest Annex, and the ECA. These provisions, for example, require transparency of decisions and that judicial and administrative proceedings be open to the public, ensure public access to legal remedy, and mandate that Peru promote public awareness of environmental laws. Like NAFTA and CAFTA-DR, the Peru Agreement contains a process for citizen submissions asserting that either party is failing to enforce its environmental laws. The Forest Annex also requires transparency in the forest concession process, the incorporation of local and indigenous views to strengthen enforcement mechanisms, and increasing public participation in forest resource planning. ECA provisions enhance the Peruvian capacity to promote public participation in environmental decision making and enforcement and require public input in defining ECA activities in both countries.

In summary, norms of effective enforcement and public participation are deeply embedded in NAFTA, CAFTA-DR, and the US-Peru PTA. The ways that these norms are articulated in these agreements are very similar to articulations in US domestic environmental law and, in many instances, are essentially replicated from one US PTA to the next. In line with existing theory, this suggests that these norms diffuse through a process of "internationalization" from US domestic policy to US PTAs (Allee and Lugg 2016; DeSombre 2000; Morin and Gold 2014). In the next section, we take a crucial next step in analyzing the extent to which these internationalized

Can Preferential Trade Agreements Diffuse Environmental Norms? 117

norms have subsequently been internalized domestically in trading-partner nations through incorporation into domestic law and policy.

US Norm Internalization in Trading-Partner Nations?

In this section, we use norm internalization (as measured through policy changes) in trading-partner nations as a proxy for the diffusion of effective enforcement and public participation norms. We do this, first, by analyzing key documents for evidence that trading-partner nations are incorporating these norms into domestic policies and practices. Second, we discuss and reject alternative explanations for the internalization (and thus diffusion) of these norms in trading-partner nations' domestic law and policy.

North American Free Trade Agreement

The internalization of effective enforcement is evidenced in several laws and policies implemented in response to NAFTA obligations. The CEC annual reports, for example, list many domestic environmental policies that were developed or revised to comply with the NAAEC. They highlight key policy changes, including Mexico's 1996 revisions to its General Law on Ecological Balance and Environmental Protection (LGEEPA) and Canada's 1999 revision of the Canadian Environmental Protection Act (CEPA), both of which strengthen effective enforcement and public participation. The LGEEPA revision recognizes the right to information and allows for third-party compliance monitoring, and the CEPA revision incorporates new provisions allowing citizens to request investigations into alleged violations of domestic environmental laws (CEC 2001; Environment Canada 1999; CEPA Part 2). Enhanced enforcement is also evidenced through the increased number of inspections and verification visits in Mexico. For example, between 1971 and 1992, an average of 1,000 inspections for pollution control took place in Mexico per year (CEC 2001). This number increased dramatically following the entry into force of NAFTA, with 13,965 such visits between September 1995 and December 1996 alone (CEC 1996)!

NAFTA's environmental cooperation activities also evidence the internalization of effective enforcement norms from the United States to Mexico. For example, in 1995, the parties established the North American Wildlife Enforcement Group to improve their collective enforcement of wildlife laws, along with the North American Working Group on Environmental

Enforcement and Compliance to help build Mexico's enforcement capacity. Subsequently, Mexico increased its inspections and seizures for compliance with wildlife laws more than threefold between 1995 and 1998 (CEC 1998).

CEC environmental cooperation activities have also catalyzed increased public participation. For example, in 1996, NAFTA parties developed the first North American Pollutant Release Inventory, modeled on the 1986 US Toxic Release Inventory. Environmental cooperation has also provided at least US$7 million for community grants, which supported a wide range of projects to engage citizens in environmental protection (CEC 2015).

Finally, in response to specific NAAEC provisions, Mexico also created several new institutions for public engagement, such as regional advisory councils, a national council, and an Advisory Council for Protected Areas, and guaranteed access to environmental information in the 1996 LGEEPA reform (CEC 2003). Canada's 1999 CEPA amendment also strengthened citizen participation and access to environmental information by providing opportunities for public input at all stages of the decision-making process (Environment Canada 1999).

Central American Free Trade Agreement
CAFTA-DR countries have implemented, adopted, or improved approximately 150 new environmental laws that enhance effective enforcement and public participation in CAFTA-DR countries, largely with US financial support (OAS 2014). For example, several parties have developed mechanisms for better enforcing wastewater permitting and have held trainings on how to conduct inspections, audits, and environmental impact assessments. They also have supported trainings for judges, prosecutors, customs agents, police, and foresters to improve enforcement actions. US-supported cooperation activities under CAFTA-DR have also helped strengthen parties' institutional capacity at multiple levels of government, improving their ability to monitor and enforce environmental laws, such as through modernizing permit systems. For example, Nicaragua, Honduras, and Costa Rica developed a web-based management system for CITES permits, and the Dominican Republic modernized their Energy Information Administration system with a geographic-information-system-based analytical tool (OAS 2014).

The United States has also worked through CAFTA-DR's cooperation activities to help Central American countries improve opportunities for public participation in environmental decision making. For example, with US support, CAFTA-DR parties have published public guides to environmental laws and developed outreach campaigns, workshops, and media events to spread awareness of environmental laws (OAS 2014). The United States has also financed a small grants program, which trained 4,500 people in public participation tools and methods through 130 workshops across the CAFTA-DR countries (OAS 2014). Finally, in response to CAFTA-DR, the Dominican Republic and other Central American countries set up advisory committees through which citizens can raise environmental issues, which additional Central American countries are currently working on as well (Art. 17.6.3).[9]

US-Peru Preferential Trade Agreement

Peru has also enacted several new domestic laws aimed at implementing public participation and effective enforcement norms as articulated in the PTA. On effective enforcement, for example, Peru has created a new Ministry of Environment with an investigatory arm to verify compliance with environmental laws, and also established an independent forestry oversight body that has already conducted thousands of forest concession audits and assessed monetary fines in cases of noncompliance. In 2008, Peru modified its penal code regarding environmental crimes to greatly strengthen criminal penalties for forest-related crimes (Peru 2013). Between 2009 and 2013, Peru more than doubled the financial resources dedicated to the National Forest Authority for institutional strengthening (Peru 2013). Furthermore, in 2013, following allegations from US environmental NGOs of Peruvian failure to adequately implement the Forest Annex, US and Peruvian officials developed an action plan to prioritize areas for further forest sector cooperation. The plan identifies five such areas, including several related to effective enforcement, such as the need to ensure timely criminal and administrative proceedings to sanction violations of Peruvian forest laws (USTR 2015b).

Unfortunately, despite these procedural improvements, illegal logging continues to be a major problem in Peru, and the country has been severely criticized for not effectively enforcing provisions in the Forest Annex in particular (Urrunaga, Johnson, and Orbegozo Sánchez 2018). These failures reflect very mixed success in terms of effective enforcement in the country. Procedural changes in Peruvian environmental law related to effective enforcement have been made, reflecting at least some normative diffusion on this issue. However, there remains much work to do to fully enforce the broad requirements of the Forest Annex, indicating that normative changes to domestic law and policy are insufficient to actually address the problem.

On public participation, parties are currently setting up a public submissions process, similar to those of NAFTA and CAFTA-DR, and Peru has made more enforcement-related information public, including forestry information and forest management plans (Peru 2013). Following major protests across the country in 2009 related to failures to adequately involve indigenous people into environmental decision making as required by the annex, Peru has revised its policies in this regard (Urrunaga, Johnson, and Orbegozo Sánchez 2018). For example, it has increased consultations with indigenous groups on new regulations that affect resources located on their traditional lands (US GAO 2014). Although far from perfect, these changes do reflect improvements in the status quo regarding Peru's domestic public participation practices.

Finally, US-funded cooperative activities are also instrumental in internalizing these norms in this case. The United States has invested approximately US$90 million into supporting implementation of the agreement's environmental provisions (US GAO 2014; USTR 2013; Urrunaga, Johnson, and Orbegozo Sánchez 2018). Peruvian officials have participated in US training sessions on forest investigation and environmental prosecution and, in cooperation with US officials, have developed an updated training module to enhance investigation techniques and rates of prosecution for forest crimes (USTR 2015c).

In summary, evidence of the internalization of effective enforcement and public participation norms is present across all three agreements. Despite these high levels of internalization, in the case of the US-Peru PTA, compliance with newly created laws and policies continues to be a significant problem, especially as it relates to illegal logging. Nevertheless, analyses of PTA implementation from the USTR, CEC, Organization of American States, and trading-partner governments support the claims that these norms have been adopted into domestic law and policy as a means of directly implementing the environmental provisions contained in NAFTA, CAFTA-DR, and the US-Peru PTA. Although additional analysis will be needed to determine the strength of internalization, the proliferation of these norms in domestic policies across agreements provides strong evidence that norm internalization is occurring.

Alternative Explanations

Norm uptake into domestic policies suggests that norms of public participation and effective enforcement (as reflected in US PTAs) are beginning to internalize in trading-partner nations. The implementation reviews cited above strongly suggest that these norms originated in domestic US politics and were subsequently implemented in trading-partner nations following PTA obligations. The US Trade Act of 2002 further reinforces this claim, with several references to public access and with effective enforcement of environmental laws identified as among the "principal negotiating objectives" on the environment (sec. 2102, para. b(11)(A)).

Nevertheless, we briefly rule out other possible explanations here. It is possible that these norms were already present in the PTAs the US trading partners had previously negotiated with other countries. First, therefore, we examined all PTAs negotiated prior to those with the United States for any discussions of effective enforcement and public participation in environmental law or policy making. If such articulations are absent, this provides even stronger evidence that such norms diffused from the US PTAs. Even if such articulations are absent, however, it remains possible that trading partners simply had not yet "internationalized" these norms. We, therefore, also examined trading partners' pre-US-PTA environmental laws for these norms. If such norms are weak or absent from such policies, this also provides strong evidence for our assertion that these norms diffused through the US PTAs and were not home-grown in the trading-partner nations.

Pre-US Preferential Trade Agreements

We found that few of the PTAs that US trading partners had entered into with other countries prior to their US PTA referenced the norms of effective enforcement or public participation. In fact, most US trading partners did not include environmental provisions in their PTAs prior to concluding an agreement with the United States at all. This appears clearly in figure 5.4 on Canadian trade agreements and figure 5.5 on Peruvian trade agreements. These figures show the number of environmental clauses on public participation and effective enforcement, as classified in the Trade Environment

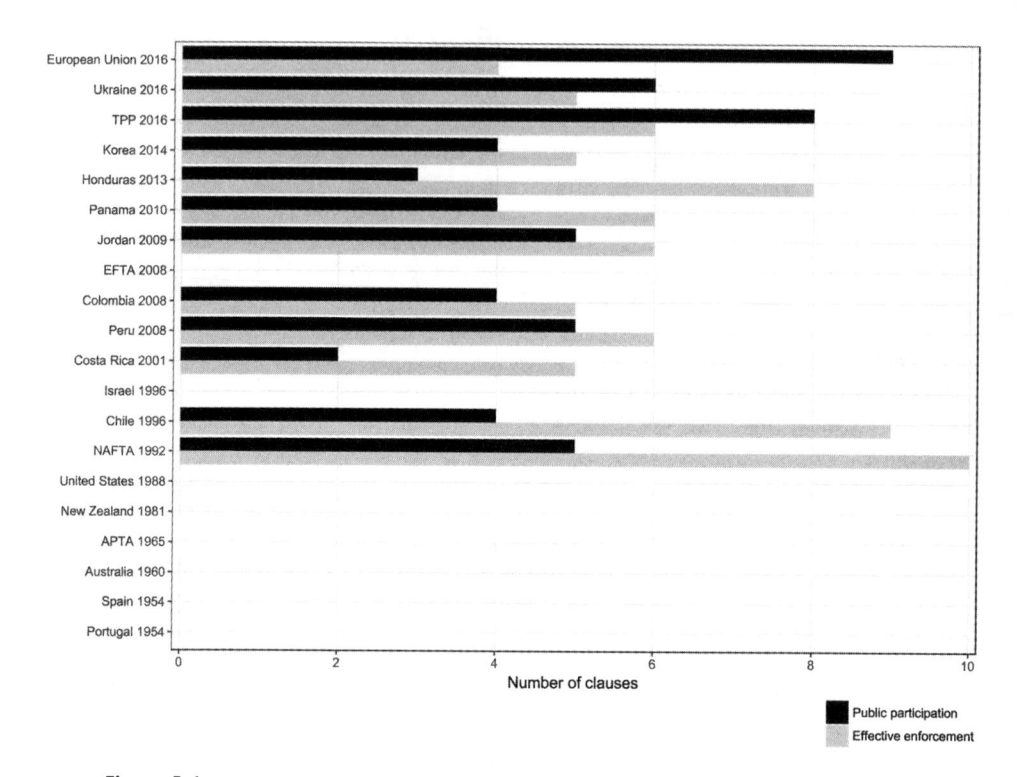

Figure 5.4
Number of environmental clauses in Canadian trade agreements (in reverse chronological order)

Database (TREND), for each trade agreement. They reveal that Canadian and Peruvian PTAs did not include such environmental clauses prior to the signature of their respective trade agreement with the United States.

Importantly, US partners often change their PTA model following their agreement with the United States and start including several environmental clauses in their subsequent PTAs. This appears clearly in figures 5.4 and 5.5, as the average number of clauses on public participation and effective enforcement increase significantly for Canada and Peru after their respective agreement with the United States. Thus, these provisions diffuse out of US agreements and reach countries that have not yet concluded an agreement with the United States. This process is illustrated in figure 5.6 below.

Can Preferential Trade Agreements Diffuse Environmental Norms? 123

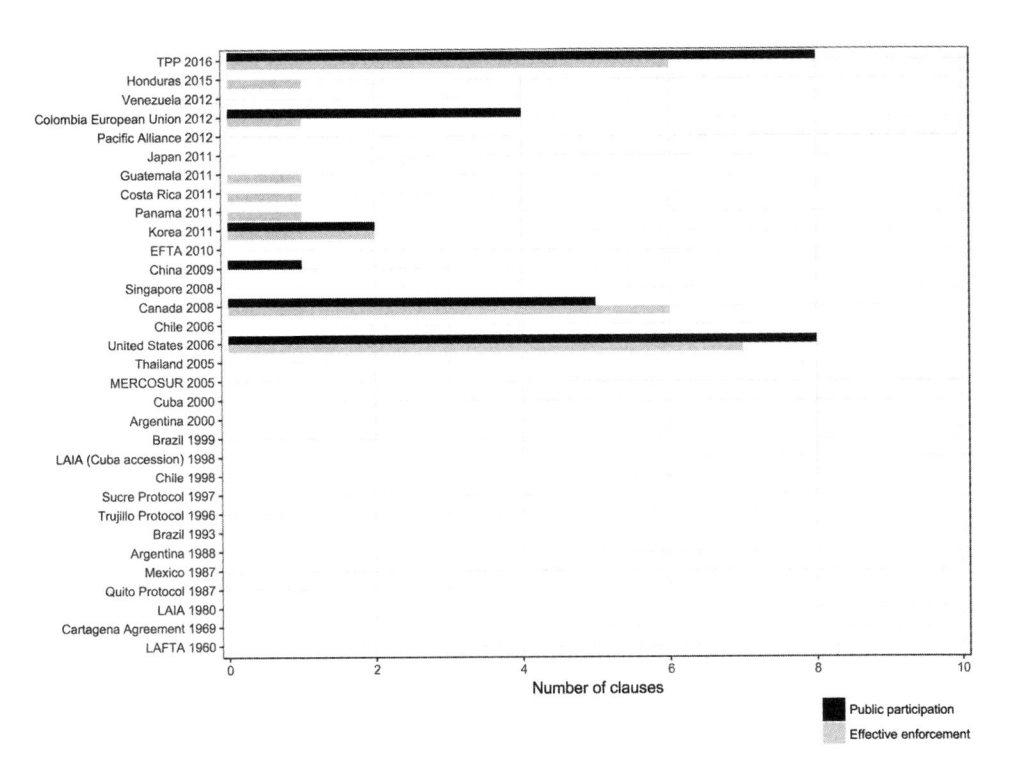

Figure 5.5
Number of environmental provisions in Peruvian trade agreements (in reverse chronological order)

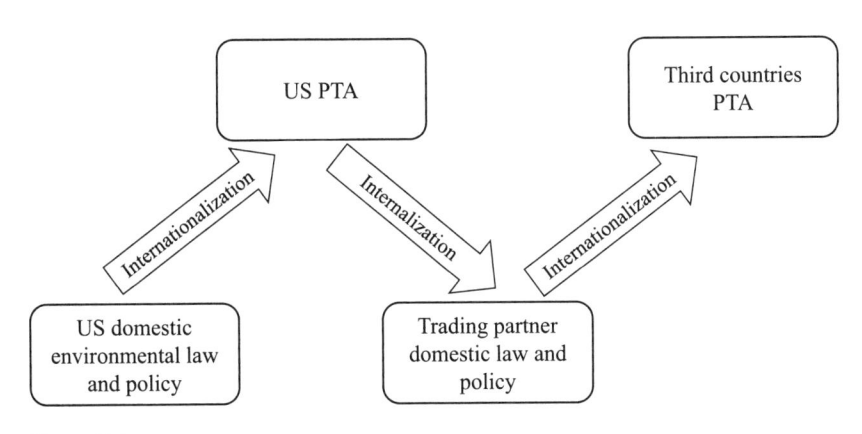

Figure 5.6
Diffusion of environmental norms through trade agreements

As a result of this diffusion, some US trading partners had concluded PTAs with clauses on public participation and effective enforcement prior to negotiating an agreement with the United States. However, all of these countries had previously signed a PTA with an earlier US trading partner. For example, Canada included provisions on public participation in environmental law making and private access to remedies in case of violations to environmental law in its 1996 agreement with Chile. These provisions were reproduced from NAFTA and its environmental side agreement. Therefore, when Chile concluded a PTA with the United States in 2003, it had already agreed to US-style norms on public participation and effective enforcement. Likewise, Costa Rica had already accepted clauses on public participation and effective enforcement in PTAs with Mexico (1994) and Canada (2001) before it concluded a trade agreement with the United States in 2004, and these earlier PTAs included US-style provisions on public participation and effective enforcement. Rather than weakening the argument of this chapter by supporting an alternative explanation, these cases of indirect diffusion further illustrate the central role of the United States in the global diffusion of these norms.

Domestic Laws
The EPA undertook a detailed review of Mexico's environmental laws prior to NAFTA. The review noted that Mexico "lacked adequate resources to construct a fully effective enforcement regime" (US EPA 1991, 5). It further noted that, prior to NAFTA, Mexico relied almost exclusively on administrative proceedings rather than the legalistic enforcement mechanisms favored by the United States (US EPA 1991). As we noted above, NAFTA required Mexico to implement more legalistic avenues for enforcement, mirroring this US enforcement approach. Prior to NAFTA, the Mexican and Canadian publics played a smaller role in environmental law enforcement (US EPA 1991; Paehlke 2000). Although Canada's overall enforcement was strong, its environmental policy was "characterized by administrative discretion and relatively closed decision-making venues" (Paehlke 2000, 169).

Prior to CAFTA-DR, USTR reviewed the environmental laws and enforcement of the Central American parties. It noted the steps they had taken to develop environmental policies and institutions, but also their limited ability to enforce such laws—due, for example, to insufficient financial and human resources (USTR 2003). Furthermore, administrative regulations and procedures lacked transparency, which limited public participation (USTR 2003). The Organization of American States noted that with CAFTA-DR, both environmental law enforcement and public participation increased, improving their ability to respond to citizen complaints (OAS 2012).

The US environmental review that preceded the Peru agreement makes clear that Peru's environmental laws had historically suffered from a lack of effective enforcement (USTR 2007b). For example, government agencies could impose only modest fines for noncompliance, and the judicial system allowed numerous opportunities for appeal (USTR 2007b). The review also noted that the PTA "has significant potential to improve environmental decision making and transparency in Peru" (USTR 2007b, 2). It explained that the PTA would improve public participation both through the public submissions process and by requiring Peru to ensure that its law and administrative proceedings would be made public and allow for public comment. This review further underscores the US role in strengthening public participation provisions through this PTA.

In summary, effective enforcement and public participation did not play an important role in the US trading-partner nations' PTAs prior to those agreed with the United States, nor in their domestic environmental laws and policies prior to their US PTAs. These factors, combined with the often-templated language on effective enforcement and public participation from US domestic law into its PTAs, strongly suggest that these norms diffused through the US PTAs.

Conclusions

Prior chapters and studies have illuminated the long history in US trade policy of pursuing environmental objectives, the strengthening of such provisions over time, and, importantly, the *potential* for such provisions to shape environmental law in trading-partner nations. This chapter extends this work by tracing those international provisions through the process of their implementation in domestic law and policy in trading-partner nations and confirming the origin of those norms in US environmental policy. We found substantial evidence of key US norms making their way through US PTAs into the domestic law and policy of parties to NAFTA, CAFTA, and the US-Peru PTA. Interview data with US government representatives strongly support this finding, with key informants stressing the US role in pushing these norms even in the face of resistance (at least initially) from some trading-partner nations. In doing so, this chapter confirms prior hypotheses in the literature that environmental linkages within PTAs are important mechanisms of norm diffusion by mapping the pathway by which this diffusion occurs. In other words, this chapter demonstrates that environmental provisions do not merely sit unimplemented in international trade agreements, but actually have diffused into domestic law and policy through internalization of these provisions abroad. Importantly, as discussed in chapter 2 and supported by interview data, this implementation has been aided by US government grants tied to PTA implementation.

We first demonstrated that the norms of effective enforcement and public participation can be traced back to US domestic law. We highlight that beginning with NAFTA in the mid-1990s, the United States has systematically "internationalized" its core environmental norms of effective enforcement and public participation into its trade agreements by replicating norms from US domestic law and policy into these international agreements. Further suggesting this directionality of diffusion, effective enforcement is identified as a primary negotiating objective in the US 2002 Trade Act, and previously these norms were notably absent in the environmental laws of many US trading partners. Furthermore, Peru, NAFTA, and CAFTA-DR countries did not incorporate these norms into their PTAs with other countries prior to their agreements with the United States (SICE 2015), and effective enforcement and public participation provisions were weak in many of these countries (US EPA 1991; Paehlke 2000; USTR 2003; USTR 2007b). As we demonstrate here, following the passage of these three US PTAs, there is substantial evidence of US norms appearing in trading-partner nations' domestic environmental law and policy. This suggests that environmental linkages within PTAs not only hold *potential* to serve as mechanisms of norm and policy diffusion, but are already serving this purpose across multiple agreements and countries.

One particularly important pathway for environmental norm diffusion through PTAs is the environmental cooperation activities undertaken to implement most US PTAs. As central features of US PTAs, environmental cooperation provisions provide a policy justification for allocating resources to trade-environment activities in trading-partner nations. Between 1995 and 2014, the United States funded more than US$196 million of trade-related environmental activities related to NAFTA, CAFTA-DR, and the US-Peru PTA (CEC 1994; US GAO 2014). Much of this work has been focused on improving effective enforcement and public participation in US trading partners through, for example, institutional capacity building. Indeed, these activities have already delivered improvements, as evidenced by CITES implementation improvements in the CAFTA-DR countries and Peru,[10] increased public access to decision making in Mexico, and major changes to Peruvian civil and penal codes.

The diffusion of environmental norms through PTAs likely reflects several existing theories of norm diffusion, especially learning and the movement of ideas. However, these cases also raise questions about how powerful states may impose their broader interests on weaker trading partners, which would reflect diffusion through coercion, a relatively understudied concept, especially in the environmental context. However, in linking environmental provisions to the coveted preferential market access promised by US PTAs, the United States may actually be coercing environmental policy changes in trading-partner nations. Although the literature has historically linked preferences for environmental provisions in PTAs with higher levels of income, recent literature suggests that developing countries don't necessarily favor environmental provisions in PTAs less than do developed countries (Bernauer and Nguyen 2015; Spilker, Bernauer, and Umaña 2018). However, developing countries likely prefer norms related to water, desertification, or indigenous communities over those emphasized by the United States. As such, the power imbalance, and potential coercion that may result, remains an important consideration in studying these negotiations.

Norm diffusion can also have important on-the-ground implications for civil society access to decision making in trading-partner nations. In discussing the public submissions mechanisms under NAFTA and CAFTA, one US government official interviewed for this study highlighted, for example, that it served as

> an outlet for [civil society] to let their governments know about concerns. There are many examples where an NGO has been trying to get an issue heard, and now they can file through [the] citizen submission process. They came kicking and screaming into it, but now all of them recognize it as a positive force in their countries. I'm really happy about that and the success of that. It's not the answer to everything but an important mechanism that didn't otherwise exist. . . . It's a way to get positive outcomes on environment that otherwise might not happen.

Finally, the nature of environmental provisions in US PTAs underscores the renewed importance of trade agreements for environmental problem solving and diplomacy writ large. The recently concluded negotiations among 11 countries on the Comprehensive and Progressive Trans-Pacific Partnership (CPTPP) is a fascinating indicator of the reach of US norms—including effective enforcement and public participation. US PTAs were the strongest influence on the CPTPP's predecessor, the 2016 TPP (Allee and Lugg 2016). Aside from important provisions related to intellectual property and investor-state dispute settlement, most of the CPTPP's provisions were adopted directly from the TPP. Therefore, although the Trump administration withdrew the United States from the TPP in 2017, US PTA provisions and norms have left their mark on the new agreement, including as related to effective enforcement and public participation. For example, the CPTPP's environment chapter is subject to a sanction-based enforcement mechanism, similar to US PTAs. The CPTPP also contains text that is templated directly from US PTAs, such as the requirement related to "judicial, quasi-judicial, and administrative proceedings," which appears in the CPTPP environment chapter verbatim from the US-Peru PTA. Particularly relevant to our discussion here, the CPTPP, like the US-Peru PTA, requires all trading partners to implement certain MEAs, such as CITES, making such provisions enforceable through the trade agreement's sanction-based enforcement mechanism. Provisions related to the elimination of certain fishery subsidies, largely intractable in preexisting WTO negotiations for decades, were similarly included and made enforceable through these means. Most importantly, the parallel trends toward the increasing geographic scope of US PTAs, coupled with the progressively strong environmental provisions contained therein, signal an important turn in the future of environmental diplomacy and the diffusion of US environmental interests: for the first time, we are beginning to see international environmental provisions with actual enforcement teeth.

6 Do US Preferential Trade Agreement Provisions Become Global Standards?

Preferential trade agreements (PTAs) are not negotiated in isolation from one another in an institutional vacuum. Each new PTA is embedded in a dense trade governance system made of existing PTAs. This institutional context surrounding PTA negotiations affects the design of the environmental provisions included in PTAs. Instead of reinventing the wheel every time they negotiate a PTA, trade negotiators tend to copy provisions from previous agreements by drawing on PTAs that they, their trading partners, or even third countries have signed (Alschner, Seiermann, and Skougarevskiy 2017; Allee and Elsig 2016; Dür, Baccini, and Elsig 2014).

Several causal mechanisms help to explain this diffusion of environmental provisions across PTAs (Dobbin, Simmons, and Garrett 2007; Milewicz et al. 2016; Morin et al. 2019). First, countries might seek to duplicate the most stringent clauses from their earlier PTAs in order to level the playing field and ensure similar regulatory conditions are imposed on their trade competitors. Second, negotiators in developing and emerging economies might draw inspiration from the PTAs that involve the most powerful countries to demonstrate their regulatory alignment and raise their profile as candidates for future PTAs and/or as leaders on environmental issues. Third, they might attempt to reduce transaction costs at the negotiation and implementation stages by simply duplicating the most common clauses in the trade system. Fourth, they might include the environmental clauses considered to be the most effective from a trade or environmental standpoint by drawing on the experience of earlier PTAs. In all likelihood, some combination of these factors explains diffusion across PTAs, and these explanations likely vary depending on the specific institutional context within which each individual PTA is negotiated.

Rather than ranking the causal weight of these mechanisms in any particular case, this chapter discusses the role of the United States in the global diffusion of environmental provisions. Chapter 5 traced the diffusion of environmental norms from US domestic law, through its PTAs, and back down to the domestic laws and policies of US trading-partner nations. This chapter goes one step further by asking whether environmental provisions that had first appeared in US PTAs were subsequently incorporated in other countries' PTAs. This chapter also asks whether provisions that were initially introduced in other countries' PTAs were replicated by the US government in its own PTAs. This analysis of diffusion flows enables us to establish whether the United States primarily plays the role of the originator or the recipient of environmental provisions in the trade governance system.

To conduct this analysis, we use the Trade and Environment Database (TREND).[1] Of the 286 categories of environmental provisions identified in TREND, we distinguish the 98 provisions that first appeared in a trade agreement to which the United States is a party from the 188 others that originate from other countries' agreements. We then track the diffusion of these two groups of provisions, paying attention to the geographical scope of their diffusion, the number of agreements that incorporate them, and their qualitative importance for the governance of the trade and environment interplay.

We find that several significant environmental clauses, which first originated in US PTAs, have found their way into US trading partners' PTAs and third countries' PTAs. In addition, our analysis demonstrates that some recent features of US PTAs were inspired by the environmental provisions of other countries' agreements. This chapter argues that this cross-fertilization is one of the driving forces behind the evolution of environmental provisions in trade agreements.

The rest of the chapter is organized as follows. The next section provides a theoretical map to understand diffusion across PTAs by presenting the trade regime as a complex adaptive system. In the following two sections, we assess respectively the diffusion of US clauses in other countries' PTAs and the diffusion of other countries' clauses in US PTAs. The fourth section presents the limits of the diffusion processes, by identifying clauses that remain unique to US PTAs, and conversely those that have not diffused to US PTAs. The chapter ends with a discussion on the specific role of the United States in the construction of global trade and environment politics.

Diffusion Within a Complex Adaptive System

In the 1990s, two scenarios emerged to predict how the diffusion of PTA environmental clauses might unfold in the future. According to the first scenario, competing models of PTA environmental chapters would be diffused from two geographic spheres of influence: the European Union and NAFTA (Steinberg 1997, 232). Steinberg predicted the "regionalization of trade-environment rules, with the European Union moving down one path, the NAFTA moving down another and the GATT/WTO barely moving at all" (1997, 265). According to the second diffusion scenario, PTA environmental clauses would converge globally and, thus, greatly facilitate the multilateralization of PTA environmental clauses within the WTO. This was the vision of Raymond Ludwiszewski, who served as EPA general counsel under William Reilly in the early 1990s. He wrote: "As GATT negotiations continue, environmentalists can be expected to press for a broad spectrum of changes to accommodate ecological issues, many of which will mirror the 'green' provisions of the NAFTA" (1993, 704).

Twenty-five years after the conclusion of NAFTA, neither scenario can fully explain the landscape of environmental provisions in global trade agreements. Although there are important differences between US and European approaches to developing PTA environmental provisions, the trade system is not fragmented into rival regional blocs who compete against each other to ensure their preferred environmental clauses prevail in trade agreements. In addition, significant heterogeneity between PTAs has emerged, making a homogenization process within the WTO very improbable. In reality, the contemporary global trade regime is somewhere in between the divergence and fragmentation of the first scenario and the convergence and centralization of the second.

Complex adaptive system theory can help us understand why environmental provisions have diffused in this way. A complex adaptive system is a "system in which large networks of components with no central control and simple rules of operation give rise to complex collective behavior" (Mitchell 2009, 13). *Complicated* systems should be distinguished from *complex* systems. In contrast to the latter, complicated systems can be understood by disaggregating the whole into its constituent parts. For example, clocks are complicated mechanical systems, but they are not complex systems. They are decomposable, linear, and inert. When part of a clock moves, it is always the predictable result of the action of a different part. In contrast, complex systems evolve on the edge of order and chaos in unpredictable ways. The collective behaviors that emerge from complex systems are greater than the sum of their parts. Some common examples of complex adaptive systems include ant colonies, brains, cities, clouds, schools of fish, and jazz bands. International relations scholars like James Rosenau (1970) and Robert Jervis (1997) have long argued that the international system can also be conceptualized as a complex adaptive system. The international system shares with other recognized complex adaptive systems nine key characteristics: multiple elements, no central coordination, heterogeneity, interdependence, self-organization, simple rules of operation, openness, multi-scale structure, and increasing complexity (Meunier and Morin 2016).

The trade governance system possesses all of these key features of a complex adaptive system (Morin and Gomez-Mera 2019). First, the trade governance system is fragmented in multiple elements, including hundreds of PTAs (Dür, Baccini, and Elsig 2014). Second, these multiple elements are not centrally coordinated by the WTO. Third, the PTAs are heterogeneous and vary significantly in breadth and depth (Horn, Mavroidis, and Sapir 2010). Fourth, PTAs are interdependent as they are negotiated, interpreted, implemented and adjudicated in the shadow of other PTAs (Gomez-Mera and Molinari 2014). Fifth, this interdependence creates self-organization in the sense that negotiators avoid blatant incompatibility between PTAs (Wolfe 2005). Sixth, trade negotiators' simple rule of operation is to apply lessons from their earlier experiences and from actions of negotiators (Skovgaard Poulsen 2014). Seventh, the trade governance system is open to its global context—as the WTO appellate body put it, it is "not to be read in clinical isolation from public international law" (WTO Secretariat 1996). Eighth, the trade system has a multi-scale structure with stable broad principles, norms that evolve slowly, and detailed rules that develop rapidly (Barton et al. 2008). And finally, the system generates an increased level of complexity, as evidenced by the growing number of PTAs, issue areas, participating countries, and obligations (Horn, Mavroidis, and Sapir 2010; Dür, Baccini, and Elsig 2014).

Complex systems incrementally expand as much as they can without undermining their internal organization (Kauffman 1993). They do so by maintaining a balance between exploration and exploitation, which keeps them on the cusp of order and chaos as they develop endogenously. Exploration refers to the efforts to create future capabilities by means of "search, variation, experimentation, and discovery" (March 1991, 102). It implies venturing into the unknown and introducing chaos to a system. Exploitation refers to the leverage of existing capabilities through activities like "reproduction, refinement, efficiency selection, and implementation" (March 1991, 71). It involves applying known strategies and imposing some order within the system. For an ant colony, the creation of a satellite nest is an exploratory strategy, while nest-mate recruitment for foraging is an exploitation strategy. In business systems, exploration can refer to research and development activities, while exploitation can take the form of scaled-up production to benefit from economy of scale. In evolutionary biology, genetic mutation is a type of exploration, while the exploitation of the genetic pool takes place with natural selection. Exploration brings more benefits to a system in the long run, while exploitation brings short-term benefits. Systems maintain a balance between the two processes. The elimination of exploration would make a system obsolete in a changing environment, while continuous exploration would prevent it from realizing potential gains from new discoveries (Duit and Galaz 2008).

In the trade governance system, exploration involves designing unprecedented rules. For example, as discussed in chapter 3, US trade negotiators were engaged in exploration activities when they came up with particularly innovative environmental provisions during the negotiations for NAFTA and the US-Peru agreement. This exploration makes the trade governance system more innovative than might be suggested by a focus on the WTO's "frozen" environmental negotiations under the Doha Declaration.[2] In the context of the trade governance system, exploitation involves replicating existing provisions from other agreements. Chapter 5 provided some examples of exploitation: environmental clauses that the United States first introduced into the trade governance system were subsequently replicated in PTAs, which US partners signed with third countries. This form of diffusion brings some order to the trade governance system. Applying complex adaptive system theory to the system implies that a certain balance is established between the processes of innovation and diffusion. Though analytically distinct, innovation and diffusion operate jointly to sustain the trade governance system's growth on the edge of order and chaos (Morin, Pauwelyn, and Hollway 2017).

Conceptualizing the trade system in this way implies that templates of PTA environmental chapters are unlikely to remain inert, since continuous diffusion makes them unstable. It also suggests that global homogenization is unlikely, given that some PTAs continue to innovate incrementally. Although PTAs duplicate environmental clauses from other agreements, continuous innovation ensures that a degree of differentiation is maintained. This means that a highly innovative country, like the United States, can influence the entire trade governance system but cannot provide a stable focal point for the global harmonization of PTA environmental clauses. The US model should not even be expected to remain unaffected by exploration conducted by other countries. Thus, as opposed to the scenarios forecasted in the early 1990s, we should observe neither an opposition of rival models nor a global harmonization around a single model. Complex system theory suggests instead a cross-fertilization process between the United States and other countries that makes the trade governance system increasingly more complex over time.

The Global Diffusion of US Environmental Provisions

This section argues that the United States is a prime explorer of the complex trade governance system and that it introduced several innovations later exploited by several other countries. As discussed in chapter 3, the United States was one of the first proponents of environmental protection in trade agreements. NAFTA and its environmental side agreement, in particular, introduced several clauses that were unprecedented in the trade governance system. Many early innovations concerned the effective enforcement of environmental law and public participation in environmental law making (see chapter 5). The United States also innovated in its subsequent PTAs: for example, for forest protection in the 2006 US-Peru agreement (see chapter 4), for illegal fisheries in the 2016 Trans-Pacific Partnership (TPP), and more recently for plastic pollution and wildlife trafficking in the 2018 United States, Mexico, and Canada Trade Agreement (USMCA). Overall, US agreements have cumulatively led to the highest number of innovative provisions (Morin, Pauwelyn, and Hollway 2017).

Trade negotiators from all over the world readily acknowledge that they look to US agreements for inspiration. In complex analysis parlance, they "exploit" environmental provisions that were first "explored" by the US government. In 2014, as part of a study commissioned by the OECD, negotiators from 10 countries completed a questionnaire about their source of inspiration for PTA provisions. When asked about precedents that have triggered the inclusion of environmental provisions specifically in their own PTAs, most respondents pointed to NAFTA (George 2014, 11). This finding is corroborated by various governmental reports that explicitly refer to precedents introduced by US PTAs as benchmarks that are used to assess their own practices or as a model to emulate (Japan 1995; Bourgeois, Dawar, and Evenett 2007; Aasen 2009). Even when non-state actors are consulted on the design of PTAs that do not involve the United States, they frequently cite US PTAs for their environmental clauses. In recent European consultations, for example, groups like Greenpeace, the Wildlife Conservation Society, Friends of the Earth, and the European Trade Union Confederations have stated that they want future European agreements to include specific clauses that appear in recent US PTAs (EU 2017a; EU 2017b; EU 2017c).

Several of the provisions first introduced by a US PTA and subsequently included in other countries' PTAs are environmental exceptions to trade commitments. These cover environmental exceptions to commitments on sanitary measures, patentability, and service liberalization. All three categories of exception were first introduced in the trade governance system by NAFTA in 1992. They were later replicated in the WTO agreements concluded in 1994 and in dozens of other PTAs (and in up to 201 PTAs, in the case of environmental exceptions relating to commitments on sanitary measures). However, it is unclear if the United States was genuinely the originator of these provisions, as NAFTA chapters on sanitary measures and intellectual property and services were modeled on the Dunkel draft of the WTO agreements (Steinberg 1997). Although the Uruguay Round was actually concluded after NAFTA, the draft WTO agreements were made available before NAFTA was signed. Thus, it is likely that the flow of influence went from the WTO to NAFTA, rather than the other way round (Steinberg 1997).

A provision that has more obvious US origins is the commitment to the effective enforcement of domestic environmental law (see chapter 5).

This provision was first introduced with NAFTA and was replicated in 14 other US PTAs. In addition, several US trading partners, including Canada, Chile, Korea, Mexico, and Peru, have adopted this provision in their own agreements with third countries. A total of 47 PTAs concluded by US partners with third countries after they had first signed their agreement with the United States include the commitment to the effective enforcement of domestic environmental law. Although this diffusion to trading partners' PTAs is interesting, it is not entirely surprising. More surprising is the diffusion beyond US trade partners: 24 PTAs that involve neither the United States nor its trade partners include the commitment to the effective enforcement of domestic environmental law. For example, most European agreements signed after 2008 require the parties to enforce their own environmental laws and prescribe state-state consultation if one party considers that the other has failed to enforce its environmental laws effectively (Morin and Rochette 2017).

Figure 6.1 shows the state of diffusion of PTAs, which include provisions on the effective enforcement of domestic environmental law for three different dates: 1995, 2005, and 2015. In all three networks, the points represent countries, and the links between them represent PTAs with clauses on effective enforcement. In 1995, the United States was one of the few countries with PTAs that included provisions on effective enforcement. At the time, Mexico had already started to diffuse this provision out of North America, and it replicated the NAFTA provision in its 1994 agreement with Costa Rica, in its 1994 agreement with Bolivia, and in the 1994 Group of Three agreement with Colombia and Venezuela. By 2005, the network had increased in density and extended considerably to include several countries that were linked through various agreements.[3] Today, the commitment to enforce environmental law effectively can be found in 71 PTAs, in addition to 15 US PTAs.

Similarly, figure 6.2 shows the state of diffusion of PTAs with provisions on public participation in environmental law making at three different times: in 1995, in 2005, and in 2015. In each of the three networks, points represent countries, and links between them represent PTAs with provisions on public participation. In 1995, the only trade agreement to include such provision is NAFTA, linking the United States, Mexico, and Canada in a triangle. The network is much denser and more extended in 2005, involving several countries linked together by various agreements. Thus,

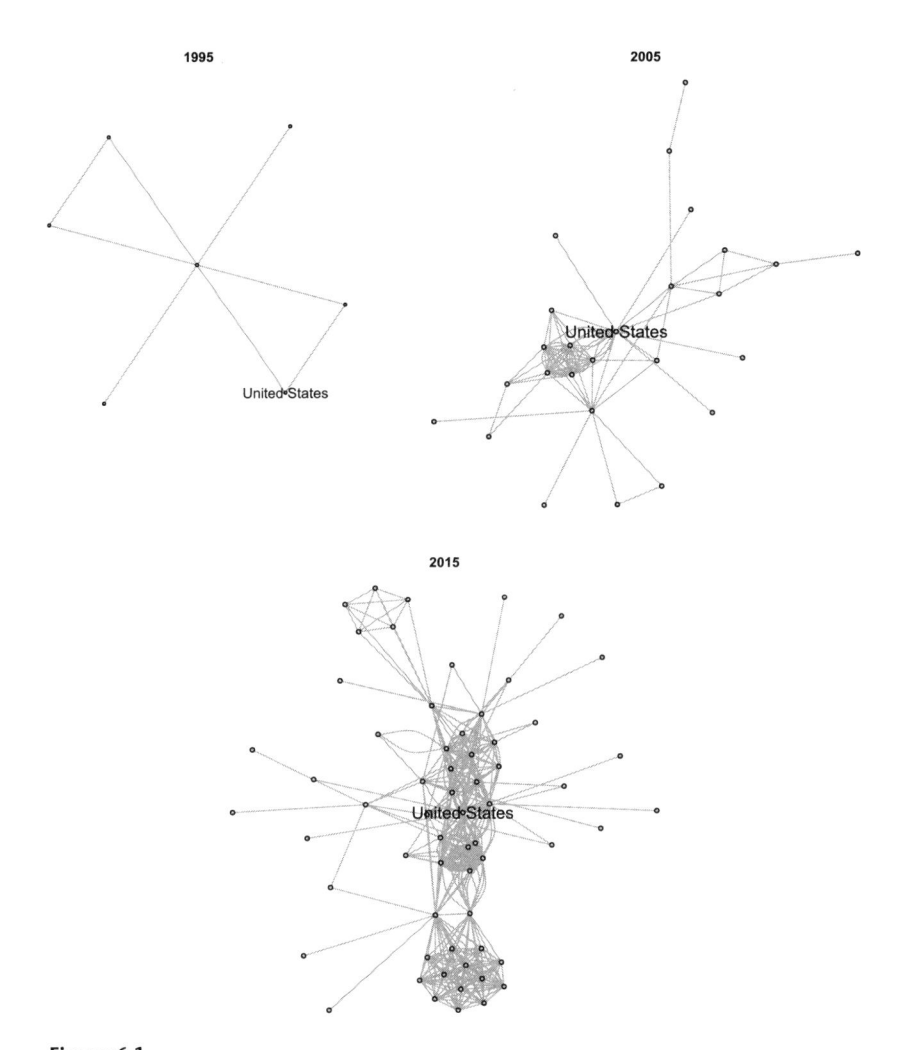

Figure 6.1
Diffusion of provisions on effective enforcement in the PTA network

several agreements other than the US PTAs now include provisions on public participation, but they all remain connected to the United States in this network of PTAs.

Another US environmental innovation, which is now frequently found in other PTAs, states that certain multilateral environmental agreements (MEAs) shall prevail in the case of inconsistency with the trade agreement. This clause was first introduced in NAFTA (Art. 104) and replicated in 19

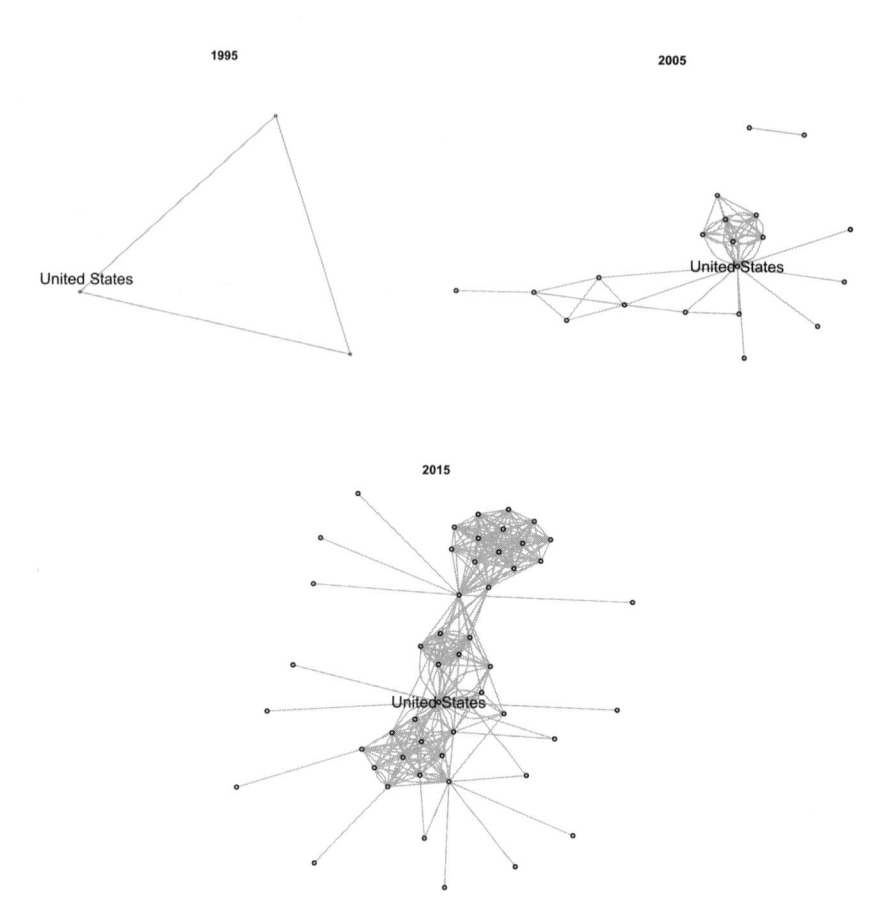

Figure 6.2
Diffusion of provision on public participation in the PTA network

agreements that US trading partners have concluded with other nations, as well as in five PTAs that involve neither the United States nor its trading partners. For example, it appears in the 2008 agreement between the Association of Southeast Asian Nations, or ASEAN, and Japan. Although the list of the most important MEAs varies slightly, it generally includes the Basel Convention on hazardous wastes, the Montreal Protocol on ozone depletion, and the Convention on International Trade in Endangered Species of Wild Fauna and Flora (CITES), which all appear in NAFTA as well. Many other PTAs explicitly state that the contracting parties are not exempt from obligations arising from other international treaties, although specific MEAs are not listed.

Other US environmental clauses that have been broadly diffused within the trade system are related to investment protection (Morin and Rochette 2017). Chapter 11 of NAFTA on investment protection states that nothing "shall be construed to prevent a Party from adopting, maintaining or enforcing any measure otherwise consistent with this chapter that it considers appropriate to ensure that investment activity in its territory is undertaken in a manner sensitive to environmental concerns" (Art. 1114.1). It further states that the parties should not waive environmental measures to attract foreign investment (Art. 1114.2). Nevertheless, following the implementation of NAFTA, some foreign investors considered that they were entitled to financial compensation under NAFTA Chapter 11, claiming that environmental regulations had an impact that was tantamount to the expropriation of their businesses (Gagné and Morin 2006). US negotiators responded by systematically inserting an annex in their subsequent PTAs to clarify that "except in rare circumstances . . . non-discriminatory regulatory actions designed and applied to protect legitimate public welfare objectives, such as health, safety and the environment, do not constitute indirect expropriation" (CAFTA-DR Art. 10.7). Dozens of PTAs that do not involve the United States now include similar terminology. For example, the European Union included a statement in its agreements with Singapore and Canada to clarify that measures designed for public welfare objectives do not constitute indirect expropriation. Thus, lessons learned from NAFTA and its safeguards, which the United States designed to limit the risk of legal challenges generated by environmental regulations, have influenced the European PTA template. Some have even argued that the clarification introduced in US PTAs helped crystallize customary international law on investment expropriation (Fauchald 2007, 4; Schwebel 2004).

Other clauses, initially introduced in US PTAs before being broadly diffused, include clauses related to public participation in the implementation of environmental provisions (33 non-US PTAs, including 12 that do not involve US partners), the protection of natural reserves (37 non-US PTAs, including 18 that do not involve US partners), the publication of domestic environmental law (30 PTAs, including seven that do not involve US partners), collaboration between stakeholders from both parties (21 non-US PTAs, including 11 that do not involve US partners), the illegal trade of endangered species (18 non-US PTAs, including six that do not involve US partners) and the illegal exploitation of forests (16 non-US PTAs, including four that do not involve US partners). In most cases, the first countries to replicate US clauses are US trade partners, such as Canada, Mexico, and Peru. Several other countries also frequently replicate US clauses, including the European Union, members of the European Free Trade Association, and China. Though the wording in the clauses differs slightly, their origin can clearly be traced back to the United States.

That said, the US model is not becoming dominant. This is because other countries also invest in exploratory strategies and introduce environmental provisions in the complex trade governance system. The next section puts the spotlight on these innovations introduced by other countries. It argues that some of these innovations successfully diffused globally, and even influence recent US PTAs.

Diffusion from Other Countries' Environmental Provisions to US Preferential Trade Agreements

This section looks at environmental innovations that were first designed by countries other than the United States. Although the United States is an important actor in the exploration of new environmental provisions, it is not the only one. As a complex adaptive system, the trade governance system is fragmented rather than centralized around a key actor. In fact, 188 of the 286 environmental provisions documented in the TREND database originate from PTAs to which the United States is not a party. These environmental provisions do not create a distinct model that would develop in disconnection or in antagonism to the US model. Instead, some of them influence the US model. As with any complex adaptive system, multiple sources of innovation that are interconnected create a productive cross-fertilization process and favor the endogenous expansion of the complex system.

Even when designing NAFTA, which was pioneering because of its environmental provisions, the United States and its NAFTA partners were heavily influenced by agreements that were negotiated outside North America. As mentioned above, several NAFTA environmental exceptions, including those relating to commitments on technical trade barriers, as well as sanitary and phytosanitary measures, were modeled after draft WTO agreements that were available at the time (Steinberg 1997, 245). Perhaps more significantly, a major General Agreement on Tariffs and Trade (GATT) dispute created the necessary political impulse for NAFTA's environmental side agreement. In the early 1990s, the United States restricted imports of tuna products from countries that failed to meet specific dolphin-protection standards. Mexico considered this restriction an unnecessary unilateral protectionist measure and filed a complaint under the GATT dispute-settlement procedure in 1991, just as NAFTA negotiations were getting underway. Although the GATT panel's report was never formally adopted, the dispute caught the attention of environmental groups and crystallized broad public opposition to further trade liberalization in the name of environmental protection. The trade dispute was arbitrated in Geneva. Had it not occurred, it is unlikely that the Clinton administration would have felt compelled to negotiate an environmental side agreement to appease critics of free trade and obtain congressional approval for NAFTA ratification (Holmer and Bello 1993).

Over and above the WTO agreements, US PTAs also appear to be influenced by European PTAs. The European Union has signed no fewer than 102 PTAs since the 1957 Treaty of Rome establishing the European Economic Community, if one includes intra-European agreements, enlargement agreements, and the association agreements. Many of these European agreements include innovative environmental provisions (see figure 2.1 in chapter 2). The Lomé II, III, and IV Conventions, in particular, are among the most innovative PTAs because they have an unprecedented number of environmental provisions (Morin, Pauwelyn, and Hollway. 2017).

One key feature of these European agreements is their sectoral approach to environmental issues (Jinnah and Morgera 2013). Instead of including only clauses related to the environment in general, several European agreements include detailed provisions on specific environmental issue areas, tailored to the particular ecological context of their trade partners. Some EU agreements cover issue areas as diverse as sustainable fisheries, deforestation, renewable energy, natural disaster management, desertification, agroecology, and climate change adaptation. This sectoral approach was subsequently adopted by the United States. The US-Peru agreement, in particular, was the first US PTA to include an eight-page long annex on forest governance, which aims to fight illegal logging and the illegal trade in wildlife. The annex includes specific and prescriptive provisions, as well as clauses regarding criminal penalties, inventories, export quotas, producer audits, and chain of custody (see chapter 4). In recent years, environmental groups pushed the US government to include an even wider set of provisions to address specific environmental issues.[4] The US government has been receptive to their suggestions (USTR 2006; 2007c). The USMCA, for example, contains several articles on specific environmental matters, including ozone depletion, ship pollution, invasive alien species, and automobile emissions and fisheries.[5] The number and specificity of these sectoral provisions, while relatively common in European agreements, are unprecedented in the TPP for a trade agreement signed by the United States.

Figure 6.3 illustrates the diffusion of sectoral provisions derived from EU PTAs. It shows the number of sectoral provisions per PTA, as classified in the TREND dataset. The first PTAs to include most of these provisions were the EU PTAs concluded in the late 1980s and early 1990s. They are represented by gray circles, as with all PTAs that involved neither the United States nor their partners. US PTAs and US partners' PTAs are represented by triangles and squares, respectively. Since several agreements are signed in the same year, the circle, triangles, and squares can be superimposed, as suggested by a darker gray hue. Figure 6.3 shows that US agreements only catch up with other PTAs in terms of the number of sectoral clauses in the 2000s.

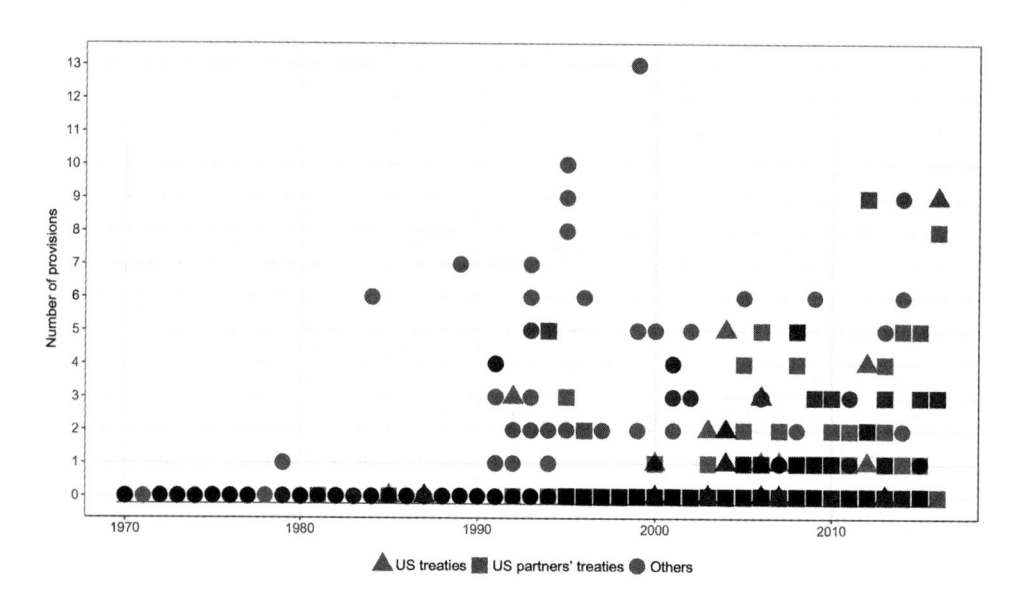

Figure 6.3
Number of provisions related to specific environmental issue areas per PTA (US, US partners, and others)

US agreements were also inspired by the European Union's special concern for policy coherence. With its structural complexity and multiple layers, policy coherence has long been a major concern for the European Union (Morin and Orsini 2014). Since the 1997 Amsterdam Treaty, achieving sustainable development is formally recognized as one of the European Union's fundamental objectives. Environmental protection must be integrated into all EU policies and activities (Marín-Durán and Morgera 2012). Accordingly, several EU trade agreements do not only bring together trade and the environment, but also seek greater policy coherence between environmental protection and various other sectors, such as agriculture, energy, mining, and tourism. Recent US agreements have emulated this practice and integrated provisions relating to policy coherence. The TPP, for example, which does not include the European Union but does include several EU trading partners, indicates that it is essential to establish coherence between the environment and other policy areas, such as mining, urban development, energy production, and industrial activities (Art. 20.15 and 20.6). Figure 6.4 shows that US trade agreements have only recently caught up with other countries in terms of the number of policy coherence provisions per PTA, as categorized by the TREND database.

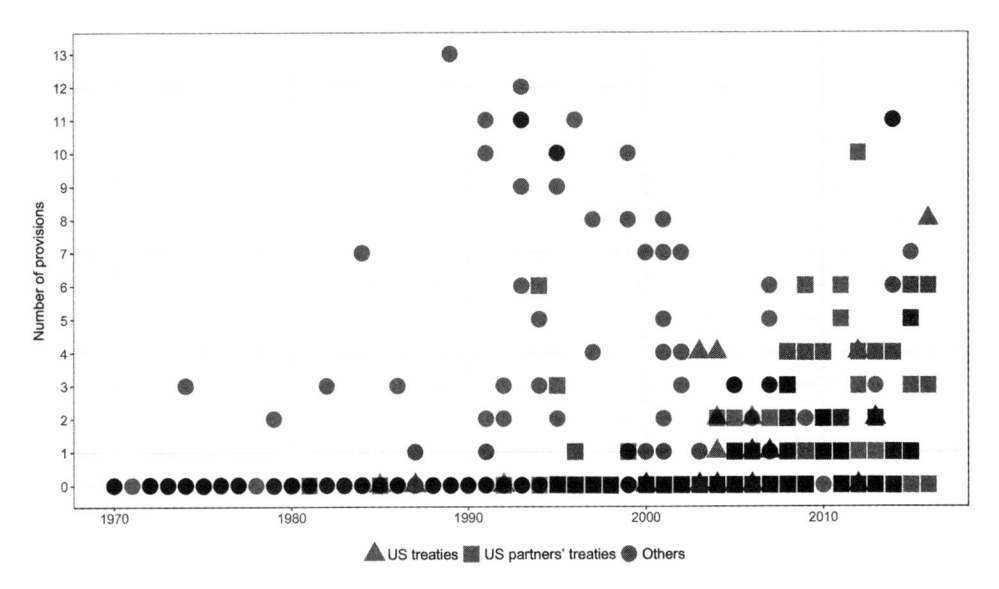

Figure 6.4
Number of provisions on policy coherence per PTA (US, US partners, and others)

The United States also drew on innovative approaches used in developing countries' PTAs, particularly for norms regarding biodiversity and genetic resources (Morin and Gauquelin 2016). Latin American PTAs were the first to include specific provisions governing access to genetic resources and the sharing of benefits derived from their use. These countries are rich in biodiversity, and they use trade negotiations as levers with respect to obligations set out in the Convention on Biological Diversity and the Nagoya Protocol on Genetic Resources. These obligations concern the protection of traditional ecological knowledge, the requirement to obtain prior informed consent before accessing genetic material, and the transfer of monetary and technological benefits to genetic resource providers. Since the conclusion of the US-Peru agreement in 2006, some obligations relating to these biodiversity issues can now be found in US PTAs as well. The US-Peru agreement, for example, includes a provision stating that the parties "recognize the importance of respecting and preserving traditional knowledge and practices of indigenous and other communities that contribute to the conservation and sustainable use of biological diversity" (18.01.03). In a side agreement, the parties also recognize the importance of obtaining informed consent before gaining access to genetic resources and of sharing the benefits derived from the use of traditional knowledge and genetic resources. It also implicitly recognizes the risk of the misappropriation of genetic resources, by underlining the importance of the quality of patent applications to ensure that the conditions of patentability are satisfied. The inclusion of biodiversity norms and principles in a US trade agreement is significant in light of the US refusal to ratify the Convention on Biological Diversity, wherein parallel provisions were in part responsible for the US recalcitrance.

This section and the previous one provided evidence of cross-fertilization between the United States and other countries. However, this cross-fertilization is not the equivalent to a global homogenization, as countries continue to explore possible new environmental provisions and selectively choose the foreign provisions they exploited. The next section discusses these limits to the diffusion process.

The Limits of Diffusion

Although the US government designs environmental provisions that diffuse to other countries' PTAs and vice versa, the global trade governance system is far from being homogenous. Some environmental provisions have never been replicated and remain the sole province of one country and its PTAs (Morin and Gauthier Nadeau 2017). Moreover, new provisions continue to emerge, maintaining the differentiation within the trade governance system.

Figure 6.5 provides a visual representation of the diversity of environmental provisions in PTAs. It compares the environmental provisions of PTAs concluded by nine countries, selected for their high number of PTAs and their political importance in the trade governance system. The comparison is conducted by measuring the Jaccard distance for all the environmental clauses included in the PTAs signed by these nine countries between 1990 and 2016. The light gray hue is associated with a high Jaccard distance, indicating that two sets of PTAs are very different. The darker gray color is associated with lower distance measures, which suggests that the PTAs' environmental provisions have similarities. Figure 6.5 shows that the environmental provisions in US PTAs are very similar to those found in the PTAs signed by US trading partners, including Australia, Canada, and Mexico. Yet the United States also shares some environmental clauses with the European Union and the European Free Trade Association, despite the

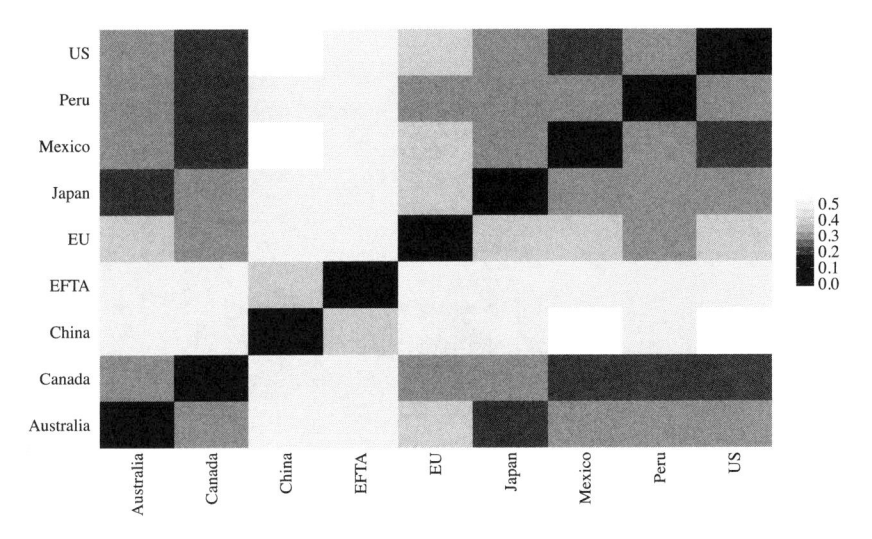

Figure 6.5
Similarity between the PTA environmental provisions of selected countries

absence of a transatlantic trade agreement. Overall, despite global diffusion processes, disparities remain between different countries' PTAs.

Figure 6.6 provides another representation of the degrees of heterogeneity of the trade governance system. Each vertical line represents a different provision, as coded in the TREND database. The color of the line indicates its distribution in US, EU, and other countries' agreements. Most provisions can be found in US, in EU, and in other countries agreements, with a varying distribution among the three groups of PTAs. Nevertheless, some provisions at the right of the figure appear exclusively in US PTAs and score 100 percent on the y-axis for the color associated to the United States. A similar number of environmental clauses can only be found in EU agreements. They score 100 percent for the color associated to the European Union and are located at the left of the figure. The provisions in light gray can only be found in PTAs that involve neither the United States nor the European

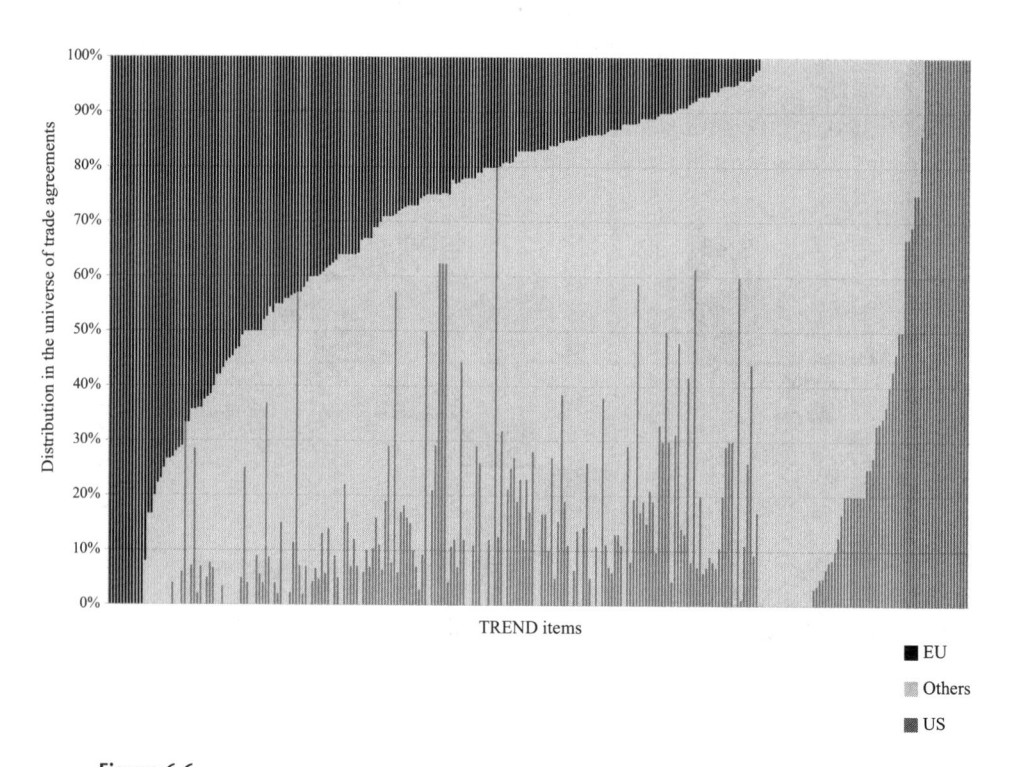

Figure 6.6
Distribution of environmental clauses in US, EU, and other countries' PTAs

Union. Overall, figure 6.6 illustrates that, despite significant overlaps and diffusion, some countries keep their specificities.

A large number of environmental provisions are actually included in a limited number of agreements. Of the 286 types of provisions covered by TREND, 56 are found in only five trade agreements or less. In comparison, 20 provisions are found in more than 100 trade agreements (Morin and Gauthier-Nadeau 2017). Agreements signed by countries such as Peru, New Zealand and Singapore include "one-hit-wonders"—that is, provisions that remain unique despite being innovative. Figure 6.7 reveals that *most* environmental provisions are not widely replicated across many trade agreements. One of the few examples of provisions that have diffused widely is the exception for the protection of life and health. Typically, these provisions that do enjoy widespread diffusion are among the first to be introduced into the trade governance system (Morin, Pauwelyn, and Hollway 2017).

One provision that has not been broadly diffused, despite its importance in environmental policymaking, is the commitment to conduct environmental assessments. It was first introduced in the NAFTA side agreement. Article 2 states that "each party shall, with respect to its territory . . . periodically prepare and make publicly available reports on the state of the environment [and] assess, as appropriate, environmental impacts." Only

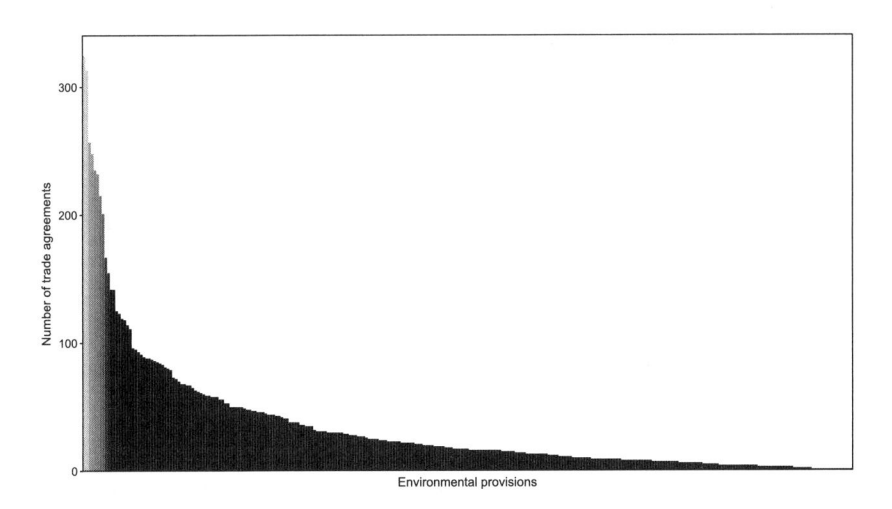

Figure 6.7
Replication of environmental provisions across trade agreements

one other PTA, the 1996 agreement between Canada and Chile, includes a similar commitment to monitor the state of the environment. Few other Canadian agreements require parties to conduct impact assessments for specific projects. For example, the environmental side agreement linked to the trade agreement between Canada and Peru states that environmental impact assessments shall be conducted for any "proposed projects, which may cause significant adverse effects on the environment with a view to avoiding or minimizing such adverse effects" (Art. 2(5)). However, this requirement has been replicated in fewer than 10 PTAs (including those signed by the United States and Canada), despite the fact that it was introduced in a PTA over 25 years ago and remains an important procedure in several countries.

Another clause that surprisingly failed to diffuse concerns the liberalization of environmental goods and services. While 51 PTAs include a vague commitment to encourage trade in environmental goods, only five actually include a specific provision on this matter. Four promote the liberalization of a small number of very specific environmental goods. The fifth and most ambitious agreement was signed by New Zealand and Taiwan in 2013. It requires parties to "eliminate all tariffs on environmental goods" (Art. 3.2.a). Considering that a multilateral agreement on trade in environmental goods has been under negotiation at the WTO since 2014, it is striking that only a few PTAs include specific provisions on this issue.

One key feature of recent US PTAs, which has not been replicated in other agreements so far, is the coverage of environmental provisions in the framework of the PTA's main dispute-settlement mechanism. The 2015 Trade Promotion Authority clearly states that environmental obligations should "be subject to the same dispute settlement and remedies as other enforceable obligations under the agreement" (sec. 102 (b)(10)(H). A resolution adopted by the European Parliament recommends following the US model by providing "recourse to a dispute settlement mechanism on an equal footing with the other parts of the agreement, with provision for fines to improve the situation in the sectors concerned, or at least a temporary suspension of certain trade benefits" (2010, para. 22c). However, even in the most recent Canadian and European PTAs, disputes on environmental provisions are only subject to government consultations. Some trade negotiators and even some environmental groups consider that dialogue and consultations are preferable to a sanction-based system because non-compliance with environmental standards often results from a lack of capacity, rather than a lack of political will and deliberate neglect (Chaytor 2009, 11; Bastiaens and Postnikov 2017; EU 2017).

Conversely, the United States has not replicated the climate-related provisions found in some EU agreements (Morin and Jinnah 2018). As figure 6.8 shows, the European Union has included various provisions related to climate change in some of its PTAs, including commitments to reduce greenhouse gas emissions and references to multilateral climate agreements. Perhaps even more significantly, in 2018, the European Union announced that it would refuse to sign trade agreements with countries that have not ratified the Paris agreement on climate change (Stone 2018). Yet several other major greenhouse gas emitters have not incorporated climate change provisions in their trade agreements. The United States, India, China, and Canada, all major players in the climate regime, have failed to include a significant number of climate change provisions in their PTAs. Some US agreements include several provisions on renewable energy and energy efficiency (as indicated in figure 6.8), but only one agreement explicitly refers to climate change, namely, the 2004 US-Australia environmental side agreement. Other climate-related clauses, such as restrictions on fossil-fuel

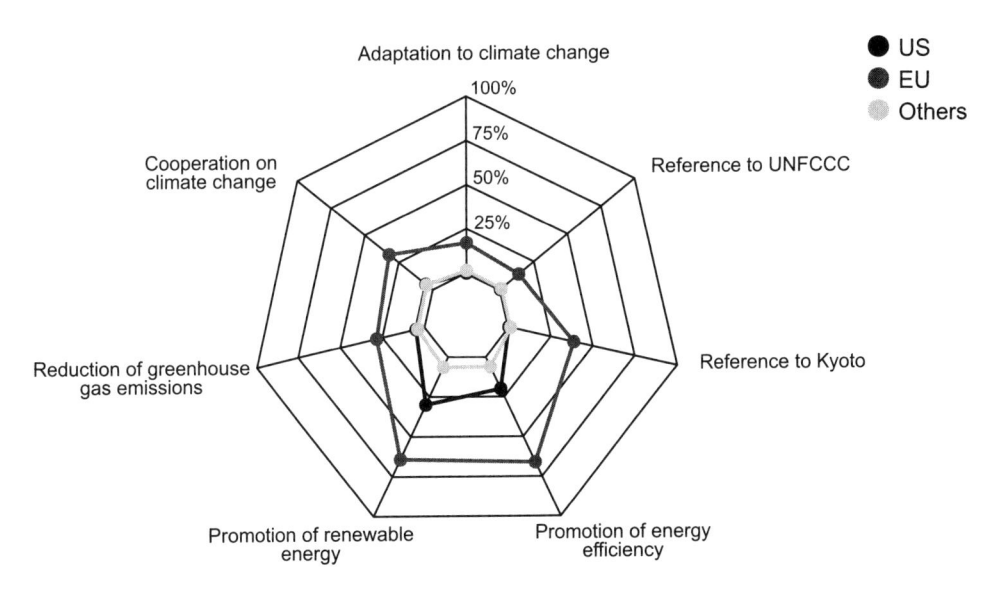

Figure 6.8
Climate-related clauses in US, EU, and other countries' PTAs

subsidies and assistance for adaptation to climate change, remain rare in the trade governance system.

Even the principles that are well established in international environmental law remain marginal and isolated in the trade governance system. The principle of common but differentiated responsibilities is a good illustration. Only two trade agreements—both signed between the European Union and Latin American countries in July 2012—explicitly acknowledge that states have a common responsibility to protect the environment. They specify that this responsibility differs as a result of the states' contribution to environmental problems and their capacity to manage them. Likewise, the precautionary principle rarely appears in non-EU agreements, apart from a modest formulation related to sanitary and phytosanitary measures. Few non-EU PTAs explicitly recognize that insufficient scientific evidence should not be used as a reason to postpone or reject environmental measures. Even the polluter-pays principle, which is normatively in line with a liberal worldview because it proposes to internalize economic externalities, is mentioned in only a handful of PTAs. It does not feature in a single US trade agreement.

In addition, some MEAs, such as the Cartagena Protocol on Biosafety, are seldom mentioned in PTAs (see figure 4.2 in chapter 4). The Cartagena Protocol has significant trade implications for the export and import of genetically modified organisms (GMOs). Yet only two European agreements mention the Cartagena Protocol and call for its implementation. The 2012 agreement between the European Union, Colombia, and Peru also includes a provision stating that "nothing in this Agreement shall limit the right of a Party to adopt or maintain measures to implement [the Cartagena Protocol]" (Art. 270.4). None of the US agreements refer to the Cartagena Protocol, and it is unlikely that US negotiators will ever follow the EU model and regulate the trade of GMOs.

The section has shown that, despite the diffusion of some environmental provisions from and to US PTAs, other provisions remain specific to a few countries. European negotiators have not followed the US leadership regarding enforcement procedures, whereas American negotiators have not emulated European examples on climate and GMOs governances. This is evidence that the global trade governance system is not converging toward a single cohesive model and that some degree of differentiation will likely remain among PTAs environmental provisions.

Conclusions

Overall, the United States has had a profound impact on the trade governance system. As a negotiating party to NAFTA and its side agreement, it established new standards that were later replicated in PTAs around the world. The United States, Canada, and Mexico duplicated NAFTA's environmental provisions in their PTAs with their subsequent trade partners, who themselves replicated these provisions in their PTAs with third countries. That said, NAFTA constitutes neither a static regional model nor a point of global convergence. Instead, it triggered a proliferation of new environmental provisions that appeared across the trade governance system. It gives rise to a Cambrian explosion of an increasingly diverse and complex set of provisions. Some of these provisions were developed by foreign countries and later emulated by US negotiators. Others remain to be included in a US agreement.

These empirical observations are consistent with a representation of trade governance as a complex adaptive system (Morin, Pauwelyn, and Hollway 2017). PTAs' environmental provisions did not coalesce into regional blocs or around a multilateral agreement, because trade negotiators kept a balance between exploration and exploitation. They explore the governance landscape by introducing novel environmental provisions, which maintain some degree of differentiation among PTAs, and they exploit the known provisions by duplicating them in other PTAs, which maintain some degree of cohesion. The trade governance system unfolds itself at this edge between chaos and order by constantly growing in complexity.

The constant cross-fertilization between PTAs can generate productive policy results. In particular, combining US enforcement procedure and the dispute-settlement mechanism with the European sector approach constitutes a promising formula. When the two approaches are integrated in the same PTA, they result in a set of environmental commitments that have a broad scope and significant depth. Countries that sign these PTAs are encouraged to increase their level of environmental protection in a variety of specific domains. They are also required to enforce their environmental standards effectively. A good example is the US-Peru trade agreement, which includes a specific commitment to endangered species and a strong compliance mechanism. The combination of the two encouraged the Peruvian government to enhance its implementation of CITES (see chapter 4).

However, the United States may not be able to influence the trade governance system much more than it has already. Recent US agreements lack innovation. Major environmental issues, such as climate change, are more directly addressed in non-US agreements. The United States is still a central player in trade politics, and its reluctance to address climate change in its PTAs could actually be slowing down the diffusion of promising climate-related innovations. As might be expected from complex system theory, the initial conditions that characterize a system have long-lasting impacts. Yet evolution is nonlinear, and just because one country was innovative in the past does not mean it will continue to be innovative in the future.

7 Conclusions

The Trump administration has pushed US trade policy into entirely new terrain, potentially tweeting us into a global trade war. He has slapped tariffs on aluminum and steel from some of his closest trading partners—the European Union, Mexico, and Canada; withdrawn the United States from the 2017 Trans-Pacific Partnership (TPP), which the Obama administration negotiated with 11 other nations; and has aggressively re-negotiated NAFTA, which he famously called on Twitter "the worst trade deal ever signed" (Trump 2017). All of these actions have implications for the environment. Perhaps most relevant to trade-environment politics, in January 2018, Trump announced tariffs of up to 30 percent on solar imports, a move that some worry will actually shackle the $28 million US domestic industry, which relies on component imports from China for 80 percent of its supply chain (Eckhouse, Natter, and Martin 2018). It is possible that these solar tariffs, coupled with those on steel and aluminum, which are used in production of renewable technologies, will greatly chill global decarbonization efforts. These efforts rely on open trade so that the renewables industry can take advantage of economies of scale and global supply chains to keep production costs down (Chemnick 2018). At the same time, if the prices of steel and aluminum go up, global production will decline, which might exert downward pressure on CO_2 emissions. Further, if Trump era policies catalyze an economic crisis, emissions may also decline in the short term. In short, the environmental implications of what is looking to be a new era in US trade policy could have mixed effects on the environment, with some being potentially devastating, particularly as it relates to climate change and decarbonization in the long term.

As this book has highlighted, however, the news is not all bleak. Rather, US trade agreements promise to continue making some important contributions to global environmental politics for years to come. Thanks to strong domestic laws, notably Trade Promotion Authority (TPA)—also called "fast-track authority"—Congress has baked in several important environmental provisions that the president must include in any newly (re)negotiated trade agreements. As detailed in chapters 2 and 3, this requirement is given in exchange for a simple up-or-down Congressional vote, without the possibility for amendment or filibuster. This promises, at least until 2021 when the current TPA expires, that any US trade agreements must, for example, require trading partners to implement their obligations under seven listed multilateral environmental agreements (MEAs) and effectively enforce their existing domestic environmental laws. Importantly, violation of these environmental provisions is also subject to the full range of dispute-settlement provisions, including, for example, monetary penalties. As we discuss in chapter 5, the ability to effectively enforce these provisions through the trade dispute-settlement procedure is far stronger than any enforcement provisions under the listed MEAs themselves.

This book has further helped us to better understand how, why, and with what implications the US government pursues environmental objectives by linking them to its trade agreements. Before delving into future trends in the field, we summarize here our key findings and core arguments in each of these three areas.

1. How does the United States link trade and environmental issues in its trade agreements?

In chapter 2, we used the Trade and Environment Database (TREND), which codes 688 global trade agreements for environmental provisions, to trace the evolution of US trade-environment linkages from 1985 (US-Israel PTA) to 2017 (TPP). This analysis illuminated a strong trend toward more prescriptive and far-reaching environmental provisions over time.

We demonstrated how environmental provisions in US preferential trade agreements (PTAs) have evolved through five distinct phases. During phase 1 (1985–1999), the United States recognized connections between trade and environmental goals by incorporating highly circumscribed environmental exceptions to trade rules rather than pursuing specific environmental objectives directly. During phase 2 (1992–1999), US trade policy began to navigate potential synergies and conflicts between environmental protection and trade liberalization by creating environmental cooperation mechanisms and by leveling the playing field to ensure that Mexico and other developing countries did not benefit economically from lower environmental standards and lax enforcement. During phase 3 (2000–2001), the United States began to integrate accountability mechanisms for environmental issues. During phase 4 (2002–2005), the US Congress further strengthened those environmental provisions through Trade Promotion Authority requirements. Finally, during phase 5 (2006-present), the United States is aggressively using trade agreements to achieve environmental goals, especially those that the United States has already committed to under other domestic and/or international environmental instruments.

Existing US domestic trade law, such as the 2015 Trade Act, articulates specific environmental provisions that the United States must pursue in all of its trade agreements. However, these domestic laws merely set a minimum baseline for which issues must be included. Aside from a prohibition on addressing climate change issues through trade agreements, domestic trade law does not provide much guidance as to the limits of PTAs in addressing environmental issues, or on how environmental issues should be framed in PTAs. These decisions are instead developed through domestic political processes that involve, for example, interagency coordination, soliciting input from NGOs, and engaging trading-partner nations in dialogue about environmental issues.

2. Why does the United States link trade and environmental issues in its trade agreements?

Chapter 3 looked to the literature on linkage politics to better understand why the United States might choose to link environmental issues to its trade agreements by including environmental provisions. One overarching theme is that these linkages tend to be what Betsill and colleagues (2015) call "catalytic" linkages, which seek to facilitate action, as opposed to those that divide labor more efficiently. For example, the provisions related to MEAs in US PTAs, and associated cooperative activities under environmental cooperation agreements (ECAs) with Peru, Colombia, and Morocco, all sought to push these trading partners into higher levels of compliance with specific MEAs. Similarly, US PTAs have successfully pushed trading-partner nations to adopt stronger domestic laws for public participation in environmental decision making, as well as to effectively enforce their preexisting environmental laws. Importantly, enhanced cooperation through ECAs has channeled funds to implement MEAs at levels that far outstrip what is available under MEAs themselves. These funds have been used to help trading-partner nations to, for example, implement legislation and train scientific authorities.

Efficiency gains are, at best, an afterthought in these US trade-environment linkages. This is in stark contrast to what the environmental-regime overlap literature has illuminated. That literature has largely focused on "division of labor" linkages, highlighting, for example, how the biodiversity conventions have worked together on conservation of common species of concern, how the chemical conventions have held major conferences together, and how the Intergovernmental Forum on Forests' agenda has been impacted by other regimes with interests in forest governance, such as the Convention on Biological Diversity and the United Nations Framework Convention on Climate Change (Jinnah 2014; Selin 2010; Rosendal 2001b).

The US case has also illuminated that motivations for linking trade and environmental politics are multifaceted. Rationales are rooted in several existing, and sometimes competing, theories in the literature. In linking trade-environment issues in its PTAs, the US government sought to minimize compliance costs by choosing issues that it has already implemented domestically and were reflected in US domestic law. It was further responsive to domestic pressures, especially from the environmental NGO community, which were central in drafting key pieces of some of these agreements, and which advised Congress on how to construct the Bipartisan Trade Deal of 2007 (the "May 10 agreement"). The latter is particularly important in that it shaped the subsequent Trade Act of 2015, which gave the US president Trade Promotion Authority (TPA) and delineated the baseline environmental terms of all US trade agreements negotiated under TPA.

The United States is also guided, at least in part, by some protectionist interests. It has sought to protect domestic timber industries from illegal trafficking of species such as mahogany and cedar. Although these policies, namely the Lacey Act, have had some success in decreasing imports of these species into the United States, exports of likely illegal Peruvian timber to

Conclusions

China, which lacks comparable legislation, are growing (EIA 2018). Interview data further suggest that US choices were also driven by temporally sensitive, contextual factors, such as data availability, NGO expertise, "hot topic" issues, and the politics of the current US administration. As one New Zealand government interviewee highlighted, the level of a country's ambition also depends greatly on who the trading partner is and who they have negotiated with in the past. These data suggest, for example, that had the US-Peru PTA been negotiated now, the environmental provisions would likely look much different than what we ended up with in the agreement, focusing for example on today's "hot topics" in the region, such as mining, rather than the PTA's actual focus on forestry issues.

3. What are the implications of the United States linking environmental issues to its trade agreements?

Chapters 4–6 explored various implications of environmental linkages in US trade agreements. Chapter 4 asked: *can trade agreements enhance the effectiveness of MEAs?* Looking through the lens of the US-Peru PTA, we argue that they can and indeed have done so. Specifically, we demonstrate how trade agreements can enhance MEA effectiveness by serving as vectors to catalyze MEA implementation and by strengthening MEA compliance mechanisms. Drawing on the regime effectiveness literature, we argue that procedural effectiveness, as measured through improvements in MEA implementation and compliance, is already being enhanced in biodiversity MEAs. Not only do many US trade agreements already incorporate provisions that require implementation of MEAs, but in the last decade, they have begun to link compliance with those MEA-relevant provisions to the trade agreement's full dispute-resolution mechanism. In complementing MEAs' historically managerial mechanisms with PTA's more legalistic ones, we argue that US PTAs can strengthen MEA compliance capacity.

We caution, however, that evidence is lacking regarding effectiveness improvements along other dimensions, such as problem solving and goal attainment. For example, in the US-Peru case, interview data and NGO reports suggest that illegal timber shipments have shifted to species not covered under the PTA and/or that trade flows may have merely shifted away from the United States and toward China (EIA 2018). This suggests that, in this case, effectiveness as measured through problem solving and/

or goal attainment is not improved and may actually have negative implications. More research is needed to fully understand these implications.

Chapter 5 asked: *can free trade agreements diffuse environmental norms?* Again, we argue here that they can and have done so. We examine this through the lens of two key norms in US environmental policy: effective enforcement and public participation. We examine these norms across three US PTAs: 1992's NAFTA, the 2004 Central American Free Trade Agreement (CAFTA-DR), and the 2006 Peru Trade Promotion Agreement. Through a detailed process-tracing analysis, we demonstrate how these two key norms have "internationalized" from US domestic environmental law and policy through environmental linkages within US PTAs, and subsequently how these norms have been "internalized" through their incorporation into domestic policy and practice in trading-partner nations (figure 7.1). We argue that in illuminating this new mechanism of environmental norm diffusion, we now better understand the potential for PTAs to shape environmental policy and practice across borders.

Importantly, we highlight how environmental cooperation activities, through environmental cooperation agreements (ECAs), are critical mechanisms for environmental norm diffusion. Largely ignored in the trade-environment literature, these findings suggest that additional attention should be paid to the potential and implications of environmental cooperation to diffuse environmental norms and policies to trading-partner nations.

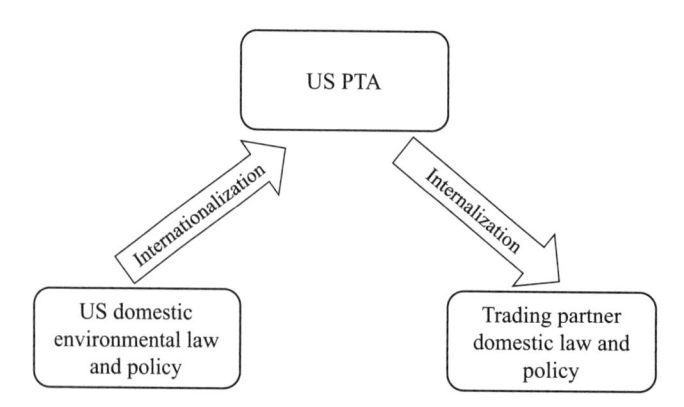

Figure 7.1
Diffusion of environmental norms through trade agreements

Conclusions 159

Chapter 5 also cautioned, however, that powerful states may coerce weaker trading partners to adopt their environmental preferences in exchange for US market access. Indeed, interview data suggested that the US-designed Forest Annex to the US-Peru PTA was "shoved down [Peru's] throat" in exchange for market access. This type of diffusion through coercion is a relatively understudied concept in the environmental context. This is not to say that developing countries favor inclusion of environmental provisions in PTAs less than developed countries do (Bernauer and Nguyen 2015). However, developing countries likely prefer provisions related to water, desertification, or indigenous communities over those emphasized by the United States. As such, the power imbalance, and potential coercion that may result, remains an important consideration in studying these negotiations.

Finally, chapter 6 asked: *do US PTA provisions become global standards?* Again, we argue that they do. More specifically, we find that several important environmental provisions, which first originated in US PTAs, have found their way into the PTAs of US trading partners and into those of third countries' PTAs. This is notably the case of environmental exceptions to commitments on investment protection. They first appeared in NAFTA and other US agreements and were subsequently replicated in PTAs that do not involve the United States. We further demonstrate that the environmental provisions of other countries' agreements inspired some recent features of US PTAs. For example, the European Union traditionally includes in its trade agreements detailed provisions on specific environmental issue areas tailored to the particular ecological context of their trade partners. Recent US agreements build on this European approach and add issue-specific provisions, especially on forestry, fisheries, and endangered species, in addition to provisions related to the environment in general. Centrally, chapter 6 argues that this cross-fertilization between the PTAs of different countries is a critical mechanism in the evolution of environmental provisions in the trade system.

Chapter 6 also identified two important limits to this cross-fertilization process. First, recent US agreements are not as innovative as NAFTA was for its time. They also borrow less from other countries. Most recent US agreements duplicated environmental provisions from earlier US agreements. This standardization will likely slow down the cross-fertilization between PTAs. Second, flows of influence are lopsided in favor of high-income countries. While some developing countries have successfully introduced some innovative environmental provisions in the trade system, notably in genetic resources and traditional knowledge, most provisions that were replicated by several countries originally come from high-income countries. This implies that some issues that are important for developing countries, such as desertification, access to fresh water, and adaptation to climate change, are rarely addressed in the context of trade negotiations.

Finally, it should be noted that non-environmental clauses can also have environmental consequences. This is partly related to negative externalities: trade liberalization creates economic effects (more production, agricultural specialization, long distance shipping, etc.), which have clear environmental consequences. Some may also argue there are also regulatory impacts, as some trade commitments limit the capacity of governments to regulate the environment, including via a "chilling effect" of sorts. On the other hand, PTAs' trade commitments might actually do more for the environment than their environmental provisions by, for example, favoring the development and diffusion of environmental technologies. These are all questions that were outside the scope of our analysis here, but demand further investigation.

Unintended Consequences and the Importance of Public Participation

Environmental provisions hold much promise for strengthening environmental governance writ large. However, if trade is used to promote environmental goals at the expense of other social issues, problems of inequity and instability can result. Power differentials between countries is a key variable to consider in this regard. Although the inclusion of both baseline and more progressive environmental provisions in US PTAs promises important environmental benefits, there are also potential risks. This is especially the case when there are power imbalances between trading partners, like between Mexico and the United States. Is it a good thing for the United States to push its environmental preferences on trading partners in exchange for market access? Not always. When domestic institutions in trading-partner nations are not adequately robust, implementation of far-reaching environmental provisions can lead to corruption, practices that further entrench existing inequalities, and even loss of life.

Conclusions

The case of the US-Peru PTA is particularly instructive in this regard. The domestic political fallout in that country in the lead up to the entry into force of its PTA with the United States resulted in social unrest and violence that have been blamed, in part, on the PTA and, especially, on the Peruvian government's use of the PTA as a political cover to push through its broader social agenda as it related to forest and land-use issues. The case therefore highlights one particularly important possible concern: trade partners' potential use of PTA requirements as a shield for implementing broader social reforms without adequate consultation processes with impacted stakeholders. Because this case is so instructive in thinking about lessons going forward, it is worth recounting the story as a cautionary tale for the future of trade-environment linkages in trade agreements. This section recounts the story in some detail and suggests some possible policy options to avoid this tragic outcome in the future.

In April 2009, one month after the US-Peru PTA was signed, indigenous communities began to block roads near Bagua, Peru, in peaceful protest of the Peruvian government's action to implement the US PTA. The protests continued until June 5, 2009, when the Peruvian government decided to clear the protesters from the "Devil's Curve," a stretch of the Belaunde Terry Highway near Bagua, approximately 600 miles north of Lima. What was a peaceful protest quickly turned violent. Official estimates report that 34 people, including 10 civilians and 24 police officers, were killed in the standoff. Hundreds more were injured. Unofficial reports suggest that several more protesters were "disappeared" (Rénique 2009), with up to 40 bodies thrown into the local river by police helicopters (Merino 2010, cited in Stetson 2012). Many suggest that what has come to be known as the "Bagua massacre" was a result of Peruvian President Alan García's circumvention of domestic laws in order to implement provisions of the PTA (de Jong and Humphreys 2016; Hughes 2010; Rénique 2009; Stetson 2012; EIA 2018). Interview data (and common sense) suggest this was in part due to strong pressures from the US government to implement the annex very quickly after it was signed, with threats that in order for the PTA to enter into force, certain implementation thresholds must be met. Specifically, following the signing of the PTA in April 2006, the Peruvian Congress granted García the authority for a 180-day period to pass a series of legislative decrees, which have come to be colloquially known as *la ley de la selva* (the law of the jungle; Escobar Torio and Tam 2017). Specifically,

Law 29157 granted García the power to "legislate on matters related with the implementation of the Agreement to promote commerce between Peru and the USA" (de Jong and Humphreys 2016, 558). García argued these decrees were necessary to bring Peruvian domestic laws into compliance with its obligations under the PTA (de Jong and Humphreys 2016; Hughes 2010; Stetson 2012).

Acting upon this authority and without any public consultation, García subsequently issued 108 legislative decrees, including a new forest law, which, among other things, opened up tropical forest land to mineral extraction and agro-industrial production and undermined collective property rights of Peru's indigenous people (Rénique 2009). For example, two of the most controversial decrees, LR No. 1064 and 1090, would together make it possible to change the legal status of 60 percent (more than 45 million hectares) of Amazonian land from forests to agricultural lands (Carlsen 2009; de Jong and Humphreys 2016). Other decrees weakened voting rights for local communities regarding lease or sale of communal lands (LD 1015) and transferred zoning authority from local communities to the central government (LD 1064; Escobar Torio and Tam 2017). That the decrees were pushed through so quickly was very problematic. As one NGO representative said, "nobody had the time to read them, much less comment on them or engage."

Following domestic and international pressure regarding the issue, including international media coverage of the Bagua massacre, García repealed two of the most controversial of the decrees (LD Nos. 1064 and 1090). The Peruvian Parliament appointed a committee to investigate the case, resulting in four official reports, which among other things accused the Peruvian Minister of Commerce Aráoz of exaggerating the possible impacts of repealing the decrees on the US-Peru PTA and declared the decrees unconstitutional because adequate consultation processes were not followed (Arse 2014; de Jong and Humphreys 2016). Although the Peruvian Congress enacted the Law of Consultation in May 2010 to require prior informed consent of indigenous communities, García refused to sign it, and it was not signed until August 2011, one month after his predecessor, President Ollanta Humala, took office (Arse 2014).

Although all of the decrees were intended to relate to the environment chapter (chapter 18) of the PTA, de Jong and Humphreys' analysis of all 108 decrees suggest that only 25 of them actually relate to environmental

Conclusions 163

issues (2016, 558). Others have further suggested that, at most, only 20 percent of the decrees relate to PTA implementation at all (de Jong and Humphreys 2016). The latter strongly suggests that the PTA was indeed used a shield by the Peruvian government to push an alternative social agenda that was at best marginally related to the PTA itself. One NGO key informant lamented that the US government did not take the NGO community's concerns about what was unfolding in Peru during this time seriously enough. That informant further underscored that s/he "continue[s] to see that what happened in Peru after the Bagua incident was the result of a really unholy mix of fierce economic interests taking advantage of that very specific circumstance that the new trade deal provided them, as well as the added bonus of a naïve [US Trade Representative (USTR)] office who at that point was very trusting of its Peruvian counterparts and didn't want to hear the warnings of the NGO community once the deal was signed." To be fair, this same informant added that:

> I don't blame Bagua on the annex; that's the wrong conclusion to derive from this story. But there is a lesson here about what the knock-on effects are when you shoehorn environmental reforms into trade agreements when institutions are not aligned on what it will take to implement them. There could have been a better process from both government and NGOs to make sure we put the right things in there.

Although the official Peruvian government position, as underscored by interviews with Peruvian government officials, is that the Bagua massacre was not related to the PTA at all, this position is widely criticized, including by NGO and US government interviewees. Rather, it is widely understood that the lack of adequate participatory processes in Peru's sweeping passage of implementing legislation for the PTA was largely responsible for massive social unrest and even loss of life.

The promise of US market access, coupled with the power differential between the United States and Peru in this case, helps to explain why Peru accepted such deeply prescriptive environmental policies in this PTA, and why it was subsequently able to push through a host of policies without adequate domestic consultation under the auspices of the PTA implementation. This combination of conditions is not unusual in US trade negotiations, nor more broadly. In order to avoid this problem in future, the United States (and other powerful countries) might consider building stronger participation requirements into its PTAs. As discussed in chapter 5, public participation in environmental decision making is already a key norm the United States incorporates into all of its trade agreements. These provisions could be strengthened to require such things as prior and informed consent from local communities who will be impacted by PTA implementation. Allowing for longer implementation periods in trading-partner nations may also help to avoid this problem in future. Peru only had 18 months to implement the Forest Annex provisions. This not only put a lot of stress on Peru to push through legislation without allowing for adequate consultations, but also provided political cover for doing so domestically. Further, the United States could benefit from additional public consultations at home, in particular with US NGOs who specialize in environmental issues in trading-partner nations, such as the Environmental Investigation Agency's expertise in forest issues in Peru. Although there are existing mechanisms to consult with such organizations, better consultation processes can both identify potential flares before they ignite and potentially avoid tragedies like we saw in Bagua in 2009. Slowing this implementation process down through consultation will also have the important benefit of ensuring that adequate

---

Box 7.1
Positive and Negative Implications of Environmental Provisions in Preferential Trade Agreements

Positive Implications

- Enhanced MEA effectiveness
- Environmental norm diffusion
- Opportunity to innovate and design new environmental standards
- Increased funds for capacity building and institution building
- Stronger mechanisms for enforcement of environmental rules

Negative Implications

- Possible coerced diffusion of environmental norms/policies
- Focus more on priorities of developed countries than on those of developing countries
- Focus more on local than on global environmental issues
- Inadequate time for robust public participation
- Trade flows of regulated products may spill over to third-party countries
- PTAs can be used as a shield for pushing through alternative social agenda

Conclusions

domestic institutions are in place to implement PTA provisions. Despite this implementation problem, one NGO interviewee highlighted a thin silver lining to the Bagua massacre: it triggered the development of robust public participation laws in Peru.

The Future of US Trade Environment Politics

The future of US trade-environment politics is somewhat uncertain. As we noted in the opening section of this chapter, in withdrawing from the TPP, demanding a renegotiation of NAFTA, and slapping tariffs on major trading partners, President Trump has destabilized global trade governance, with uncertainty about how these decisions will impact many things, among them the environment. Yet, as we argue below, these actions are actually unlikely to weaken environmental protection. The TPP, and its environmental agenda, will continue without the United States under another name, and the renegotiated NAFTA has actually resulted in some stronger environmental provisions (Laurens et al. 2019). We flesh out these arguments below. We further point to some other emerging areas of trade-environment politics that are likely to be, or in our view should be, important in the years to come. These include the utilization of trade agreements to pursue climate change interests and an emerging cadre of disputes within the WTO surrounding renewable energy technologies. We conclude with a list of core policy recommendations that we suggest should guide governments in developing trade-environment linkages going forward.

Comprehensive and Progressive Trans-Pacific Partnership

Following the US withdrawal from the TPP in 2017, the remaining 11 countries maintained the agreement, with very few changes, and renamed it the Comprehensive and Progressive Trans-Pacific Partnership (CPTPP).[1] The CPTPP was agreed on March 8, 2018 and entered into force on December 30, 2018. As a result, the US thumbprint remains clearly visible on the CPTPP's environmental provisions. Notably, the CPTPP's environment chapter contains an article on Conservation and Trade that explicitly addresses the Convention on International Trade in Endangered Species of Wild Fauna and Flora (CITES)—a hallmark of US trade policy since 2009. The CPTPP requires parties to "adopt, maintain, and implement" CITES among several other managerial-style enforcement requirements, such as sharing information, strengthening forest management capacity domestically, and better involving NGOs in implementation. Like other recent US PTAs, CPTPP also subjects the environment chapter to the same dispute-resolution procedures as the rest of the Agreement, including through sanctions. Notably, however, as it relates to CITES implementation, the CPTPP requires that a violation can only be established if a Party's failure to "adopt, maintain, or implement" CITES is done in a manner that affects trade or investment between the parties (Art. 20.17, fn. 23). This sets a comparatively high bar for demonstrating CITES violation in comparison to the US-Peru TPA, which did not require a violation to impact trade or investment.

CPTPP contains several other environmental provisions that are clearly derived from US trade policy. For example, the agreement requires parties to: enforce their domestic environmental laws; enhance mechanisms for public participation; provide for judicial, quasi-judicial, or administrative proceedings for enforcement; establish public submissions processes; develop environmental cooperation frameworks; and critically, all such provisions are fully enforceable through dispute settlement—a hallmark of US trade policy that has not been adopted by CPTPP countries otherwise, apart from their earlier PTA with the United States.

As is standard practice in US trade policy, these environmental provisions reflect US efforts to "level the playing field," and would not have been new obligations for the United States. In other words, that the United States will no longer be required to implement the CPTPP's environmental provisions may not really matter that much, because it has already implemented most of them. The environmental provisions were largely designed for other countries to implement. There are some exceptions, of course. For example, interview data suggest that the biodiversity provisions were largely pushed by Peru. Similarly, the CPTPP requires parties to cooperate on transitions to a low emissions economy (without explicitly mentioning climate change), which was also pushed by other countries. However, such provisions are weak and unenforceable, and would have been unlikely to result in any important policy change in the United States regardless.

There is, however, one exception, which will likely result in negative environmental impacts following the US withdrawal. This is related to the removal of a provision in the 2016 TPP that mirrored the US Lacey Act, which required countries to respect domestic laws of foreign countries with respect to trade in endangered species. That is, the provision would have made it illegal for all parties to import a species from another country if that species was taken illegally from its country of origin and is particularly relevant to illegal timber trade. The United States fought hard, supported and pushed by key environmental NGOs, to include this Lacey Act language in the TPP. They were opposed strongly by Chile, Malaysia, New Zealand, and Vietnam on the grounds of practical difficulties, especially concerning knowledge of foreign countries' domestic law. Unsurprisingly then, when the United States withdrew from TPP, the "Lacey language" was removed. Some commentators underscore the missed opportunity this watering down of anti-illegal logging language from CPTPP presents for the world's forests and the people whose livelihoods depend on them (Barber and Li 2018).

As such, aside from the so-called Lacey Act provisions, which were removed after the United States withdrew, the environmental impacts of the CPTPP are unlikely to change much as a result of the US withdrawal. Rather, as the CPTPP parties begin to implement their environmental obligations, it will present another interesting empirical case of norm and policy diffusion to examine. Similarly, if we observe enhanced implementation of CITES and other listed MEAs in connection with CPTPP implementation, we may have additional evidence of the role PTAs can play in enhancing some dimensions of MEA effectiveness.

United States, Mexico, and Canada Trade Agreement

Another important contemporary development catalyzed by the Trump administration is its initiation of the renegotiation of the 1994 NAFTA on August 16, 2017. The renegotiation was based on a set of publicly available negotiating objectives, which were developed and revised by the USTR based on hundreds of hours of consultations with members of Congress, private sector representatives, labor representatives, NGOs, and others (USTR 2017b). Given Trump's hostile track record on environmental issues, some might have expected his administration to water down NAFTA's landmark environmental provisions. However, the United States, Mexico, and Canada Trade Agreement (USMCA) not only brings most environmental provisions into the core of the agreement, rather than in a side agreement as in NAFTA, but it also contains more environmental provisions than the original agreement, notably on domestic levels of environmental protection, environmental cooperation, coherence between environmental policies and non-environmental issues, public participation, and environmental exceptions to trade commitments (Laurens et al. 2019). Figure 7.2 shows that the most striking difference between USMCA and its predecessor is the number of specific environmental issues they each address.

In fact, the only categories where NAFTA includes more environmental provisions than USMCA are environmental principles. Unlike NAFTA, USMCA does not refer to the prevention principle—and dispute settlement. Indeed, the North American Agreement on Environmental Cooperation (NAAEC) included a specific dispute-settlement mechanism in case of failure to enforce domestic environmental laws (part V), whereas USMCA addresses disputes in which a party does not comply with the environmental provisions of the agreement.

What explains these strengthened environmental provisions in the USMCA? The answer is actually fairly straightforward. Because NAFTA was

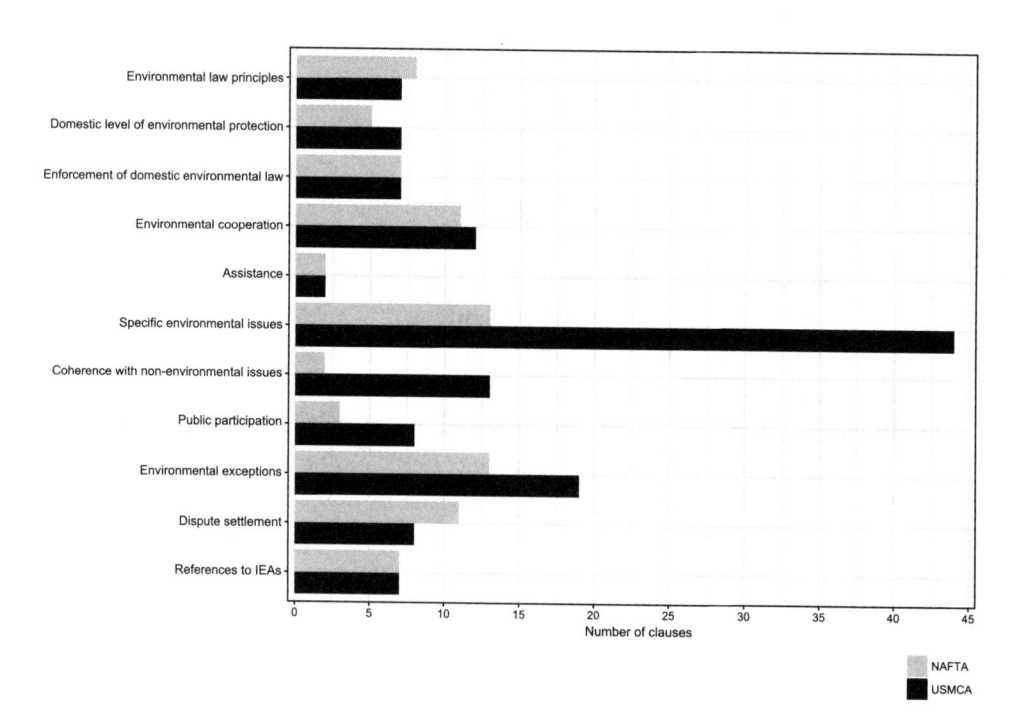

Figure 7.2
Number of environmental provisions in NAFTA and USMCA

renegotiated under Trade Promotion Authority (TPA), the US administration had a strong incentive to include all environmental provisions required by TPA-2015. These include, for example, requiring trading partners to implement specific multilateral environmental agreements, among several other requirements, detailed in chapter 2. Although the 1994 NAFTA was progressive on environmental issues for its time, the environmental provisions required by TPA are much more far-reaching. Further, the USMCA article on wildlife trafficking (Art. 24.22(7)b) reflects the Trump administration's demonstrated interest in ensuring effective enforcement, including with respect to wildlife trafficking, as evidenced through his 2017 Executive Order on Enforcing Federal Law with Respect to Transnational Criminal Organizations Preventing International Trafficking,[2] as well as through his administration's block of illegally harvested timber in Peru, even if the motivation may have been to protect the US domestic timber industry. The illegal, unreported, and unregulated fishing and fisheries subsidies provisions (USMCA Art. 24.20) are also reflective of long-standing negotiations on these issues within the WTO (Campling and Havice 2017).

Climate-Progressive Trade Agreements and Missed Opportunities
The failure to address climate change directly in the context of US PTAs is a significant limit to US efforts to reconcile trade liberalization and environmental protection. In principle, PTAs hold great potential to enhance climate change governance (Morin and Jinnah 2018). In contrast to multilateral negotiation on climate, PTAs involve fewer parties at the bargaining table, they are supported by strong enforcement mechanisms, and they allow for policy experimentation. Yet, by and large, trade negotiations have not seized this opportunity.

Some US agreements include modest provisions on renewable energy and energy efficiency. The European Union addresses climate change more directly in its PTAs. Some European PTAs include commitments to reduce greenhouse gas emissions and references to multilateral climate agreements. In 2018, the European Union announced that it would refuse to sign trade agreements with countries that have not ratified the Paris Agreement on climate change (Stone 2018). A few months later, the PTA between the European Union and Japan became the first trade agreement to include an explicit reference to the Paris Agreement. Yet, even EU agreements do not include specific and enforceable provisions on issues at the very heart of trade—climate linkages, including carbon taxes, fossil-fuel subsidies, carbon credits, and emission trading (Morin and Jinnah 2018).

One of Canada's objectives for the renegotiation of the NAFTA was to "fully support efforts to address climate changes" (Freeland 2017). However, USMCA does not break new ground on the climate front. US TPA specifically prohibits the president from including in its trade agreements commitments to any "greenhouse gas emissions measures, including obligations that require changes to United States laws or regulations or that would affect the implementation of such laws or regulations, other than those fulfilling the other negotiating objectives in this section" (Section 914 para. (b)). As explained in chapter 2, this drastically circumscribes the potential of US trade agreements to address climate change in a meaningful way.

Renewable Energy Disputes in the WTO

Another important emerging area of trade-environment politics surrounds a spate of disputes in the WTO challenging subsidies for renewable energy. Interestingly, although fossil-fuel subsidies outnumber those for renewables subsidies by a ratio of 4:1, to date, only renewables have been challenged under the WTO dispute-settlement mechanism (Asmelash 2015; Van de Graaf and van Asselt 2017). The first such renewable energy dispute was filed in 2010 by Japan, later joined by the European Union, challenging Canada's use of the feed-in tariff in Ontario, which guaranteed minimum electricity prices for solar and wind sources if a baseline domestic content requirement was met (Van de Graaf and van Asselt 2017; WTO 2013). In that dispute, the WTO dispute-settlement body ruled against Canada, not because the subsidy was deemed non-compliant with the WTO Agreement on Subsidies and Countervailing Measures, but because the policy violated national treatment obligations under the General Agreement on Tariffs and Trade (GATT) and the Agreement on Trade-Related Investment Measures. A similar outcome resulted from a case involving a US challenge to domestic content requirements in an Indian power purchase agreement with solar producers (WTO 2016).

There have since been at least eight more cases filed challenging domestic support of, for example, solar, wind, and biofuels industries in WTO member states. Most of those have not yet been resolved, leaving much uncertainty about the future compatibility of renewable energy subsidies in WTO member states. As more and more states are turning to renewables as a source of decarbonization, these disputes are likely to increase into the future. As Joanna Lewis cogently argues, this underscores the importance of navigating the fundamental tension between the political economy of domestic renewable energy support (i.e., creating jobs and ensuring domestic technological development) with the basic principles of the global trade regime (i.e., reducing barriers and non-discrimination), before any negative implications for global decarbonization are realized (Lewis 2014). PTAs can play a role in navigating these tensions if the United States and others major players can begin to delineate rules under which renewables support is permissible. Although there are challenges for the United States in particular for including such provisions due to TPA's prohibition on including measures related to greenhouse gas emissions, renewables rules need not necessarily conflict with TPA if such rules are geared toward securing other environmental benefits. For example, renewables policies could be developed under the auspices of decreasing emissions of criteria pollutants (that largely correlate with greenhouse gas emissions) for the purpose of protection of public health.[3]

Environmental Goods and Services

Finally, another important ongoing issue in trade-environment politics is the negotiations surrounding a possible new plurilateral agreement on environmental goods within the WTO. These negotiations began in July 2014, currently among 46 WTO members, to negotiate a system of tariff reductions for environmental goods. Although there was hope that these negotiations would conclude in December 2016, ministers were unable to reach agreement and the future of the Environmental Goods Agreement remains uncertain.

One reason it has likely lost steam, and why the United States hasn't pursued this issue within its PTAs, is that environmental goods have been the center of a trade war between the United States, European Union, and China. Closely related to the renewables discussion above, these three countries have slapped tariffs and countervailing duties on one another's environmental goods, including on solar panels, wind turbines, and biofuels. This trade war appears to be driven at least in part by domestic manufacturers of renewable energy technologies in those countries (Brewster, Brunel, and Mayda 2016) and has likely resulted in a chilling of interest in the United States in pursuing environmental goods discussions within its PTAs.

Recommendations Going Forward

Finally, our analysis and findings point to a series of policy lessons for trade negotiators in the United States and more broadly, as well as for others involved in developing and/or lobbying for linking trade and environmental policies. These recommendations are based on our core position that, when very carefully designed, trade agreements can serve as powerful tools to pursue environmental objectives. This is in part because trade agreements have stronger mechanisms for enforcement, such as dispute settlement, and are better positioned to secure adequate funds for implementation. In addition, PTAs can bring together like-minded countries, can use linkages to advance negotiation objectives, and can facilitate regulatory innovation. Further, linking trade and environmental policies makes sense. This is not only because of the intimate connection between global economic growth, including through international trade, and increased environmental degradation, but also because of the potential for international trade to enhance environmental protection through, for example, reducing barriers to trade in environmental goods. It's not that trade agreements are a panacea for environmental problems; we recognize that the unsustainable consumption patterns that trade agreements support are arguably antithetical to solving environmental problems at all. However, when considering the socio-economic system within which we currently operate, trade agreements can and should be considered as part of a multifaceted response to environmental problems.

In this final section, we lay out the most important policy lessons from our research, which are largely transferrable across countries and environmental policy priorities.

1. Develop baseline environmental provisions for PTAs secured through domestic legislation to ensure environmental priorities are maintained over time.

US Trade Promotion Authority has been instrumental in securing a baseline of environmental action through trade agreements that ensures politically negotiated environmental priorities do not get lost over time when,

Conclusions

for example, a less environmentally friendly administration takes office, or environmental priorities are negotiated away for seemingly more central trade issues. This approach further ensures some level of predictability for industry and can help to secure meaningful action on environmental issues that often take multiple years, or even decades, to address effectively.

Clearly, this is not something that can be easily transplanted to other countries. The US Congress has unique power in trade compared with other parliaments. Yet one case where the TPA experience could be useful is in the European Union. The European Parliament does not have a similar procedure in place to influence the negotiation process conducted by the European Commission, but it can adopt resolutions to express its views in the course of negotiations. A resolution adopted by the European Parliament recommended trade negotiators strengthen environmental provisions by providing for "recourse to a dispute settlement mechanism on an equal footing with the other parts of the agreement, with provision for fines to improve the situation in the sectors concerned, or at least a temporary suspension of certain trade benefits" (European Parliament 2010). Also, the Council of the European Union, on behalf of member states, can provide the European Commission a "negotiating mandate" with clear directives for trade negotiations. The negotiating mandate provided for the Transatlantic Trade and Investment Partnership was similar to the TPA in many ways: it asked negotiators to provide clauses on the enforcement of domestic environmental laws, to promote trade in environmental goods and services, and to require the implementation of a set of MEAs. Parliamentarians in other countries can also put pressure on trade negotiators to address environmental issues seriously.

2. Include provisions in future PTAs that require trading partners to utilize adequate participatory democratic processes throughout the implementation phase and in developing implementing legislation *prior* to entry into force of the PTA.

Trading partners are often expected to implement certain aspects of their PTAs as a condition of the agreement entering into force. This can create an incentive, especially when timelines are short, to push legislation through quickly, without adequate consultation with stakeholders. Most agree this was the case in Peru following the agreement of its PTA with the United States. A confluence of factors contributed to the Bagua massacre in Peru at that time. Among these factors was a failure on behalf of the US government to recognize the Peruvian government's disregard for democratic participatory processes in implementing the PTA through a series of 100 executive decrees, which were pushed through in as many days without adequate consultation with relevant stakeholders. This is not to say it was the fault of the United States; Peru is, of course, a sovereign state and made those decisions internally. However, governments should be mindful of power and capacity differentials between trading partners and the incentives these may create to circumvent democratic processes in less powerful countries in the name of securing access to large markets. Central to avoiding this in the future is allowing trading partners adequate time to implement such legislation through democratic participatory channels. Depending on the specific domestic political contexts in trading-partner nations, as well as the extent of the changes required by the PTA, this may involve allowing more time for implementing legislation to be in place before the PTA enters into force.

3. Build on existing MEAs, including requirements to ratify and implement MEAs.

Linking trade-related MEAs (e.g., the seven listed MEAs in US PTAs) to PTAs can be especially important in securing important environmental and trade benefits, such as protecting domestic markets from illegal timber while simultaneously protecting endangered tree species from illegal logging. The United States and others should continue to pursue MEA ratification and implementation through PTAs. These provisions should also be forward looking, including requirements to participate in ongoing multilateral negotiations, making adjustment to PTAs as new MEAs are adopted or amended, and so on. Caution should be used, however, to ensure that any PTA commitment to implement MEAs be required in the context of adequate domestic institutions, including consultation processes, in trading-partner nations. This can be done through consultations with credible NGOs and other governmental ministries/departments who have strong in-country experience in trading-partner nations, as well as through targeted capacity building provisions within PTAs themselves and any associated environmental cooperation agreements (ECAs).

Conclusions

4. Utilize environmental cooperation agreements under PTAs to enhance capacity building and diplomatic relations.

Trade agreements are able to secure far more political attention and implementation funding than is typically available for environmental issues. As such, utilizing ECAs to identify potential areas for environmental cooperation between trading partners can yield important benefits for environmental protection and enhancing diplomatic relations between countries, especially at the sub-ministerial level, where implementation occurs. Central to securing these benefits is support from more powerful trading partners to ensure that less powerful countries have adequate capacity to actually implement MEA-related provisions within PTAs. This might include assistance in setting up core institutions, such as ministries of environment, training national scientific authorities, and/or institutional support in developing systems of criminal penalties for violation of PTA-environmental provisions domestically. This assistance should be specific with clear targets and timeframes, and all funding should be structured as additional aid (i.e., that which is not diverted from other funding streams and/or represents a rebranding of existing aid efforts).

5. Strong action on environmental cooperation should be complemented by strong enforcement provisions, such as providing access to full dispute-settlement options for environmental provisions.

Environmental cooperation has delivered myriad benefits and allows for great flexibility in addressing environmental issues, which may be less central to core trade liberalization priorities. These provisions, which involve large cash and in-kind transfers for capacity building on environmental issues, should be pursued as win-wins for both training partners. Complementing these softer provisions, however, should be stronger enforcement measures to secure compliance with environmental provisions in trade agreements. Such provisions were long excluded from access to full dispute settlement until 2009 in the US case, and continue to be excluded from PTAs in most other parts of the globe, such as from EU PTAs. However, if environmental issues are seen as important enough to include in trade agreements, there is no acceptable prima facie rationale for excluding them from the full range of enforcement provisions. The US case suggests that important environmental benefits can be secured in doing so, without yet having to formally access the dispute-settlement provisions. Working together, effective enforcement and environmental cooperation can yield important benefits for both trade and environmental goals.

6. Monitor environmental innovations in non-US and non-EU agreements with a view toward enhancing cross-fertilization between countries.

Some lesser-known agreements include interesting environmental provisions, which may be attractive to US negotiators and others looking to innovate in this area. For example, PTAs from some Latin American countries contain innovative provisions related to genetic resources and traditional knowledge. Another example is the 2001 agreement establishing the Caribbean Community, which innovates in asking for the international recognition of the Caribbean Sea as a "Special Area requiring protection from the potentially harmful effects of the transit of nuclear and other hazardous wastes, dumping, pollution by oil or by any other substance carried by sea or wastes generated through the conduct of ship operations" (Revised Treaty of Chaguaramas, supra note 42, Art. 141). Such developments should be systematically monitored and considered for adoption.

Notes

Chapter 1

1. In addition to their core trade liberalizing function, PTAs serve as instruments of regional integration, vehicles for strategic market access and security, and as tactical tools to influence multilateral negotiations. Recent trends in PTA structure reflect an increase in cross-regional (particularly North-South) and bilateral free trade areas (as opposed to regional customs unions). Many of these recent agreements mirror the WTO's existing framework policies, while also increasingly providing reciprocal preferential treatment.

2. Our list of PTAs relies on the collection of the Design of Trade Agreements (DESTA) project (Dür et al 2014). This list of PTAs includes free trade agreements, customs unions, and partial scope agreements. Some of them are in force, but others were never ratified. The DESTA list is more comprehensive than the WTO list, as it includes agreements that were concluded by countries that are not WTO members as well as agreements that WTO members have failed to notify the WTO secretariat of.

3. These tariffs are called "production process method," or PPM, tariffs. For more on PPMs, see Charnovitz (2002a).

4. See Bernasconi-Osterwalder et al. (2006) for a detailed history of how these environmental provisions have been interpreted by the WTO's dispute-settlement body.

5. Several European agreements have a low number of environmental provisions. This is because the European Economic Community concluded several PTAs prior to the 1990s, when trade agreements typically included few environmental provisions. If one looks only at PTAs concluded in the last 15 years, the European Union and the United States have a similar median number of environmental provisions per PTA.

6. The TPP was signed by 12 countries, including the United States, in February 2016. The remaining 11 CPTPP countries are New Zealand, Australia, Brunei Darussalam, Canada, Chile, Japan, Malaysia, Mexico, Peru, Singapore, and Vietnam.

7. See Steinberg (2002) for a summary of how other regional trade organizations have addressed environmental issues.

8. Interpretations of Article XX were similar, if not more narrow, under the 1947 GATT. For a description of the 1947 GATT decisions and an analysis of political factors influencing them, see Kelemen (2001).

9. Only final adopted decision is reflected in table 1.1. Article XX disputes heard under the GATT prior to the establishment of the WTO are not reflected. All summary data in table 1.1 is drawn from WTO Secretariat (2019 and 2002).

10. Canada-Renewable Energy, Canada-FIT, China Wind Power Equipment, US-Countervailing Measures *(China)*, India-Solar Cells, EU-Biodiesel, EU-Renewable Energy Generation Sector, and US-Renewable Energy.

11. These negotiations built on similar negotiations under the Asia Pacific Economic Cooperation, or APEC, which identified a list of 54 environmental goods on which tariffs would be reduced by 2015.

12. We unpack this particular question in greater depth in chapter 3.

13. Technically, the Doha issues are discussed in the CTE in special session (CTESS), which was established to negotiate these issues.

14. See Kent (2014) and Shaffer (2002) for more comprehensive assessments of the CTE's work and the literature assessing it.

15. Although see Morin and Gauquelin (2016) for a discussion of how Latin American countries have been surprisingly influential in securing the inclusion of biodiversity provisions in US PTAs to which they are party.

16. This collection of PTAs was borrowed from the DESTA project (Dür, Baccini, and Elsig 2014).

17. Officially titled the Dominican Republic–Central America–United States Free Trade Agreement.

Chapter 2

1. It should also be noted that Bourgeois and colleagues' phases refer to US trade policy broadly, not specifically to environmental linkages.

2. See chapter 1 for a discussion of TREND.

Notes

3. The history of Article XX dispute settlement is more complex than we can cover here. For a detailed interpretation of the first 20 reports interpreting Article XX, see Moran (2017).

4. The US-Vietnam agreement was also negotiated during this time. It is an anomaly among US PTAs in that it contains very few environmental provisions. This exception resulted from the fact that the agreement is not a full-fledged free trade agreement. It is modest in all trade dimensions. It was concluded by the Clinton administration for political reasons, before the wave of PTAs concluded under the Bush administration.

5. Fast-track authority, also known as Trade Promotion Authority, expired on July 1, 2007. However, the agreements with Peru (2006), Colombia (2006), Korea (2007), and Panama (2007) were signed in time to be considered under fast-track authority as well. Because these agreements contain important new innovations, they are discussed in more detail in the third phase of US trade-environment politics below.

6. The final agreement stipulates that the provisions must also be applied to Colombia.

7. It should be noted that there were deep divisions between Latin American countries on these issues, and some Andean civil society groups regard the inclusion of biodiversity and traditional knowledge provisions in a PTA as an attempt at privatizing resources that have historically belonged to the Andean commons and are in contravention to Andean Community law. See, e.g., Toro Perez (2009).

Chapter 3

1. Chapter 2 fleshes out the specifics of the Forest Annex in great detail.

2. Peruvian government officials contest this characterization, highlighting that the Annex also reflected their interests in forest conservation.

Chapter 4

1. See Esty (1994) for a comprehensive overview of these positions.

2. For a discussion on environmentalists' criticisms of free trade, see Daly (1993). On the issue of the regulatory capacity of states involved in trade negotiations, see Hudec (1992).

3. European PTAs are more likely to refer to climate change conventions, including the UNFCCC, the Kyoto Protocol, and the Paris Agreement. For their part, Latin American countries refer frequently to the Convention on Biological Diversity in their trade agreements. Yet a greater share of US PTAs refer to CITES and the

Montreal Protocol than European PTAs refer to the UNFCCC and Latin American PTAs refer to the Convention on Biological Diversity.

4. It is important to look at date of agreement rather than entry into force, as parties may wish or be required to begin implementation of multilateral environmental agreement provisions prior to (or as a condition of) entry into force of the PTA.

5. It should be noted that the US-Peru provisions related to CITES almost exclusively focus on improving Peru's performance in this regard. We therefore only look at implementation improvements in Peru.

6. The literature tends to describe the latter as an "enforcement"-based model. As both models describe enforcement approaches, we find this distinction confusing and therefore refer to this model as a "legalistic" one.

7. As we argue below, this is beginning to shift in the US context.

8. The same analysis could be used to compare compliance strength across PTAs.

9. Author interview with US government official, January 2010.

10. Conversion factors are used to convert specimens (i.e., sawn wood) into number of individual trees, and have been highly contentious in CITES negotiations because some see them as a way to obscure actual species take.

11. Under CITES, range states must publish export quotas for Appendix-II listed species, which should be based on scientific evidence confirming that quota does not threaten the survival of the species.

12. At time of writing, USTR has not yet formally evaluated Peru's progress on the action plan.

13. Inside US Trade, "USTR Comes under Fire for Weak Oversight of Peru FTA Logging Rules," June 12, 2015.

14. The Environmental Investigation Agency has been heavily involved in monitoring Peru's implementation of the environment chapter, and very critical of Peru's efforts. (See, for example, EIA 2015.)

15. Author interview with NGO representative, January 2010.

16. This excludes a massive spike in 2014, when the quota rose to 811,143 m^3. We have excluded this year from the graph because we think it may be a data entry error.

17. All data is collected from the CITES Trade Database and the CITES's Secretariat's reporting of export quotas at www.cites.org.

18. Author interview with CITES secretariat staff, speaking in his/her personal capacity, February 2010.

Notes

Chapter 5

1. Building on our definition of legalistic enforcement mechanisms in chapter 4, this definition is adapted from the NAAEC Article 45.1(b) (NAAEC 1993) and TPP Article 20.3.5 (TPP 2015).

2. Officially titled the Dominican Republic–Central America–United States Free Trade Agreement.

3. See also chapter 2.

4. Legalization is characterized by the degree of obligation, delegation, and precision. See chapter 4 for a discussion of legalization and how it is measured.

5. The various types of clauses on public participation and effective enforcement are documented in appendix 1.

6. Officially titled the Agreement Among the Governments of Costa Rica, the Dominican Republic, El Salvador, Guatemala, Honduras, Nicaragua, and the United States of America on Environmental Cooperation.

7. See chapter 3 for a detailed discussion of all the new environmental provisions contained in this agreement.

8. See chapter 4 for detailed discussion of the Forest Annex and in particular its links to multilateral environmental agreements.

9. See RD Será Sede de la Séptima Reunión del Consejo de Asuntos Ambientales del DR-CAFTA, *El Nacional* (Dominican Republic), May 6, 2013.

10. See chapter 4 on this point.

Chapter 6

1. See chapter 1 for a description of the TREND database.

2. Paragraph 31 of the Doha Declaration outlines the WTO's negotiating mandate on environmental issues during the contemporary negotiating round. Although it has made some incremental progress on issues related to environmental goods and services, the other topics have seen little progress.

3. Milewicz et al. (2016) studied closed triads of countries, which signed agreements that included non-trade issues. They note that most of the agreements were initiated by the United States and conclude that the United States plays a central role in the diffusion of non-trade issues in PTAs.

4. See Trade and Environment Policy Advisory Committee reports on US FTAs.

5. Although the United States withdrew from the TPP in 2017, it was an active participant in the negotiations and agreed to the final text of the TPP under the Obama administration in 2016.

Chapter 7

1. For a list and analysis of the 22 changes made, see New Zealand Ministry of Foreign Affairs and Trade, n.d.

2. Exec. Order. No. 13773, 82 Fed. Reg. 10691 (February 9, 2017), Available online at: https://www.federalregister.gov/documents/2017/02/14/2017-03113/enforcing-federal-law-with-respect-to-transnational-criminal-organizations-and-preventing. Accessed August 27, 2018.

3. GATT Article XX, which provides protection for environmental policies that would otherwise conflict with WTO rules, includes exemptions for the protection of human health.

References

Aasen, Marianne. 2009. March 18 CMP Report on Environmental Policies and Labour Standards in FTAs. Committee of Members of Parliament of the EFTA Countries, p. 20. http://www.efta.int/media/documents/advisory-bodies/parliamentary-committee/reports-eea-joint-committee/Report-Labour-Environment.pdf. Accessed August 26, 2018.

Abbott, Kenneth W., Robert O. Keohane, Andrew Moravcsik, Anne-Marie Slaughter, and Duncan Snidal. 2000. The Concept of Legalization. *International Organization* 54 (3) (Summer):401–19.

Acharya, Amitav. 2004. How Ideas Spread: Whose Norms Matter? Norm Localization and Institutional Change in Asian Regionalism. *International Organization* 58 (2) (April):239–275.

Aggarwal, Vinod K., and Kristi Govella, ed. 2013. *Linking Trade and Security, The Political Economy of the Asia Pacific*. New York: Springer Science+Business Media.

Allee, Todd, and Andrew Lugg. 2016. Who Wrote the Rules for the Trans-Pacific Partnership? *Research and Policy* (July-September):1–9.

Allee, Todd, and Manfred Elsig. 2016. Are the Contents of International Treaties Copied-and-Pasted? Evidence from Preferential Trade Agreements. World Trade Institute Working Paper No 8.

Alschner, Wolfgang, Julia Seiermann, and Dmitriy Skougarevskiy. 2017. Text-as-Data Analysis of Preferential Trade Agreements: Mapping the PTA Landscape. UNCTAD Research Paper No. 5, UNCTAD/SER.RP/2017/5. United Nations Conference on Trade and Development.

Andresen, Steinar, and Shardul Agrawala. 2002. Leaders, Pushers and Laggards in the Making of the Climate Regime. *Global Environmental Change* 12 (1):41–51.

Arce, Moisés. 2014. *Resource Extraction and Protest in Peru*. Pittsburgh, PA: University of Pittsburgh Press.

Arda, Mehmet. 2000. "Being the Environmental Stick": An Improper Role for International Trade. *Environment and Development Economics* 5 (4) (October):483–529.

Asmelash, Henok Birhanu. 2015. Energy Subsidies and WTO Dispute Settlement: Why Only Renewable Energy Subsides are Challenged. *Journal of International Economic Law* 18 (2) (June):261–285.

Axelrod, Mark. 2011a. Savings Clauses and the Chilling Effect. In *Managing Institutional Complexity: Regime Interplay and Global Environmental Change*, ed. Sebastian Oberthür and Olav Schram Stokke. Cambridge, MA: MIT Press.

Axelrod, Mark. 2011b. Climate Change and Global Fisheries Management: Linking Issues to Protect Ecosystems or to Save Political Interests? *Global Environmental Politics* 11 (3) (August):64–84.

Axelrod, Robert, and Robert O. Keohane. 1985. Achieving Cooperation Under Anarchy: Strategies and Institutions. *World Politics* 38 (1) (October):226–254.

Baccini, Leonardo, Andreas Dür, and Manfred Elsig. 2015. The Politics of Trade Agreement Design: Revisiting the Depth-Flexibility Nexus. *International Studies Quarterly* 59 (4) (December):765–775.

Baccini, Leonardo, and Johannes Urpelainen. 2014. Before Ratification: Understanding the Timing of International Treaty Effects on Domestic Policies. *International Studies Quarterly* 58 (1) (March):29–43.

Baghdadi, Leila, Inmaculada Martínez-Zarzoso, and Habib Zitouna. 2013. Are RTA Agreements with Environmental Provisions Reducing Emissions? *Journal of International Economics* 90 (2) (July):378–390.

Barber, Charles V., and Bo Li. 2018. With US Out of TPP, So Are Measures to Curb Illegal Logging. Washington, DC: World Resources Institute. March 14, 2018. https://www.wri.org/blog/2018/03/us-out-tpp-so-are-measures-curb-illegal-logging. Accessed August 2, 2019.

Barton, John H, Judith L. Goldstein, Timothy E. Josling, and Richard H. Steinberg. 2008. *The Evolution of the Trade Regime: Politics, Law, and Economics of the GATT and the WTO*. Princeton, NJ: Princeton University Press.

Bastiaens, Ida, and Evgeny Postnikov. 2017. Greening Up: The Effects of Environmental Standards in EU and US Trade Agreements. *Environmental Politics* 26 (5):847–869.

Bättig, Michèle B., and Thomas Bernauer. 2009. National Institutions and Global Public Goods: Are Democracies More Cooperative in Climate Change Policy? *International Organization* 63 (2) (April):281–308.

Baver, Sherrie. 2011. NAFTA, CAFTA and the Environment: The Role of Institutions. *IdeAs: Idées d'Amériques* 1. https://ideas.revues.org/73. Accessed August 25, 2018.

References

Bechtel, Michael M., Thomas Bernauer, and Reto Meyer. 2012. The Green Side of Protectionism: Environmental Concerns and Three Facets of Trade Policy Preferences. *Review of International Political Economy* 19 (5) (December):837–866.

Bernasconi-Osterwalder, Nathalie, Daniel Magraw, Maria Julia Oliva, Elisabeth Tuerk, and Marcos Orellana. 2006. *Environment and Trade: A Guide to WTO Jurisprudence*. London: Earthscan.

Bernauer, Thomas, and Quynh Nguyen. 2015. Free Trade and/or Environmental Protection? *Global Environmental Politics* 15 (4) (November):105–129.

Betsill, Michele M. 2007. Regional Governance of Global Climate Change: The North American Commission for Environmental Cooperation. *Global Environmental Politics* 7 (2):11–27.

Betsill, Michele, and Elisabeth Corell. 2008. *NGO Diplomacy: The Influence of Nongovernmental Organizations in International Environmental Negotiations*. Cambridge, MA: MIT Press.

Betsill, Michele, Navroz Dubash, Matthew Paterson, Harro Van Asselt, Antto Vihma, and Harald Winkler. 2015. Building Productive Links between the UNFCCC and Broader Global Climate Governance Landscape. *Global Environmental Politics* 15 (2):1–10.

Bettiza, Gregorio, and Fillipo Dionigi. 2014. How Do Religious Norms Diffuse? Institutional Translation and International Change in a Post-Secular World Society. *European Journal of International Relations* 20 (3):1–26.

Bhagwati, Jagdish. 1995a. U.S. Trade Policy: The Infatuation with Free Trade Areas. In *The Dangerous Drift to Preferential Trade Agreements*, ed. Jagdish Bhagwati and Anne O. Krueger. Washington, DC: American Enterprise Institute Press.

Bhagwati, Jagdish. 1995b. Trade Liberalisation and "Fair Trade" Demands: Addressing the Environmental and Labour Standards Issues. *The World Economy* 18 (6) (November):745–759.

Bhagwati, Jagdish. 2008. *Termites in the Trading System: How Preferential Agreements Undermine Free Trade*. New York, NY: Oxford University Press.

Blomquist, Robert F. 2002. Ratification Resisted: Understanding America's Response to the Convention on Biological Diversity, 1989–2002. *Golden Gate University Law Review* 32 (4) (Spring):493–586.

Blümer, Dominique, Jean-Frédéric Morin, Clara Brandi, and Axel Berger. n.d. Environmental Provisions in Trade Agreements: Defending Regulatory Space or Pursuing Offensive Interests. Unpublished manuscript.

Bourgeois, Jacques, Kamala Dawar, and Simon J. Evenett. 2007. A Comparative Analysis of Selected Provisions in Free Trade Agreements. DG Trade 1–212. http://

trade.ec.europa.eu/doclib/docs/2008/march/tradoc_138103.pdf. Accessed May 10, 2018.

Brandi, Clara, Dominique Blümer, and Jean-Frédéric Morin. Forthcoming. When Do International Treaties Matter for Domestic Environmental Legislation? *Global Environmental Politics*.

Brewster, Rachel, Claire Brunel, and Anna Maria Mayda. 2016. Trade in Environmental Goods: A Review of the WTO Appellate Body's Rules in US-Countervailing Measures (China). *World Trade Review* 15 (2) (April):327–349.

Busch, Per-Olof, Helge Jörgens, and Kerstin Tews. 2005. The Global Diffusion of Regulatory Instruments: The Making of a New International Environmental Regime. *Annals of the American Academy of Political and Social Science* 598 (1) (March): 146–167.

CAFTA-DR. 2006. Dominican Republic–Central America–United States Free Trade Agreement. http://1.usa.gov/1ZrHmy7. Accessed August 25, 2018.

Campling, Liam, and Elizabeth Havice. 2017. Small Vulnerable Economies and Fisheries Subsidies Disciplines: Issues, Debates and Alliances. *Commonwealth Trade Hot Topics* 142. Commonwealth Secretariat.

Carlsen, Laura. 2009. Trade Agreement Kills Amazon Indians. *Foreign Policy in Focus*. https://fpif.org/trade_agreement_kills_amazon_indians/. Accessed March 28, 2018.

CEC. 1994. *Council Resolution 94–01*. Montreal, Canada: Commission for Environmental Cooperation.

CEC. 1996. *Annual Report: 1996*. Montreal, Canada: Commission for Environmental Cooperation.

CEC. 1998. *Annual Report: 1998*. Montreal, Canada: Commission for Environmental Cooperation.

CEC. 2001. *Report by the North American Working Group on Enforcement and Compliance Cooperation*. Montreal, Canada: Commission for Environmental Cooperation.

CEC. 2003. *Summary of Environmental Law in Mexico*. www.cec.org/lawdatabase/mx05.cfm?varlan=english. Accessed April 21, 2015.

CEC. 2015. *North American Fund for Environmental Cooperation. Commission for Environmental Cooperation*. www.cec.org/Page.asp?PageID=749&SiteNodeID=374. Accessed April 21, 2015.

Charnovitz, Steve. 1994. The NAFTA Environmental Side Agreement: Implications for Environmental Cooperation, Trade Policy and American Treaty Making. *Temple International and Comparative Law Journal* 8 (2) (Fall):257–314.

References

Charnovitz, Steve. 2002a. The Law of Environmental "PPMs" in the WTO: Debunking the Myth of Illegality. *Yale Journal of International Law* 27 (1) (Winter):59–110.

Charnovitz, Steve. 2002b. Triangulating the World Trade Organization. *American Journal International Law* 96:28–55.

Charnovitz, Steve. 2007. The WTO's Environmental Progress. *Journal of International Economic Law* 10 (3) (August):685–706.

Chasek, Pamela S. 2007. US policy in the UN Environmental Arena: Powerful Laggard or Constructive Leader? *International Environmental Agreements: Politics, Law and Economics* 7 (4):363–387.

Chasek, Pamela S., David L. Downie, and Janet Welsh Brown. 2018. *Global Environmental Politics*. New York, NY: Routledge.

Chaytor, Beatrice. 2009. *Environmental Issues in Economic Partnership Agreements: Implications for Developing Countries*. Geneva: International Centre for Trade and Sustainable Development.

Chemnick, Jean. 2018. Renewable Energy Sees Trump's Tariffs as Fresh Blow. ClimateWire. March 8, 2018. https://www.eenews.net/climatewire/2018/03/08/stories/1060075781. Accessed July 13, 2018.

Clinton, William J. 1999. Executive Order 13141—Environmental Review of Trade Agreements. November 16, 1999. Online by Gerhard Peters and John T. Woolley, *The American Presidency Project*. http://www.presidency.ucsb.edu/ws/?pid=56947. Accessed August 20, 2018.

Colyer, Dale. 2011. *Green Trade Agreements*. New York, NY: Palgrave MacMillan.

Conca, Ken. 2000. The WTO and the Undermining of Global Environmental Governance. *Review of International Political Economy* 7 (3) (Autumn):487–496.

Cooper, Marc. 1999. Teamsters and Turtles: They're Together at Last. Los Angeles Times. http://articles.latimes.com/1999/dec/02/local/me-39707. Accessed May 24, 2018.

Daly, Herman E. 1993. The Perils of Free Trade. *Scientific American* 269 (5) (November):50–57.

Davis, Christina L. 2004. International Institutions and Issue Linkage: Building Support for Agricultural Trade Liberalization. *American Political Science Review* 98 (1) (February):153–169.

De Bièvre, Dirk, Ilaria Espa, and Arlo Poletti. 2017. No Iceberg in Sight: On the Absence of WTO Disputes Challenging Fossil Fuel Subsidies. *International Environmental Agreements: Politics, Law and Economics* 17 (3) (June):411–425.

De Jong, Wil, and David Humphreys. 2016. A Failed Social Licence to Operate for the Neoliberal Modernization of Amazonian Resource Use: The Underlying Causes of the Bagua Tragedy of Peru. *Forestry: An International Journal of Forest Research* 89 (5) (October):552–564.

Deere, Carolyn, and Daniel Esty. 2002. *Greening the Americas: NAFTA's Lessons for Hemispheric Trade*. Cambridge: MIT Press.

Del Gatto, Filippo, Bernardo Ortiz-von Halle, Braulio Buendía, and Chen Hin Keong. 2009. Trade Liberalization and Forest Verification: Learning from the US-Peru Trade Promotion Agreement. Verifor Briefing Paper.

DeSombre, Elizabeth R., and J. Samuel Barkin. 2002. Turtles and Trade: The WTO's Acceptance of Environmental Trade Restrictions. *Global Environmental Politics* 2 (1) (February):12–18.

DeSombre, Elizabeth. 2000. *Domestic Sources of International Environmental Policy: Industry, Environmentalists, and US Power*. Cambridge, MA: MIT Press.

Dobbin, Frank, Beth Simmons, and Geoffrey Garrett. 2007. The Global Diffusion of Public Policies: Social Construction, Coercion, Competition, or Learning? *Annual Review of Sociology* 43 (August):449–472.

Duit, Andreas, and Victor Galaz. 2008. Governance and Complexity—Emerging Issues for Governance Theory. *Governance* 21 (3) (July):311–335, at 318.

Dür, Andreas, Leonardo Baccini, and Manfred Elsig. 2014. The Design of International Trade Agreements: Introducing a New Dataset. *Review of International Organizations* 9 (3) (September):353–375.

Eckersley, Robyn. 2004. The Big Chill: The WTO and Multilateral Environmental Agreements. *Global Environmental Politics* 4 (2) (May):24–50.

Eckhouse, Brian, Ari Natter, and Chris Martin. 2018. Trump's Tariffs on Solar Mark Biggest Blow to Renewables Yet. *Bloomberg*. January 22, 2018. https://www.bloomberg.com/news/articles/2018-01-22/trump-taxes-solar-imports-in-biggest-blow-to-clean-energy-yet. Accessed July 13, 2018.

EIA. 2015. Implementation and Enforcement Failures in the US-Peru Free Trade Agreement (FTA) Allow Illegal Logging Crisis to Continue. June 2015 Briefing Paper. Environmental Investigation Agency. https://s3.amazonaws.com/environmental-investigation-agency/posts/documents/000/000/325/original/Implementation_and_Enforcement.pdf?1468593199. Accessed August 22, 2018.

EIA. 2018. Destination China: A Companion Briefing to Moment of Truth. Environmental Investigation Agency. https://eia-global.org/reports/destination-china-a-companion-briefing-to-moment-of-truth. Accessed May 17, 2019.

References

Environment Canada. 1999. A Guide to Understanding the Canadian Environmental Protection Act. Environmental Investigation Agency. http://bit.ly/1UmeUtA. Accessed August 25, 2018.

EO 13141. 1999. White House Executive Order. https://www.govinfo.gov/content/pkg/FR-1999-11-18/pdf/99-30346.pdf. Accessed August 1, 2019.

Escobar Torio, Jeremy John, and Chui-Ling Tam. 2017. Indigenous Power Struggles in the Peruvian Amazon: A Spatio-cultural Analysis of Communication. *Environmental Communication* 12 (4):480–494.

Esty, Daniel. 1994. *Greening the GATT: Trade, Environment, and the Future*. Peterson Institute.

Esty, Daniel. 2002. The World Trade Organization's Legitimacy Crisis. *World Trade Review* 1 (1) (March):7–22.

EU. 2017. Trade and Sustainable Development (TSD) Chapters in EU Free Trade Agreements (FTAS). European Commission Non-Paper, July 11, 2017.

EU. 2017a. Update on EU-Indonesia Trade Negotiations. European Commission. December 15, 2017. http://trade.ec.europa.eu/doclib/docs/2017/december/tradoc_156522.pdf. Accessed August 26, 2018.

EU. 2017b. Civil Society Dialogue on EU-Japan Economic Partnership Agreement. European Commission. July 18, 2017. http://trade.ec.europa.eu/civilsoc/meetdetails.cfm?pastyear=2017&meet=11500. Accessed May 17, 2019.

EU. 2017c. Meeting on Trade and Sustainable Development. European Commission. July 3, 2017. http://trade.ec.europa.eu/doclib/docs/2017/july/tradoc_155846.pdf. Accessed August 26, 2018.

European Parliament. 2010. Resolution of 25 November 2010 on Human Rights and Social and Environmental Standards in International Trade Agreements. http://www.europarl.europa.eu/sides/getDoc.do?type=TA&language=EN&reference=P7-TA2010-434. Accessed August 7, 2017.

Fauchald, Ole Kristian. 2007. International Investment Law and Environmental Protection. *Yearbook of International Environmental Law* 17 (1):3–47, at 4–5.

Finnemore, Martha. 1993. International Organizations as Teachers of Norms: The United Nations Educational, Scientific and Cultural Organization and Science Policy. *International Organization* 47 (4) (Autumn):565–597.

Finnemore, Martha, and Sikkink, Kathryn. 1998. International Norm Dynamics and Political Change. *International Organization* 52 (4) (Autumn):887–917.

Fiorino, Daniel. 1990. Citizen Participation and Environmental Risk: A Survey of Institutional Mechanisms. *Science, Technology and Human Values* 15 (2) (August): 226–243.

Freeland. 2017. Address by Foreign Affairs Minister on the Modernization of the North American Free Trade Agreement (NAFTA). Government of Canada. https://www.canada.ca/en/global-affairs/news/2017/08/address_by_foreignaffairsminister onthemodernizationofthenorthame.html. Accessed August 27, 2018.

Gagné, Gilbert, and Jean-Frédéric Morin. 2006. The Evolving American Policy on Investment Protection: Evidence from Recent FTAs and the 2004 Model BIT. *Journal of International Economic Law* 9 (2) (June):357–382.

Gallagher, Kevin. 2004. *Free Trade and the Environment: Mexico, NAFTA, and Beyond*. Palo Alto, CA: Stanford University Press.

George, Clive. 2014. Environment and Regional Trade Agreements: Emerging Trends and Policy Drivers. *OECD Trade and Environment Working Papers*, 2014/02. OECD Publishing.

Gomez-Mera, Laura, and Andrea Molinari. 2014. Overlapping Institutions, Learning, and Dispute Initiation in Regional Trade Agreements: Evidence from South America. *International Studies Quarterly* 58 (2) (June):269–281.

Gopinathan, Unni, Nick Watts, Alexandre Lefebvre, Arthur Cheung, Steven J. Hoffman, and John-Arne Røttingen. 2018. Global Governance and the Broader Determinants of Health: A Comparative Case Study of UNDP's and WTO's Engagement with Global Health. *Global Public Health*.

Gresser, Edward. 2010. Labor and Environment in Trade Since NAFTA: Activists Have Achieved Less, and More, Than They Realize. *Wake Forest Law Review* 45 (2): 491–525.

Guzman, Andrew T. 2002. A Compliance-Based Theory of International Law. *California Law Review* 90 (December):1823–1888.

H.R. 30009. 2002. Trade Act of 2002. http://1.usa.gov/1c9qQ11. Accessed August 25, 2018.

Haas, Ernst B. 1980. Why Collaborate? Issue-Linkage and International Regimes. *World Politics* 32 (3) (April):357–405.

Harrison, Kathryn. 1995. Is Cooperation the Answer? Canadian Environmental Enforcement in Comparative Context. *Journal of Policy Analysis and Management* 14 (2):221–244.

Hodas, David R. 1995. Enforcement of Environmental Law in a Triangular Federal System: Can Three Not Be a Crowd When Enforcement Authority Is Shared by the United States, and Their Citizens. *Maryland Law Review* 54:1552–1657.

References

Hogenboom, Barbara. 1998. *Mexico and the NAFTA Environment Debate: The Transnational Politics of Economic Integration*. Utrecht, The Netherlands: International Books.

Holmer, Alan F., and Judith H. Bello. 1993. Trade and the Environment: A Snapshot from Tuna/Dolphins to the NAFTA and Beyond. *The International Lawyer* 27 (1) (Spring):169–176.

Horn, Henrik, Petros C. Mavroidis, and André Sapir. 2010. Beyond the WTO? An Anatomy of EU and US Preferential Trade Agreements. *World Economy* 33 (11) (November):1565–1588.

Housman, Robert F., and Paul M. Orbuch. 1993. Integrating Labor and Environmental Concerns into the North American Free Trade Agreement: A Look Back and a Look Ahead. *American University Journal of International Law & Policy* 8 (4) (Summer):720–815.

Howse, Robert. 2002. The Appellate Body Rulings in the Shrimp/Turtle Case: A New Legal Baseline for the Trade and Environment Debate. *Columbia Journal of Environmental Law 27* (2):491–521.

Hudec, Robert. E. 1992. Circumventing Democracy: The Political Morality of Trade Negotiations. *New York University Journal of International Law and Politics* 25 (Winter):311–322.

Hufbauer, Gary Clyde. 2000. *NAFTA and the Environment: Seven Years Later*. Washington, DC: Peterson Institute.

Hughes, Llewelyn, and Jonas Meckling. 2017. The Politics of Renewable Energy Trade: The US-China Solar Dispute. *Energy Policy* 105 (June):256–262.

Hughes, Neil. 2010. Indigenous Protest in Peru: The "Orchard Dog" Bites Back. *Social Movement Studies* 9 (1):85–90.

Husted, Brian, and Jeanne Logsdon. 1997. The Impact of NAFTA on Mexico's Environmental Policy. *Growth and Change* 28 (1) (December):24–48.

Inside US Trade. 2015. USTR Evaluating Potential Case against Peru Environmental Law Changes. 3 (10):1–3.

Jacobson, Harold K., and Edith Brown Weiss. 1998. A Framework for Analysis. In *Engaging Countries: Strengthening Compliance with International Environmental Accords*, ed. Harold K Jacobson and Edith Brown Weiss. Cambridge, MA: MIT Press.

Japan. 1995. Harmonizing Environment and Trade Policies. Advisory Group on Global Environment Problems, Special Sub-Group on Environment and Trade. Report submitted to the Environment Agency of Japan. http://www.env.go.jp/en/earth/iec/hetp/index.html. Accessed August 26, 2018.

Jervis, Robert. 1997. *System Effects: Complexity in Political and Social Life*. Princeton, NJ: Princeton University Press.

Jinnah, Sikina. 2003. Emissions Trading Under the Kyoto Protocol: NAFTA and WTO Concerns. *Georgetown International Environmental Law Review* 15 (1):709–761.

Jinnah, Sikina. 2010. Overlap Management in the World Trade Organization: Secretariat Influence on Trade-Environment Politics. *Global Environmental Politics* 10 (2) (May):54–79.

Jinnah, Sikina. 2011. Strategic Linkages: The Evolving Role of Trade Agreements in Global Environmental Governance. *Journal of Environment and Development* 20 (2):191–215.

Jinnah, Sikina. 2014. *Post-Treaty Politics: Secretariat Influence in Global Environmental Governance*. Cambridge, MA: MIT Press.

Jinnah, Sikina. 2017. Makers, Takers, Shakers, Shapers: Emerging Economies and Normative Engagement in Climate Governance. *Global Governance* 23 (2) (April-June):285–306.

Jinnah, Sikina, and Abby Lindsay. 2016. Diffusion Through Issue Linkage: Environmental Norms in US Trade Agreements. *Global Environmental Politics* 16 (3) (August):41–61.

Jinnah, Sikina, and Elisa Morgera. 2013. Environmental Provisions in American and EU Free Trade Agreements: A Preliminary Comparison and Research Agenda. *Review of European, Comparative & International Environmental Law* 22 (3) (November):324–339.

Johnson, Tana. 2015. Information Revelation and Structural Supremacy: The World Trade Organization's Incorporation of Environmental Policy. *Review of International Organizations* 10 (2) (June):207–229.

Johnson, Tana, and Johannes Urpelainen. 2012. A Strategic Theory of Regime Integration and Separation. *International Organization* 66 (4):645–677.

Katzenstein, Peter J. 1996. Security: Norms and Identity in World Politics. In *The Culture of National Security: Norms and Identity in World Politics*, ed. Peter J. Katzenstein, 1–32. New York: Columbia University Press.

Kauffman, Stuart. 1993. *The Origins of Order*. Oxford, UK: Oxford University Press.

Keck, Margaret K., and Kathryn Sikkink. 1998. *Activists Beyond Borders: Advocacy Networks in International Politics*. Cambridge: Cambridge University Press.

Kelemen, R. Daniel, and David Vogel. 2010. Trading Places: The Role of the United States and the European Union in International Environmental Politics. *Comparative Political Studies* 43 (4):427–456.

References

Kelemen, R. Daniel. 2001. The Limits of Judicial Power: Trade-Environment Disputes in the GATT/WTO and the EU. *Comparative Political Studies* 34 (6) (August):622–650.

Kent, Avidan. 2014. Implementing the Principle of Policy Integration: Institutional Interplay and the Role of International Organizations. *International Environmental Agreements: Law, Policy and Economics* 14 (3) (September):203–224.

Kulovesi, Kati. 2011. *The WTO Dispute Settlement System: Challenges of the Environment, Legitimacy and Fragmentation.* Alphen aan den Rijn, The Netherlands: Kluwer Law International.

Kulovesi, Kati. 2014. International Trade Disputes on Renewable Energy. *Review of European Comparative & International Environmental Law* 23 (3) (November):342–353.

Laurens, Noémie, Zachary Dove, Jean-Frédéric Morin, and Sikina Jinnah. 2019. NAFTA 2.0: The Greenest Trade Agreement Ever? *World Trade Review.* doi: 10.1017/S1474745619000351.

Lechner, Lisa. 2016. The Domestic Battle Over the Design of Non-Trade Issues in Preferential Trade Agreements. *Review of International Political Economy* 23 (5):840–871.

Lewis, Joanna. 2014. The Rise of Renewable Energy Protectionism: Emerging Trade Conflicts and Implications for Low Carbon Development. *Global Environmental Politics* 14 (4) (November):10–35.

Lewis, Joanna. 2015. The Rise of Renewable Energy Protectionism: Emerging Trade Conflicts and Implications for Low Carbon Development. *Global Environmental Politics* 14 (4) (November):10–35.

Ludwiszewski, Raymond B. 1993. Green Language in the NAFTA: Reconciling Free Trade and Environmental Protection. *The International Lawyer* 27 (3) (Winter): 691–706.

March, James G. 1991. Exploration and Exploitation in Organizational Learning. *Organization Science* 2 (1):1–147, at 71.

Marín-Durán, Gracia, and Elisa Morgera. 2012. *Environmental Integration in the EU's External Relations: Beyond Multilateral Dimensions.* Oxford, UK: Hart Publishing.

Markell, David L., and John H. Knox. 2003. *Greening NAFTA: The North American Commission for Environmental Cooperation.* Redwood City, CA: Stanford University Press.

Marsh, David, and J. C. Sharman. 2009. Policy Diffusion and Policy Transfer. *Policy Studies* 30 (3):269–288.

Martínez-Zarzoso, Inmaculada, and Walid Oueslati. 2016. Are Deep and Comprehensive Regional Trade Agreements Helping to Reduce Air Pollution? Discussion Paper 292, Center for European Governance and Economic Development Research.

Matisoff, Daniel C. 2010. Are International Environmental Agreements Enforceable? Implications for Institutional Design. *International Environmental Agreements: Politics, Law and Economics* 10 (3) (September):165–186.

Mejía, Elena, Ximena Buitrón, Marielos Peña-Claros, and James Grogan. 2008. Big Leaf Mahogany (Swietenia Macrophylla) in Peru, Bolivia, Brazil. Geneva: CITES Secretariat.

Meunier, Sophie and Jean-Frédéric Morin. 2016. No Agreement Is an Island: Negotiating TTIP in a Dense Regime Complex. In *The Politics of Transatlantic Trade Negotiations: TTIP in a Globalized World*, ed. Jean-Frédéric Morin, Tereza Novotná, Frederik Ponjaert and Mario Telò. London: Routledge.

Meyer, Timothy. 2017. Explaining Energy Disputes at the World Trade Organization. *International Environmental Agreements* 17 (3) (June):391–410.

Milewicz, Karolina, James Hollway, Claire Peacock, and Duncan Snidal. 2016. Beyond Trade. The Expanding Scope of the Nontrade Agenda in Trade Agreements. *Journal of Conflict Resolution* 62 (4):743–773.

Mitchell, Melanie. 2009. *Complexity: A Guided Tour*. Oxford, UK: Oxford University Press.

Mitchell, Ronald. 1994. Regime Design Matters: Intentional Oil Pollution and Treaty Compliance. *International Organization* 48 (3) (Summer):425–58.

Mitchell, Ronald. 2018. Data from Ronald B. Mitchell 2002–2018. International Environmental Agreement Database Project Version 2018.1 http://iea.uoregon.edu. Accessed May 22, 2018.

Moran, Niall. 2017. The First Twenty Cases Under GATT Article XX: Tuna or Shrimp Dear? In *International Economic Law*, 3–21. Berlin: Springer.

Morin, Jean-Frédéric. 2008. The Strategic Use of Ethical Arguments in International Patent Lawmaking. *Asian Journal of WTO and International Health Law and Policy* 3 (2) (September):505–537.

Morin, Jean-Frédéric. 2014. Paradigm Shift in the Global IP Regime: The Agency of Academics. *Review of International Political Economy* 21 (2):275–309.

Morin, Jean-Frédéric, and Guillaume Beaumier. 2016. TPP Environmental Commitments: Combining the US Legalistic and the EU Sectoral Approaches. *Biores*. April 29, 2016. Geneva: International Center for Trade and Sustainable Development.

Morin, Jean-Frédéric, and Corentin Bialais. 2018. Strengthening Multilateral Environmental Governance Through Bilateral Trade Deals. Center for International Governance Innovation.

References

Morin, Jean-Frédéric, Dominique Blümer, Clara Brandi, and Alex Berger. 2019. Kick-Starting: Explaining the Varying Frequency of PTAs' Environmental Clauses by Their Initial Condition. *World Economy*.

Morin, Jean-Frédéric, Andreas Dür, and Lisa Lechner. 2018. Mapping the Trade and Environment Nexus: Insights from a New Dataset. *Global Environmental Politics* 18 (1) (February):122–139.

Morin, Jean-Frédéric, and Mathilde Gauquelin. 2016. Trade Agreements as Vectors for the Nagoya Protocol's Implementation. CIGI Papers 115. Center for International Governance Innovation.

Morin, Jean-Frédéric, and Rosalie Gauthier Nadeau. 2017. Environmental Gems in Trade Agreements: Little-Known Clauses for Progressive Trade Agreements. CIGI Papers 148. Center for International Governance Innovation.

Morin, Jean-Frédéric, and Edward Richard Gold. 2014. An Integrated Model of Legal Transplantation: The Diffusion of Intellectual Property Law in Developing Countries. *International Studies Quarterly* 58 (4) (December):781–792.

Morin, Jean-Frédéric, and Laura Gomez-Mera. 2019. The Evolution of Governance Systems: The Case of the Trade Regime. *International Studies Review* viz005:15–20.

Morin, Jean-Frédéric, and Sikina Jinnah. 2018. The Untapped Potential of Preferential Trade Agreements for Climate Governance. *Environmental Politics* 27 (3):541–565.

Morin, Jean-Frédéric, Nicolas Michaud, and Corentin Bialais. 2016. Trade Negotiations and Climate Governance: The EU as a Pioneer, But Not (Yet) a Leader. IDDRI, Issue Brief No. 10/2016, September.

Morin, Jean-Frédéric, and Amandine Orsini. 2014. Policy Coherency and Regime Complexes: The Case of Genetic Resources. *Review of International Studies* 40 (2) (April):303–324.

Morin, Jean-Frédéric, Joost Pauwelyn, and James Hollway. 2017. The Trade Regime as a Complex Adaptive System: Exploration and Exploitation of Environmental Norms in Trade Agreements. *Journal of International Economic Law* 20 (2) (June):365–390.

Morin, Jean-Frédéric, and Myriam Rochette. 2017. Transatlantic Convergence of PTAs' Environmental Clauses. *Business and Politics* 19 (4) (December):621–658.

NAAEC. 1993. *North American Agreement on Environmental Cooperation*. www.cec.org/Page.asp?PageID=1226&SiteNodeID=567. Accessed April 22, 2015.

Nascimento, Nathan. 2018. Let Trade Promotion Authority Renewal Move Ahead. The Hill. http://thehill.com/opinion/international/385829-let-trade-promotion-authority-renewal-move-ahead. Accessed July 11, 2018.

Neumayer, Eric. 2004. The WTO and the Environment: Its Past Record Is Better Than Critics Believe, But the Future Outlook Is Bleak. *Global Environmental Politics* 4 (3) (August):1–8.

Neumayer, Eric. 2017. *Greening Trade and Investment: Environmental Protection without Protectionism.* London, UK: Earthscan.

New Zealand Ministry of Foreign Affairs and Trade. n.d. Despite Similarities between the CPTPP and the TPP, There Will Also Be Some Significant Differences to Aspects that Were of Concern to New Zealanders the First Time Around. https://www.mfat.govt.nz/en/trade/free-trade-agreements/free-trade-agreements-concluded-but-not-in-force/cptpp/tpp-and-cptpp-the-differences-explained/#dates. Accessed July 16, 2018.

OAS. 2012. *Monitoring Progress of the Environmental Cooperation Agenda in the CAFTA-DR Countries: Third Evaluation Report.* Washington, DC: Organization of the American States.

OAS. 2014. *Monitoring Progress of the Environmental Cooperation Agenda in the CAFTA-DR countries: Fourth Evaluation Report.* Washington, DC: Organization of the American States.

Oberthür, Sebastian, and Thomas Gehring. 2006. Institutional Interaction in Global Environmental Governance: The Case of the Cartagena Protocol and the World Trade Organization. *Global Environmental Politics* 6 (2) (May):1–31.

OECD. 2007. Regional Trade Agreements and Environment. Document COM/ENV/TD (2006)47/FINAL. http://www.oecd.org/officialdocuments/publicdisplaydocumentpdf/?doclanguage=en&cote=com/env/td(2006)47/final. Accessed June 1, 2018.

Paehlke, Robert. 2000. Environmentalism in One Country: Canadian Environmental Policy in an Era of Globalization. *Policy Studies Journal* 28 (1) (February):160–175.

Parker, Charles F., and Christer Karlsson. 2018. The UN Climate Change Negotiations and the Role of the United States: Assessing American Leadership from Copenhagen to Paris. *Environmental Politics* 27 (3):519–540.

Pavoni, Riccardo. 2010. Mutual Supportiveness as a Principle of Interpretation and Law-Making: A Watershed for the "WTO-and-Competing-Regimes" Debate? *European Journal of International Law* 21:649–679.

Peru. 2013. *Matriz de Cumplimiento del Anexo Forestal del Acuerdo de Promocion Comercial (APC) Peru-Estados Unidos.* Lima, Peru: Ministerio de Comercio Exterior y Turismo.

Poletti, Arlo, and Daniela Sicurelli. 2015. The European Union, Preferential Trade Agreements, and the International Regulation of Sustainable Biofuels. *Common Market Studies* 54 (2) (July):249–266.

References

Putnam, Robert D. 1988. Diplomacy and Domestic Politics: The Logic of Two-Level Games. *International Organization* 42 (3):427–60.

Raustiala, Kal. 1995. The Political Implications of the Enforcement Provisions of the NAFTA Environmental Side Agreement: The CEC as a Model for Future Accords. *Environmental Law* 25:31–56.

Raustiala, Kal. 1997. States, NGOs, and International Environmental Institutions. *International Studies Quarterly* 41 (4) (December):719–40.

Raustiala, Kal. 2003. Citizen Submissions and Treaty Review in the NAAEC. In *Greening NAFTA: The North American Commission for Environmental Cooperation*, ed. David L. Markell and John H. Knox, 256–273. Stanford, CA: Stanford University Press.

Rénique, Gerardo. 2009. Law of the Jungle in Peru: Indigenous Amazonian Uprising Against Neoliberalism. *Socialism and Democracy* 23 (3):117–135.

Rosenau, James N. 1970. Foreign Policy as Adaptive Behavior: Some Preliminary Notes for a Theoretical Model: *Comparative Politics* 2 (3) (April):365–387.

Rosendal, Kristin G. 2001a. Impacts of Overlapping International Regimes: The Case of Biodiversity. *Global Governance* 7 (1) (January-March):95–117.

Rosendal, Kristin G. 2001b. Overlapping International Regimes: The Case of the Intergovernmental Forum on Forests (IFF) between Climate Change and Biodiversity. *International Environmental Agreements* 1 (4) (December):447–468.

Salzman, James. 2001. Executive Order 13, 141 and the Environmental Review of Trade Agreements. *The American Journal of International Law* 95 (2) (April):366–380.

Schwebel, Stephen M. 2004. The Influence of Bilateral Investment Treaties on Customary International Law. *Proceedings of American Society of International Law Annual Meeting* 28:27–30.

Seattle Police Department. 1999. After Action Report—World Trade Organization Ministerial Conference, Seattle Washington. November 29–December 3, 1999. http://media.cleveland.com/pdextra/other/Seattle%20PD%20after%20action%20report.pdf. Accessed May 24, 2018.

Selin, Henrik. 2010. *Global Governance of Chemicals: Challenges of Multi-Level Management.* Cambridge, MA: MIT Press.

Selin, Henrik, and Stacy D. VanDeveer. 2003. Mapping Institutional Linkages in European Air Pollution Politics. *Global Environmental Politics* 3 (3) (August):14–46.

Shaffer, Gregory. 2002. The Nexus of Law and Politics: The WTO's Committee of Trade and Environment. In *The Greening of Trade Law: International Trade Organizations and Environmental Issues*, ed. Richard H. Steinberg, 81–117. Oxford: Rowman and Littlefield.

SICE. 2015. Foreign Trade Information System. OAS Foreign Trade Information System. www.sice.oas.org/agreements_e.asp. Accessed August 25, 2018.

Skodvin, Tora, and Steinar Andresen. 2006. Leadership Revisited. *Global Environmental Politics* 6(3):13–27.

Skovgaard Poulsen, Lauge N., 2014. Bounded Rationality and the Diffusion of Modern Investment Treaties. *International Studies Quarterly* 58 (1) (March):1–14.

Smith, Carolyn. 2011. Trade Promotion Authority and Fast-Track Negotiating Authority for Trade Agreements: Major Votes. *Congressional Research Service*. https://fas.org/sgp/crs/misc/RS21004.pdf. Accessed March 22, 2018.

Spilker, Gabriele, Thomas Bernauer, and Víctor Umaña. 2018. What Kinds of Trade Liberalization Agreements Do People in Developing Countries Want? *International Interactions* 44 (3):510–536.

Spyke, Nancy. 1999. Public Participation in Environmental Decision-Making at the New Millennium: Structuring New Spheres of Public Influence. *Boston College Environmental Affairs Law Review* 26:263–313.

State Secretariat for Economic Affairs. 2010. Background Information: Conclusion of EFTA Work on Trade, Environment and Labour Standards. World Trade Organization. August 30, 2010:1–3.

Steinberg, Richard. 1997. Trade-Environment Negotiations in the EU, NAFTA, and WTO: Regional Trajectories of Rule Development. *American Journal of International Law* 91 (2) (April):231–267.

Steinberg, Richard. 2002. *The Greening of Trade Law: International Trade Organizations and Environmental Issues*. Boulder: Rowman and Littlefield.

Stetson, George. 2012. Oil Politics and Indigenous Resistance in the Peruvian Amazon: The Rhetoric of Modernity Against the Reality of Coloniality. *The Journal of Environment and Development* 21 (1) (February):76–97.

Stilwell, Matthew and Tuerk, Elizabeth. 1999. *Trade Measures and Multilateral Environmental Agreements: Resolving Uncertainty and Removing the WTO Chill Factor*. Geneva: World Wide Fund for Nature and Center for International Environmental Law.

Stokke, Olav Schram. 2000. Managing Straddling Stocks: The Interplay of Global and Regional Regimes. *Ocean and Coastal Management* 43 (2–3) (February):205–234.

Stokke, Olav Schram. 2001. The Interplay of International Regimes: Putting Effectiveness Theory to Work. Fridtjof Nansen Institute Report 14.

Stone, Jon. 2018. EU to Refuse to Sign Trade Deals with Countries that Don't Ratify Paris Climate Change Accord. *Independent*. https://www.independent.co.uk/news/world/europe/eu-trade-deal-paris-climate-change-accord-agreement-cecilia-malmstr-m-a8206806.html. Accessed August 26, 2018.

References

Strange, Michael. 2015. Implication of TTIP for Transnational Social Movements and International NGOs. In *The Politics of Transatlantic Trade Negotiations: TTIP in a Globalized World*, ed. Jean-Frédéric Morin, Tereza Novotna, Frederik Ponjaert, and Mario Telò, 81–92. Farnham, UK: Ashgate.

Subramanian, Arvind. 1992. Trade Measures for Environment: A Nearly Empty Box? *The World Economy 15* (1) (January):135–152.

Susskind, Laurence, and Saleem H. Ali. 2015. *Environmental Diplomacy: Negotiating More Effective Global Agreements*. Oxford University Press.

Toro Perez, Catalina. 2009. Biodiversity in the FTAS with the USA and Europe: The Crisis of the Andean Integration Process. *Resvista Semillas*, 40–41. Translated by bilaterals.org. https://www.bilaterals.org/?biodiversity-in-the-ftas-with-the. Accessed March 29, 2018.

Trachtman, Joel. 2018. WTO Trade and Environment Jurisprudence: Avoiding Environmental Catastrophe. *Harvard International Law Journal* 58 (2):1–38.

Trans-Pacific Partnership (TPP). 2015. Chapter 20 Environment. https://medium.com/the-trans-pacific-partnership/environment-a7f25cd180cb. Accessed August 25, 2018.

Trump, Donald, J. 2017. We are in the NAFTA (worst trade deal ever made) renegotiation process with Mexico & Canada. Both being very difficult, may have to terminate? Twitter. August 27, 2017, 6:51am.

UNEP. 2012. *Global Environmental Outlook 5—Environment for the Future We Want*. Nairobi, Kenya: United Nations Environment Program.

Urrunaga, Julia, Andrea Johnson, and I. Dhayneé Orbegozo Sánchez. 2018. The Moment of Truth: Promise or Peril for the Amazon as Peru Confront Illegal Timber Trade. Washington DC: Environmental Investigation Agency.

US Department of State. 2012. CAFTA-DR Environmental Cooperation Regional Program Highlights. https://www.state.gov/documents/organization/142902.pdf. Accessed August 25, 2018.

US EPA. 1991. *Mexican Environmental Laws, Regulations and Standards*. Washington, DC: US Environmental Protection Agency.

US EPA. 2014. *Fiscal Year 2014 Enforcement and Compliance Annual Results*. Washington, DC: US Environmental Protection Agency.

US GAO. 2014. U.S. Trade Representative Should Continue to Improve Its Monitoring of Environmental Commitments. GAO-15–161. Washington, DC: US Government Accountability Office.

USTR and CEQ 2000. Guidelines for Implementation of Executive Order 13141. https://ustr.gov/sites/default/files/guidelines%20for%2013141.pdf. Accessed March 23, 2018.

USTR. 2003. *Interim Environmental Review: U.S.-Central America Free Trade Agreement.* Washington, DC: Office of the United States Trade Representative.

USTR. 2006. The U.S.-Columbia Trade Promotion Agreement. https://ustr.gov/archive/assets/Trade_Agreements/Bilateral/Colombia_FTA/Reports/asset_upload_file265_9824.pdf. Accessed August 26, 2018.

USTR. 2007a. Bipartisan Trade Deal—Trade Facts. https://ustr.gov/sites/default/files/uploads/factsheets/2007/asset_upload_file127_11319.pdf. Accessed August 1, 2019.

USTR. 2007b. *Final Environmental Review United States–Peru Trade Promotion Agreement.* http://1.usa.gov/1Umf2Jn. Accessed May 11, 2015.

USTR. 2007c. The U.S.-Panama Trade Promotion Agreement. https://ustr.gov/archive/assets/Trade_Agreements/Bilateral/Panama_FTA/Reports/asset_upload_file953_11245.pdf. Accessed August 26, 2018.

USTR. 2013. US-Peru PTA Strengthening Forest Sector Governance in Peru. https://ustr.gov/sites/default/files/2013-Progress-under-the-Forest-Annex.pdf. Accessed August 22, 2018.

USTR. 2014a. 2014–2017 United States-Colombia Work Program for Environmental Cooperation. https://ustr.gov/sites/default/files/USColombiaWorkPlanSigned.pdf.

USTR. 2014b. U.S.-Panama Environmental Cooperation Commission 2014–2017 Work Program. https://ustr.gov/sites/default/files/Panama-US-Env-Coop-Work-Program-2014-2016_DRAFT%2001292014-English.pdf. Accessed July 14, 2018.

USTR. 2015a. Standing Up for the Environment: Trade for a Greener World. Special Report. https://ustr.gov/sites/default/files/USTR-Standing-Up-for-the-Environment-2015-Report.pdf. Accessed August 21, 2018.

USTR. 2015b. Review of 2012 EIA Petition Regarding Bigleaf Mahogany and Spanish Cedar Exports. https://ustr.gov/sites/default/files/EIA%20Review%20Summary.pdf. Accessed April 22, 2015.

USTR. 2015c. *United States–Peru Trade Promotion Agreement: Strengthening Forest Sector Governance in Peru (2013 Progress Under the Forest Annex).* https://ustr.gov/sites/default/files/2013-Progress-under-the-Forest-Annex.pdf. Accessed April 22, 2015.

USTR. 2017a. Summary of Objectives for the NAFTA Renegotiation. https://ustr.gov/sites/default/files/files/Press/Releases/NAFTAObjectives.pdf. Accessed March 23, 2018.

References

USTR. 2017b. USTR Releases Updated NAFTA Negotiating Objectives. Press Release. Office of the United States Trade Representative. November. https://ustr.gov/about-us/policy-offices/press-office/press-releases/2017/november/ustr-releases-updated-nafta. Accessed July 18, 2018.

USTR. 2018. Environmental Reviews. https://ustr.gov/issue-areas/environment/environmental-reviews. Accessed March 23, 2018.

Van de Graaf, Thijs, and Harro van Asselt. 2017. Introduction to the Special Issue: Energy Subsidies at the Intersection of Climate, Energy, and Trade Governance. *International Environmental Agreements: Politics, Law and Economics* 17 (3) (June):313–326.

Vivas-Eugui, David. 2009. Landmark Biodiversity, TK Provisions Accompany EFTA-Colombia FTA. *Biores* 3 (2). https://www.ictsd.org/bridges-news/biores/news/landmark-biodiversity-tk-provisions-accompany-efta-colombia-fta. Accessed May 10, 2018.

Vogel, David. 1995. *Trading Up: Consumer and Environmental Regulation in a Global Economy.* Cambridge, MA: Harvard University Press.

Vogel, David. 2012. *The Politics of Precaution: Regulating Health, Safety, and Environmental Risks in Europe and the United States.* Princeton, NJ: Princeton University Press.

Vogler, John, and Hannes R. Stephan. 2007. The European Union in Global Environmental Governance: Leadership in the Making? *International Environmental Agreements: Politics, Law and Economics* 7 (4):389–413.

Weiss, Edith Brown, and Harold Karan Jacobson. 2000. *Engaging Countries: Strengthening Compliance with International Environmental Accords.* Cambridge, MA: MIT Press.

Wolfe, Robert. 2005. See You in Geneva? Legal (Mis)Representation of the Trading System. *European Journal of International Relations* 11 (3) (September):339–365.

WTO. 2013. Appellate Body Report on "Canada—Certain Measures Affecting the Renewable Energy Generation Sector" (DS412 and DS426).

WTO. 2016. Appellate Body Report on "India–Certain Measures Relating to Solar Cells and Solar Modules" (DS456).

WTO Secretariat. 2002. *GATT/WTO Dispute Settlement Practice Relating to GATT Article XX, Paragraphs (b), (d) and (g).* Document No. WT.CTE/W/203. Geneva, Switzerland: World Trade Organization.

WTO Secretariat. 1996. *United States—Standards for Reformulated and Conventional Gasoline. Report of the Appellate Body.* Document No. WT/DS2/AB/R. Geneva, Switzerland: World Trade Organization.

WTO Secretariat. 2019. *WTO Dispute Settlement: One-Page Case Summaries (1995–2018).* Geneva, Switzerland: World Trade Organization.

Wu, Mark, and James Salzman. 2013. The Next Generation of Trade and Environment Conflicts: The Rise of Green Industrial Policy. *Northwestern University Law Review*. 108 (2) (Winter):401–474.

Yamin, Farhana. 2001. NGOs and International Environmental Law: A Critical Evaluation of Their Roles and Responsibilities. *Review of European Community & International Environmental Law* 10 (2) (July):149–62.

Yoo, In Tae, and Inkyoung Kim. 2016. Free Trade Agreements for the Environment? Regional Economic Integration and Environmental Cooperation in East Asia. *International Environmental Agreements: Politics, Law and Economics* 16 (5) (October): 721–738.

Young, Oran R. 1991. Political Leadership and Regime Formation: On the Development of Institutions in International Society. *International Organization* 45(3): 281–308.

Young, Oran R. 1994. *International Governance: Protecting the Environment in a Stateless Society*. Ithaca, NY: Cornell University Press.

Young, Oran R. 1996. Institutional Linkages in International Society: Polar Perspectives. *Global Governance* 2 (January-April):1–24.

Young, Oran. 2002. *The Institutional Dimensions of Global Change: Fit Interplay and Scale*. Cambridge, MA: MIT Press.

Zhou, Li, Xi Tian, and Zhengyi Zhou. 2017. The Effects of Environmental Provisions in RTAS on PM2.5 Air Pollution. *Applied Economics* 49 (27):2630–2641.

Index

Note: page numbers followed by *f, t,* or *b* refer to figures, tables, or boxes, respectively.

Agreement on the Application of Sanitary and Phytosanitary Measures, 13

Bipartisan Agreement on Trade Policy (May 10 Agreement), 35–36, 67–68
Bipartisan Congressional Trade Priorities and Accountability Act (TPA-2015), 37, 39
Bush, George H. W., 9, 30
Bush, George W., 34–35, 67

Canadian Environmental Protection Act (CEPA), 117–118
Cartagena Protocol, 150
Central American Free Trade Agreement (CAFTA-DR), 113–115, 118–119
Clinton, William, 9, 30, 32
Commission on Environmental Cooperation (CEC), 31
Complex adaptive system theory, 131–134, 140, 151–152
Comprehensive and Progressive Trans-Pacific Partnership (CPTPP), 6, 38–39, 128, 165–167
Congress (US), 79
  PTA/MEA funding appropriations, 96, 98
  Trade Act of 2002, 14
  trade power, 173
  2007 Bipartisan Trade Deal, May 10 Agreement, 67
  US Trade Promotion Authority (TPA), 67, 154
Convention on Biological Diversity (CBD), 99
Convention on International Trade in Endangered Species of Wild Fauna and Flora (CITES), 5, 64, 165–166. *See also* US-Peru PTA
  compliance management, COP, 86–87
  linkages, PTAs and MEAs, 73–74

Diffusion. *See* Norm, policy diffusion
Doha Development Agenda, 14

Environmental cooperation agreements (ECAs), 70–71
Environmental provisions evolution, US trade agreements, 23–24, 25*t*, 26, 29*t*. *See also* US PTAs, global policy diffusion
EU-Malaysia Preferential Trade Agreement (PTA), 62
Executive Order 13141 (Clinton administration), 32

Executive Order 13773 (Trump administration), 69–70

Fast-track authority. *See* Trade Promotion Authority (TPA)

Garcia, Alan, 161–162
General Agreement on Tariffs and Trade (GATT), 3, 26, 140–141
General Law on Ecological Balance and Environmental Protection (LGEEPA), Mexico, 117
Greening the GATT (Daniel Esty), 8

Innovative trade agreements, unprecedented environmental provisions, 31, 32f

Linkage politics. *See also* PTA-MEA linkages
democracy level, environmental clauses in PTAs, 60f
domestic pressure, 60–61, 65
ECAs, 70–71
EU-Malaysia PTA, 62
interagency process, US, 63–65
NGO involvement, 65–66
protectionist interests, 61, 68
study of, 53–55
trade, security regimes, 55
trading partner interests, 68–69
transnational crime and, 6 9–70
Trump administration, 69–70
typologies, international politics, 56–58, 59t
US-Peru PTA, 62, 66
US PTAs, 63–70, 65f

May 10 Agreement. *See* Bipartisan Agreement on Trade Policy (May 10 Agreement)

Montreal Protocol, 69
Multilateral environmental agreements (MEAs). *See* PTA-MEA linkages

NAFTA (North American Free Trade Agreement), 30–32, 104
Clinton administration, 9, 30
environmental provisions, 112–113, 168–169, 168f
investor-state dispute settlement, 9
norm, policy diffusion, 112–113
norm internalization, 117–118
Trump administration, 165, 167–168
US PTAs, global diffusion, 131, 135, 151
Norm, policy diffusion. *See also* US PTAs, global policy diffusion
CAFTA-DR, 113–115
counterfactual analysis, 110–111
domestic laws, 124–125
enforcement, 103, 108–112, 109f, 114–116, 124–125
environmental clauses, 121–122, 122f, 123f, 124
issue linkage and, 11f, 104–107
mechanisms, 106–108, 129
NAAEC, 112–113
NAFTA, 112–113
policies, international treaties and, 105
process tracing, 107
public participation, 103, 108–115, 109f, 124–125
tactical linkages, 106–107
US-Peru PTA, 115–117
US PTAs, environmental norms, 112, 125–128
US role, causal mechanisms, 129
US trade agreement influence, 104
Norm internalization
alternative explanations, 120–124
CAFTA-DR, 118–119

Index

NAFTA, 117–118
public participation, 118–119
US-Peru PTA, 119–121
North American Agreement on Environmental Cooperation (NAAEC), 9, 31–32, 112–113

Paris Agreement (2015), 41
Peru, Annex on Forest Sector Governance, 36–37
PTA-MEA linkages
 back-door environmental governance, 99
 CITES, 5, 64, 73–74, 78, 78f, 85–88, 93–94, 97–98
 commitment within, 77
 compliance measures, 80, 82t
 effectiveness, measurement, 78–85, 79t
 frequency, 76–77, 77f
 indirect benefits, 100
 managerial vs. legalistic model, 80–84, 82t, 83t, 96
 overview, 74–78, 75f, 77f, 78f
 trade liberalization, environmental protection vs., 73
 unintended consequences, 101
 US leadership, 76–77, 77f
PTAs. *See also* US PTAs, global policy diffusion
 environmental provisions, 3–4, 4f
 environmental provisions, implications, 3–4, 164b
 growth, 1–2, 2f
 innovations per country, 5, 5f
 regional integration, 177
 United States vs. EU, Japan, China, 5–6, 6f

Renewable energy disputes, WTO, 170–171
Research methods, questions, findings, 17–18, 20–21, 22t

Shrimp-turtle dispute (WTO), 10, 10f

Trade and Environment Policy Advisory Committee (TEPAC), 65–66
Trade-environment politics, scholarly literature, 14–17
Trade Expansion Act (1962), 63
Trade Policy Review Group, 63–64
Trade Policy Staff Committee, 63–64
Trade Promotion Authority (TPA), 154, 169
Trans-Pacific Partnership (TPP), 6, 38, 99, 103–104, 128, 142–143, 165–167
TREND, 20–21, 31, 32f, 130
Trump administration
 environmental provisions, US trade agreements, 24
 Executive Order 13773, 69–70
 linkage politics, 69–70
 NAFTA and, 165, 167–168
 tariffs, trade war, 153
Tuna/dolphin dispute (WTO), 8–9

United Nations Framework Convention on Climate Change (UNFCCC), 68
United States, Mexico, and Canada Trade Agreement (USMCA), 14, 24, 64, 167–169, 169f
US-Israel PTA, 26, 30
US-Jordan PTA, 23, 33, 34
US Marine Mammal Protection Act, 8–9
US-Peru PTA, 62, 69
 Annex on Forest Service Governance, 87–88, 90–91, 100–101
 CITES and, 73–74, 85–88, 93–94, 97–98
 compliance measures, 80–81, 82t, 85
 compliance mechanisms of precision, delegation, obligation, 88–91
 domestic political fallout, 161–162

US-Peru PTA (cont.)
  enforcement, dispute settlement, 34–36, 114–116
  Environmental Investigation Agency (EIA) critique, 96–97
  environmental measures, limitations, 48–49f
  environmental provisions, categories, 27–28t
  environmental provisions, distribution by country: 1985–2018, 42–43f
  environmental provisions, evolution, 29t
  environmental provisions, overview, 26
  GATT/WTO disputes, US as respondent, 28, 29t, 30
  implementation, 80
  implementation, domestic policy change, 91–94
  joint institutions, 50–51f
  mahogany exports, 92–93, 93f
  missed opportunities, future improvements, 41
  norm, policy diffusion, 115–117
  norm internalization, 119–121
US PTAs, global policy diffusion, 130, 135
  agreement implementation, 45–47f
  beyond US trading partners, 136
  catalytic linkages, 155–156
  climate-related clauses, 149–150, 149f
  cross-fertilization, 130, 141, 144, 151, 159–160
  diffusion, causal mechanisms, 129, 158f
  diffusion, complex adaptive systems, 131–134
  diffusion limits, 144–150
  dispute-settlement mechanisms, 148–149
  effective enforcement, 137f
  environmental clauses distribution, 146–147, 146f
  environmental exceptions, 135, 159
  environmental impact assessments, 147–148
  environmental provisions, replication across trade agreements, 146–147, 147f
  environmental provisions evolution, five phases, 26–40, 145f, 154–155
  European Union agreements, 131, 135, 141
  global diffusion, causal mechanisms, 129
  goods and services liberalization, 148
  homogenization, innovation, 134, 152
  investment protection, 139
  Latin American PTAs, 144
  MEAs and, 139–138, 155–157
  NAFTA and, 131, 135, 151
  policy coherence provisions per PTA, 143, 143f
  public participation, 138f, 139, 156, 161–163
  sectoral provisions per PTA, 142–143, 142f
  through coercion, 159
  unintended consequences, 160–161
US Trade Act (2002), 21, 34, 63
US trade environmental politics future, 165
US trade-environment linkages
  phase one: 1985–1991, 26–30
  phase two: 1992–1998, 30–32
  phase three: 1999–2001, 32–33
  phase four: 2002–2005, 34–35
  phase five: 2006–present, 35–40
US Trade Promotion Authority (TPA), 67, 154. *See also* Trade Promotion Authority (TPA)
US Trade Representative (USTR), 63–64
US-Vietnam PTA, 32, 179

Index

World Intellectual Property Organization, 54
WTO (World Trade Organization), 1–2
  dispute settlement, environmental provisions, 9–11
  environmental exemptions, 2–3
  Environment Goods Agreement, 171–172
  GATT Artical XX, environmental exemptions, 11, 12–13t, 14, 26, 28
  relevance, 1
  renewable energy disputes in, 170–171
  shrimp-turtle dispute, 10
  tuna/dolphin dispute, 8–9